My Journey as a Religious Pluralist

My Journey as a Religious Pluralist

A Christian Theology of Religions Reclaimed

ALAN RACE

Foreword by Jim Kenney

RESOURCE *Publications* • Eugene, Oregon

MY JOURNEY AS A RELIGIOUS PLURALIST
A Christian Theology of Religions Reclaimed

Copyright © 2021 Alan Race. All rights reserved. Except for brief quotations in critical publications or reviews, no part of this book may be reproduced in any manner without prior written permission from the publisher. Write: Permissions, Wipf and Stock Publishers, 199 W. 8th Ave., Suite 3, Eugene, OR 97401.

Resource Publications
An Imprint of Wipf and Stock Publishers
199 W. 8th Ave., Suite 3
Eugene, OR 97401

www.wipfandstock.com

PAPERBACK ISBN: 978-1-7252-9823-1
HARDCOVER ISBN: 978-1-7252-9822-4
EBOOK ISBN: 978-1-7252-9824-8

05/27/21

Dedicated to
My loving wife, the Reverend Sonya J. Wratten,
whose journey in interreligious dialogue and understanding has
contributed significantly to mine,
and whose constant encouragement has helped
this book come to fruition,
and to
My dear friend, Professor Harold Kasimow,
whose trusting compassion over many years has been a delight
and source of spiritual joy.

FOR PONDERING . . .

The Infinite a sudden Guest
Has been assumed to be –
But how can that stupendous come
Which never went away?
Emily Dickinson

In that world—of global supply chains, instantaneous capital transfers, social media, transnational terrorist networks, climate change, mass migration, and ever-increasing complexity—we will learn to live together, cooperate with one another, and recognize the dignity of others, or we will perish.
Barack Obama

The problem to be faced is: how to combine loyalty to one's own tradition with reverence for different traditions?
Abraham Joshua Heschel

Without a global revolution in the sphere of human consciousness, nothing will emerge for the better in the sphere of our being as humans.
Vaclav Havel

The pluralism and the diversity of religions, colour, sex, race and language are willed by God in his wisdom, through which God created human beings.
His Holiness Pope Francis and The Grand Imam of Al-Azhar, Ahmad Al-Tayyeb

In the particular is contained the universal.
James Joyce

Interreligious theology is very likely to shape, in the long run, the style of all theology.
Perry Schmidt-Leukel

The opposite of a correct statement is a false statement. But the opposite of a profound truth may well be another profound truth.
Niels Henrik David Bohr

In the otherness of my religious friend I find differences that I will never be able to include neatly in my limited categories, but at the same time I can talk with, learn from, and respond to this stark otherness. In the face of the religious other I see or sense the face of the Other that shines within and beyond us all. Pluralists affirm this. And I trust that persons in all the religious communities of our world can affirm it as well.
Paul Knitter

Another world is not only possible, she is on her way. On a quiet day, I can hear her breathing.
Arundhati Roy

So the world religions really are different forms of cosmic optimism.
John Hick

Contents

Foreword by Jim Kenney — xi
Acknowledgments — xv
Introduction — xix

PART ONE: CRITICAL FOUNDATIONS

1. Christianity: 2000 Years of Inventiveness — 3
2. Quarrying Tradition — 28

PART TWO: CONSTRUCTIVE THEORY

3. Truth is Many-Eyed — 39
4. The Dialogue of Religions: Pragmatic Necessity or Providential Opportunity? — 51
5. Can There be a Christian Pluralism? — 67
6. Christ and the Scandal of Particularities — 79

PART THREE: ETHICS IN DIALOGUE

7. Hospitality is Good, But How Far Can It Go? — 95
8. 9/11 and Choices for Dialogue — 103
9. Religious Absolutism, Violence, and the Public Square — 115
10. Taking Democracy into a Global Ethic: The Christian Next Step — 129
11. A Spirituality for Ecological Awareness: Contemplative Vision and Prophetic Discernment — 141

PART FOUR: EPILOGUE

12	No Avoiding the Inevitable	157
13	"Whose God is it anyway?"	180

Bibliography	187
Index	197

Foreword

I AM FORTUNATE TO bring some 40 years of experience in interreligious and intercultural dialogue to the very pleasant task of reading this remarkable book, *My Journey as a Religious Pluralist: A Christian Theology of Religions Reclaimed*, and the signal honor of writing the *Foreword*. I also bring a long and cherished friendship with the author. Alan's penetrating insight, deep knowledge of scripture, theology, and interfaith relations has made him an invaluable partner in shared ventures too numerous to list. We continue to relish our disputations, our shared inquiries, hunches, and occasional certainties.

This book, which I find exhilarating, celebrates the radical fact of human cultural, religious, and spiritual diversity and lifts up the now somehow controversial idea of religious pluralism as the most rewarding pathway to interreligious understanding. Alan offers a compelling four-part weave of some thirty years of published work with some very new reflections on a Christian theology of religions, illuminating the whole with a stirringly fresh analysis that somehow makes the reader feel as if every chapter were just written.

In the first stage of *My Journey*, we encounter the notion, compelling and yet almost playfully offered, of 2,000 years of Christian "inventiveness." That process has been in turns marvelous and problematic, as the author usefully illustrates with glimpses of key moments in Christian history, from the forging of the gospel tradition itself, through the melding of Greek philosophy and Hebrew ethical monotheism, to the transformation of Christian thought under the influence of the western Enlightenment. We are reminded, though, that "integrating historical change into Christian consciousness still comes as a massive shock to the Christian system."

Intriguingly linked with the litany of invention is the author's critical inquiry into the renascence of the role of "tradition" in current Christian theological discussion. If Christian life and thought vary with the flow of historical currents, then "it is small wonder many now feel that tradition has become an unstable concept" that can no longer be captured in the language of consistent organic unfolding or validated by reference to the Church Fathers. The appeal to tradition, now more and more often encountered, "masks the real nature and extent of theological innovation and diversification that has gone on throughout history."

"Imaginative innovation" emerges in this view as a more apt characterization of the nature of tradition than "ideological authority." Here, the author offers the refreshing image of tradition as "quarry." One immediately feels the evocative force of the metaphor. Older templates and familiar patterns endure on all sides, inspiring and challenging; but new possibilities beckon, new shapes not yet cut free from the matrix.

As we move on to part two, the stage is set for a thorough revalorization of a Christian pluralistic approach to the experience of the religious other. The development of new modes of relation to other religious traditions (forms of encounter and, especially, *dialogue*) has gradually urged the Christian world away from mere competitiveness toward a *modus vivendi* more in keeping with the spirit of the Second Vatican Council in the 1960s. Now each well-chosen essay helps the reader get to "yes" with respect to interreligious dialogue as an essential tool for shaping authentic Christian pluralism. The dialogical experience can even bring the thoughtful Christian to the exploration of the stunningly powerful notion of Christ as "a parable of God," a view that can remain open to "other parables" without losing a Christological mooring.

In the book's third major section, Alan sets out to map the transformative potential of pluralistically oriented religious encounter, dialogue, and engagement with the world. He brings dialogical skills and the pluralistic vision to bear on some of our most urgent global presenting problems, from the democratic project and the elusiveness of a Global Ethic, to absolutism and violence in the name of religion, to the most urgent challenge of all, the ecological and existential threat of anthropogenic climate change. Calling the reader's attention to the phenomenon of a new (or, perhaps, revitalized) *denialism*, driven by the desire "for something not to be true," he suggests that a response akin to the religious idea of conversion, of "seeing and acting aright" is demanded. Here the author's suggestion is visionary: "We need a combination of *contemplative wisdom* and *prophetic discernment*." The first will allow us to take in the interdependent complexity of existence itself and the second will help us discern our individual and societal roles within that organic whole.

Much of the power of this book derives from the respectful and, indeed, dialogical way in which Alan Race addresses one after another of the learned opponents (Schleiermacher might have said, "the cultured despisers") of the evolutionary mindset that gives rise to and is nurtured by religious pluralism. He brings that process to a head in the fourth and final part, as he responds to criticisms of the "exclusivism, inclusivism, pluralism" typology and of his own advocacy of pluralism.

I found *My Journey's* conclusion quite compelling, in some measure because my own work plays a small role in Alan's analysis, but also because the chapter offers a somewhat overdue response to critics of his seminal typology of three primary responses to the fact that many religions coexist in the world. The "exclusivism-inclusivism-pluralism" model first set out in 1983, in *Christians and Religious Pluralism*, has long shaped debates about a Christian theology of religions. In recent years, the typology has increasingly been critiqued, perhaps most often by scholars ill-at-ease with the idea and practice of religious pluralism.

First, the author calls up the compelling suggestion by the late Ewert Cousins that our time might be witnessing, or birthing, a "Second Axial Period." The *First* (identified by Karl Jaspers with the laying of the foundations, in the first millennium BCE, of the great modern religions) saw the human emergence from "tribal" to "individual" consciousness. The *Second*, Cousins argued, is marked by the movement into "global" consciousness, and the evolutionary advance of religious and spiritual understanding and engagement toward a pluralist vision of religion and spirituality.

Alan then references my own argument that the evolution of human culture (and cultures) is real and is therefore a meaningful subject for inquiry and analysis. My book on the subject (*Thriving in the Crosscurrent: Clarity and Hope in a Time of Cultural Sea Change*, 2010) also draws on Ewert Cousins and cites his description of a new turning on the religious axis as a persuasive example of the reality and power of *cultural evolution*. The cultural evolutionary dynamic, in this view, is a steady, occasionally accelerated movement of our dominant values toward a closer fit with complex, interdependent reality.

If cultures truly evolve, Alan suggests, rather than merely change, then "*Cultural Evolution* forms the wider background against which Christian faith and other religious traditions must face the realities of plurality." I would add that in an interdependent culture or cosmos the refinement of a pluralist mindset and a compassionate openness to the other is the only rational strategy. If human values indeed evolve in synchrony with our deepening understanding of one another and the complex world in which we make our way, then second axial global consciousness and hopeful, pluralist intentionality are to be expected, not merely aspired to.

The final sections of the concluding chapter address the range of critiques of the tripartite typology, of the very project of a theology of religions, and of pluralism itself, demonstrating in the process that most objections are reactions against pluralism's challenge to Christian absolutism. We are reminded that liberal theological thought may have lost some luster in the academy and the church, but we are invited, at the same time to consider some very persuasive arguments for that liberality. Race argues convincingly that a theology of religions, like the typology itself, must bend toward pluralism, but he does so by guiding the reader first through a litany of alternative approaches to dialogue and interreligious relations. (This process actually takes place throughout the book but is most concisely and cogently laid out in the last chapter.) The variations on the "anything but pluralism" theme are all there: dialogue as hospitality, the dynamic of tradition and its invitation to ideological thinking, supersession, the fulfilment of every religious path in Jesus Christ, and—more recently—comparative theology. The book touches repeatedly and at some depth on each one, but in the end, none really succeeds as a way to answer the question posed by the religious other, "What I really want to know is what you think of my religion?"

This is a critically important concern in the context of interreligious encounter and in an age on which awareness of the plurality of religions has descended. It seems to me, however, that the question suggests a vital reciprocal phrasing. "What do I think of *your* religion? And how do those thoughts change me?"

Jim Kenney

Acknowledgments

As a MY JOURNEY book many of the chapters have been published previously, but some appear here in modified form. I would like to acknowledge the provenance of the chapters as follows:

Chapter 1: *Christianity: 2000 Years of Inventiveness* was first given as the Fourth Geza Vermes Lecture (Millennium Lecture) at the Centre for the History of Religions, Inter-Faith Dialogue and Pluralism, University of Leicester, UK, in 2000, and published in *Encounters, the Journal of Inter-Cultural Perspectives*, Vol. 6, No. 1, March 2000, Markfield Islamic Foundation, Leicester. 'A Muslim Critique' by Maryam Jameelah and my 'A Response to Maryam Jameelah' were published in Encounters, Vol. 6, No. 2, September 2000. The journal *Encounters* has since been discontinued. I am grateful to the Markfield Islamic Foundation for permission to re-publish.

Chapter 2: *Quarrying Tradition* was first published in the British journal *Theology* for September/October, 1990, No. 755. I am grateful to SPCK for permission to re-publish.

Chapter 3: *Truth is Many-Eyed* was first published in *God's Truth: Essays to celebrate the twenty-fifth anniversary of Honest to God*, edited by Eric James, London: SCM, 1988. It is republished by permission. rights@hymnsam.co.uk.

Chapter 4: *The Dialogue of Religions: Pragmatic Necessity or Providential Opportunity?* was first presented to the annual Modern Churchpeople's Union Conference, 2001, the theme of which was Providence.

Chapter 5: *Can There be a Christian Pluralism?* appeared in an earlier form in *Buddhist and Christian Attitudes to Religious Diversity*, eds., Hans-Peter Grosshans, Samuel Ngun Ling, and Perry Schmidt-Leukel, Ling's

Family Publication, 2017, and was presented at a Buddhist-Christian colloquy in preparation for the edited book.

Chapter 6: This chapter was originally published in *Many Mansions: Interfaith and Religious Intolerance*, London: Bellew 1992, edited by Dan Cohn-Sherbok.

Chapter 7: *Hospitality is Good, But How Far Can It Go?* was first published in *Current Dialogue*, Issue 45, July, 2005, as a comment on "Religious Plurality and Christian Self-Understanding," which was a joint statement issued by the three constituencies of the World Council of Churches—Faith & Order, Conference on World Mission and Evangelism, and the Office on Interreligious Relations and Dialogue.

Chapter 8: *9/11 and Choices for Dialogue* was published in an earlier version in *Interreligious Insight*, 8 2 July 2010.

Chapter 9: *Religious Absolutism, Violence, and the Public Square* was published in *Beyond the Dysfunctional Family: Jews, Christians and Muslims in Dialogue With Each Other and With Britain*, edited by Tony Bayfield, Alan Race, Ataullah Siddiqui, London: The Manor House Abrahamic Dialogue Group, 2012.

Chapter 10: *Taking Democracy into a Global Ethic: The Christian Next Step*, was published in an earlier version in *Religions in Dialogue: From Theocracy to Democracy*, edited by Alan Race and Ingrid Shafer, Aldershot: Ashgate, 2002.

Chapter 11: *A Spirituality for Ecological Awareness: Contemplative Vision and Prophetic Discernment* is a significantly revised version of an earlier paper that was presented to the Globalisation for the Common Good Conference, "Our Sacred Earth: Spiritual Ecology, Values-led Economics, Education and Society Responding to Ecological Crisis," Lucca, Italy, 2018.

Chapter 12: *Whose God is it anyway?* was first given as a sermon preached at Great St. Mary's University Church, Cambridge, on Sunday 10th May 1987.

I am most grateful to Jim Kenney, formerly Global Director of the Parliament of the World's Religions and now adult educator through the online Global Lecture Hall Forum, for writing the Foreword to this book. His expansive way of interpreting the world offers hope to everyone who engages with it. We have known one another for many years, learned from one another, shared many conference platforms, and, together with Cetta Kenney, have shared the production and editing of the celebrated journal, *Interreligious Insight*. I count him and Cetta among the best of my friends. They have been wonderful hosts at their home over many visits to Lake Forest, Illinois.

I am grateful also to my good friend Professor Perry Schmidt-Leukel for reading this manuscript during preparation, for offering corrective guidance, and for writing an endorsement. With another good friend, Professor Paul Knitter, I was thrilled to co-edit a book of essays (*New Paths for Interreligious Theology*, 2019) by religious scholars responding to Perry's groundbreaking development of what he calls "a fractal interpretation of religious diversity." Perry and Paul are two of the most outstanding theologians of religious pluralism.

Thanks are due also to Wesley Ariarajah, Kusumita Pedersen, and Sharida Sugirtharajah for their endorsements and friendship over many years, each of them, in their own right, highly significant contributors to reflections interpreting religious diversity in the context of the global twenty-first century.

I am pleased to dedicate this book to a dear friend, Harold Kasimow, now professor emeritus at Grinnell University, Iowa, and whom I first met at the Parliament of the World's Religions gathered at Cape Town, South Africa, in 1999. That whole occasion was inspirational, not least because of the discovery of the liberal, generous, and humane approach to religious diversity that Harold espoused. We edited together a collection of interreligious responses to the dialogical outlook of Pope Francis in our book, *Pope Francis and Interreligious Dialogue: Religious Thinkers Engage With Recent Papal Initiatives* (2018), and together with Sonya Wratten, my wife, delivered a copy of the book's cover to Pope Francis in person at an unforgettable audience in St. Peter's Square at the Vatican.

I would also like to recall with loving gratitude the friendship of two generous souls, whose recent deaths are mourned by many—Dr. Ataullah Siddiqui and Raficq Abdulla. In their different ways both have left their mark on me and I remain profoundly grateful for their gifts of openness and thoughtfulness. I have included two of Raficq's poems in this book as a mark of tribute.

Finally, *"My Journey"* first began with the postgraduate supervision of my teacher and mentor, Professor John Hick, whose interpretation of religious pluralism remains, in my view, unbeatable. I am indebted to his keen intellect and support of my own theological endeavours. I was most moved to have been invited to speak at the memorial event following his death in 2012.

Introduction

THIS BOOK IS IN full agreement with the observation and aspiration signalled by the following remarks from Ewert Cousins (1927–2009), one of the most prophetic scholars of religious studies and spirituality, renowned theologian, and pioneer in interreligious dialogue:

> All the religions and all the peoples of the world are undergoing the most radical, far-reaching, and challenging transformation in history. The stakes are high: the very survival of life on our planet; either chaos and destruction, or creative transformation and the birth of a new consciousness. Forces, which have been at work for centuries, have in our day reached a crescendo that has the power to draw the human race into a global network and the religions of the world into a global spiritual community.[1]

Some might consider these remarks to be exaggerated, unnecessarily captive to an apocalyptic dualism, or crafted simply for dramatic effect, but lacking empirical and analytic perspective. Yet as we enter the third decade of the twenty-first century there is nothing to suggest that the stakes have been lowered. There is no escape from the human race's global network and the alarm bells of the climate emergency are surely evidence enough of how high the stakes continue to rise. If anything, Cousins's clarion call is more pertinent than ever.

My interest in Cousins's call relates to how the religions of the world might make their own transitions into the expectant "global spiritual community." An integral part of any such transition involves a theological appraisal of a religious community's place in a world of significant religious

---

1. Cousins, "Religions of the World," 9.

diversity. In short, the question can be stated succinctly: from my limited perspective how do I interpret the fact of religious plurality? If I trust that my religion—in my case the Christian religion—is a gateway to the truth of the human condition and to a life-giving spiritual relationship with transcendent or sacred reality, what can be said about other communities of trust, other gateways? Why are there so many religions and what is their theological status? Exploring this question forms the task known as the theology of religions.

This book collates essays, papers and lectures concerned with explorations in the Christian theology of religions stretching over more than thirty years. They are not arranged in date order but in a loose systematic format, following the pattern of Foundations, Constructive Theory, and Ethics in Dialogue. In other words, although some chapters have been published previously through various outlets, they are not randomly chosen but are brought together with other essays to form the impression of a developing coherent narrative. Time can occasionally play tricks, such that earlier arguments when revisited later in the day can seem as fresh as when they were first formulated. This is largely my conviction here.

What holds these essays together can also be captured poetically as a quest and an intuition. The following poem by a Sufi interested Muslim friend summarises for me the ethos—the aspirations, pitfalls, wrong turns, and hoped-for insights and joys—of what is sometimes called interreligious theology:

Serious Pursuit

Admit it. When you close your eye, shutting
Down the over-stimulated mind, you are in the
Dark. The diversity, richness, obscurity,
Profundity, foolishness of all religions
Flash like meteoric slingshots thudding
Against your eyeballs. But if you ignore
This celestial shower, and extend your hands,
You feel, presenting themselves for touch-
Testing, the limbs, tails, snouts, tentacles
Of a number of animals or a composite beast.
You need not choose one version of reality
Amongst many, but accept that reality as a
Whole is a variegated creature that you must
Hunt with the dedication and meticulous
Attention of the scientist, an Ahab transformed
By love, searching the vast ocean for the moment

Of still communion when the eyes are
Opened and not blinded.²

Raficq Abdulla

The poem speaks of a confusion of religious impressions that is ambiguous in terms of its helpfulness to human beings—a "richness" coupled with "obscurity," a "profundity" accompanied by "foolishness," and all "thudding against your eyeballs." This ambiguity has a ring of truth about it. Philosophers have used the confusion as evidence of the impossibility of discerning the truthfulness of any religion. As the philosopher David Hume (1711–1776) put it, in a court of law none could demonstrate their obvious superiority and so all must be false.³ But there are other ways of thinking. Why accept only one version of reality?, wonders the poet. Then, in an echo of the well-known Buddhist parable of the blind men and the elephant, the poet invites us to contemplate the option that "reality as a whole is a variegated creature."⁴ Why should the religious truth about human experience be consolidated in one version only? This is the question at the heart of all theorizing in theology of religions. Finally, the poet anticipates that what interreligious interrogation is properly about is that "moment of still communion," residing within human reach, no matter how much dedication to "searching the vast ocean" might be required. It is not that the cacophony of religions should be set aside for universal enlightenment to dawn, but that the cacophony itself should be subjected to the "meticulous attention of the scientist" and be trained to pursue the goal of the religious quest itself "when the eyes are opened and not blinded."

A great deal of the debates in theology of religions have been taken up with the question of whether the "moment of still communion" is arrived at by setting aside the particulars of religious beliefs and practices or by awakening to its potential abiding at the heart of the world's religious particularities as such. These essays lean towards the latter approach: we learn of the universal "moment of still communion" by way of culturally shaped journeys, commitments, and specificities. "In the particular is contained the universal"—so learned the musician and poet, Kae Tempest, from James Joyce.⁵

That said, all theorizing has roots and influences, some even unconscious, and it is instructive to bring these into the open. My first encounter

---

2. Abdulla, "Serious Pursuit," 75.
3. Hume, *Enquiries*, 121.
4. See Schmidt-Leukel, "*Religious Pluralism and Interreligious Theology,*" 72, for an informative comment on the parable.
5. Tempest, "Words on a page," 142.

with people of religious commitments different from my own Christian journey was in the English Yorkshire city of Bradford. This was not the city now remembered for the disruptions known as The Rushdie Affair in 1989, when the public burning of Rushdie's book, *The Satanic Verses* (1988), ignited angry protests that spread around the world, or with the violent communal and ethnic disturbances of the summer of 2001, when white (inspired by the white supremacist National Front) and south Asian youths faced one another in a stand-off—but the city of my undergraduate years when I was studying for a university degree in Natural Sciences (Chemistry) in the early 1970s. Demographic change, however, was becoming evident, as immigrants mainly from rural Pakistan, Bangladesh, and India were beginning to establish themselves in Bradford in large numbers.

As a student with a full study programme, I did not really get to know the Muslims who were the dominant immigrant group. But the impact of change on the city was highly visible and the Islamic otherness (as I learned to call it later, though less so now) was both intriguing and puzzling. The intrigue and puzzle were filtered, for example, through the experience of observing Muslim families where the father (often with the eldest son) walked along the street several steps ahead of the mother and remaining children. There was also the impact of new minarets rising in the places where mill chimneys had once belched out thick black smoke generated by the woollen textiles industry. Over my four years in the city, black smoking chimneys were beginning to be replaced by minarets with the sonorous voices of the muezzin calling the faithful to prayer.

When I came to study Christian theology during my seminary years in the mid-1970s prior to ordination in the Anglican Church, I realised by the end of my study and formation that a whole area of enquiry for Christian reflection was missing from the curriculum: the presence in our world of the great religions of humankind. Subsequently, I embarked on a journey to learn of them, and to investigate Christian responses to them from the past and in the present. It led me to writing a book,[6] and to an intellectual quest that continues to stretch for as long as any winding road might. The book became a key reference text for courses in the theology of religions worldwide.

Perhaps in the near background of my decision to research theology of religions were the intrigue and puzzlement from my first impressions of that Muslim immigration to Bradford. But there was also the presence in the theological college of the visiting Buddhist student from one of Japan's new religious movements. He had come to learn about Christianity and thought

---

6. Race, *Christians and Religious Pluralism*, 1983. (Revised and enlarged, 1993).

that a seminary was as good a place as any to learn about it. In addition to his quiet presence, I remember him mainly as a result of two impressions: first, for citing the Christian Nicene Creed in the college chapel more loudly than any of the seminarians; and second, for asking, following an erudite exposition in a college seminar of the Christian experience and doctrine of grace, what precisely was the meaning of the Christian experience and doctrine of grace! It was my first realization that the language-game of one religion might not be readily accessible to those nurtured in other language-games.

The collision of language-games in religion sets up what I call "strangeness with resonance" in the encounter between religions. Let me illustrate this through my own experience with two examples from a number of years spent in the British multireligious city of Leicester.

My first example concerns the city's earliest Hindu temple, Sri Sanatan Mandir, which is a building re-configured, internally and externally, from what was once a Baptist Church.[7] The unfamiliar sights, ambience, and reference points fill me with feelings of strangeness: they do not immediately connect with what I have been trained to expect from religious devotion. There are the murtis (images, statues—wrongly called idols) or revelatory figures expressing an aspect of divinity, some of which may be animal-looking and belong within a scripture story not of my repertoire. There are symbols of reproduction, in the simple form of the shiva-lingam (stylised phallus and vagina) which in one interpretation is said to represent the divine as Creator, Protector and Destroyer. There are practices of libation and offerings of fruit before the murtis; there is fire which purports to communicate divine energy between worshipper and worshipped. And much more. The overall impression can be one of bewildering multiple encounters, where facets of the divine blessing on the world assume many expressions. And yet there is resonance with my own experience: there is devotional intensity on the faces of the devotees; there is the giving of the human self and the lifting of the human heart, enacted before a variety of imaginative forms; there is the openness to receive blessing for the leading of a more spiritual and compassionate life; there is chanting; there is divine-human connection as the veil between the two is pierced.

My second example concerns the city's Jain temple, named the Jain Samaj of Europe, which also exhibits a transformed exterior and interior from having once been a Congregational Church. The strangeness is

---

7. Sri Sanatan Mandir was formerly the Carey Baptist Church, first erected in recognition of William Carey (1761–1834), the pioneer missionary to Bengal, India, where he founded a mission at Serampore. The irony of this mandir is that the Baptist Church in honor of a Christian missionary to India has itself been "converted" into a Hindu temple, in a reverse order of mission!

reflected in the traditional architecture of hand-carved pillars originally shipped from India, demarcating an inner shrine which houses images of tirthankaras (ford-crossers) sat in lotus positions. The priest makes devotional offering before the tirthankaras, revelatory representations of idealized teachers who have achieved the goal of enlightenment and who therefore blaze a trail for the rest of humanity. The ethos of Jainism is non-theistic, indicating a universe which is believed to be eternal, without final distinction between divinity and humanity. But what catches the eye in this building and resonates the most is the transformation of the former church's stained-glass windows into a visual outline presentation of the life of Mahavira, the final tirthankara of the present age. There is his miraculous birth, temptation by the power of evil and its overcoming, depiction of an ascetic life, the bestowing of blessings on others through receiving their feeding, teaching scenes, and eventually the achievement of enlightenment. Although the metaphysical background is quite different from that assumed in Christianity, the resonant parallels with the life of Christ are remarkable. One can think of the windows as a western material form displaying an eastern religious narrative, a unique syncretic variation on visual religious symbolism, and one unknown in Jainism's Indian place of origins.

Other encounters have increased both the strangeness and the resonance. First, encounters that alerted me to strangeness: I think of the Buddhist who was scandalised at my throwaway reference to "creation" as a cat walked across the front of our seminar circle; I remember the initial shock from the scholarly Jew who suggested to a dialogue group of Jews and Christians that Christianity was founded on a mistake; there was the Hindu who informed me that the doctrine of reincarnation was as obvious to reason as waking up in the morning. Second, balancing these encounters with flashes of resonance: I marvelled at the Muslim scholar who told me that all religions have a book (holy scripture) and it is the Muslim view that all you have to do is "rejoice in your book and get on with it"; I smiled at the infectious joy of the Hindu priest who delighted in the fact that the figure of Jesus was painted in his temple's ceiling alongside other key founders or revelatory figures from numerous traditions; I warmed to the Baha'i who reminded me in the magnificent lotus-shaped Baha'i temple of Delhi that the idea of the sacred was more universal than any of us might care to have imagined.

Now, I marvel at the human religious project called diversity. The experiences of strangeness with resonance could be multiplied. But what lesson do we draw from such a tally of religious profit and loss? My hunch has always been this: no matter the strangeness we need not be alien to one another; and no matter the resonance we need not imagine that we are variations on the same theme. But each side of the equation deserves both honouring and interrogating. This is the task of theology of religions.

In recent years, however, theology of religions has become closely allied with the rise in dialogue between religions, or strictly speaking, between religious people. But dialogue is a far from being a simple endeavour: it spans the range of encounters from an everyday conversation with someone from a different religious pathway about life in the local neighbourhood to exploring self-consciously the philosophies and theologies of many different traditions. At the more theological end of the range, for dialogue to become productive it will rely at least on (a) basic respect between parties, (b) a desire to learn, and (c) a willingness to be changed. These conditions become more demanding the deeper the dialogue progresses. Moreover, dialogue is undertaken with different purposes in mind, in formal and informal settings, by enquiring individuals and official faith-community representatives, and so on, involving many contextual factors. At the very least it signals a commitment to one another, that amounts to what the doyen of dialogue, Leonard Swidler, has named as "a whole new way of thinking, a way of seeing and reflecting on the world and its meaning."[8]

My own understanding of theological dialogue is summed up in the following proposal:

> We probably learn more from each other as human beings, even as religious human beings, and understand God better, when instead of marking off our positions from each other by verbal encounters, we go on questioning together, seeking together—fully conscious of our differences and yet, at the same time, as if these differences, so to speak, did not exist—what the truth might be.[9]

In other words, dialogue is what transpires in the space between thinking that "we're all the same behind our outward appearances" and believing that "we're all different because of our outward appearances."

Dialogue yields surprises and is never simply an exchange between de-historicised religious traditions. I recall from several years ago the pertinent observation of a Jewish contributor to a Christian-Jewish meeting that there is always a third but often unspoken partner present in the room, and that is secularism. By this he meant forms of critical thinking which interrogate tradition. At a later and different Christian-Jewish dialogue group I pressed the case for the religious abandonment of absolutism or finality

---

8. Swidler, *After the Absolute*, xi.

9. Ott, "Dialogue Between Religions," 195. The en rules in this citation are my own addition, placed in order to clarify the translation from German.

in order for our dialogue to become more honest.[10] But this proved a step too far for most of the Christian participants: anger was unleashed, and it was as though I had committed some act of religious treason. Jewish colleagues, meanwhile, looked on completely mystified as to why crossing this line was so mutinous. The experience taught me that dialogue stirred up religious emotions as well as religious reasoning. After all, Christian mainstream churches and academic theology, in the light of holocaust studies, critical thinking, and dialogue itself, have long surrendered the doctrine of supersessionism—the view that Jesus and the church has superseded Judaism—and has therefore effectively laid aside Christian finality, at least in relation to Jews and Judaism, so what had I uncovered in the psyche of my Christian partners? I have been pondering that puzzle ever since. Existential commitment it seemed was deeply encoded in theological absolutism.

The experience reinforced my belief that there is a relationship between dialogue and critical thinking in theology. Dialogue need not require a pluralist conviction in theology of religions for it to be productive, but if productivity is to flourish a self-conscious critical "theology for dialogue" seems unavoidable; otherwise, we simply respond to one another from a place of unconscious bias. Such a theology will embrace an epistemology that is prepared to be more provisional in tone than what comes to us from times prior to the rise of historical consciousness, linguistic analysis, colonial studies, and scientific understanding; and it will be more open to revision in the light of new knowledge and critical understanding. Interreligious dialogue adds a further ingredient to the armoury of critical thinking, and a self-critical theology will be more in tune with the spirit of dialogue when the absolutisms that wall us off from one another are abandoned as part of a developing understanding of religious faith in the present. Moreover, personal commitment in faith does not necessarily depend on absolutism in theology (perhaps this is what was at stake for the accusers of my religious treason). My case is simply that there are formulations of Christian faith and theology that facilitate the dialogue more readily than others. For why would Jews, Buddhists, Muslims, and so on, want to enter into dialogue if it is already assumed that Christians have the final truth necessary for the awakening/salvation/liberation of all people?

In dialogue, we might celebrate shared ethical rapprochement, mutually agonize over the continuing relevance of offensive texts from the past, agree on mutual respect, learn from comparative scriptural reasoning and comparative theology, but if the clinging to absolutism persists then, it

---

10. Race, "Rethinking," 175–188.

seems to me, the dialogue will finally flounder. The potential within dialogue's "What the truth might be" will remain unfulfilled.

The essays in this book are offered in the spirit of self-conscious, self-critical thinking.

They set out why the encounter between religions represents a new moment in the unfolding Christian story, why it cannot be ignored, and why it struggles to gain traction in both church and academy. The format of the book shaped as a theological pathway is triggered through experience and shaped in relation to critical thinking. It should not be read as a journey in time but as a theological trajectory laying out methodological and epistemological assumptions, adumbrating constructive proposals, and sketching some ethical areas where interreligious dialogue and cooperation seems most urgently needed today.

The book explains why theology of religions cannot be simply the result of the exegesis of scripture and tradition alone but must accept new data from interfaith encounters and critical approaches to sacred text and past formularies. It recalls the typological outlook—the broad options in Christian responses to religious plurality of exclusivist, inclusivist, or pluralist—first sketched in my *Christians and Religious Pluralism* (1983), which achieved the status of a classic and has provided a reference point for many commentators in the field since, even if that reference acts as a point of departure or disagreement. Speaking Christianly, to be exclusivist is to imagine that Christian faith is the sole locus of religious truth and salvation; to be inclusivist is to recognize that "other traditions" contain elements of religious truth and salvation but are "fulfilled" in the Christian dispensation; to be pluralist is to accept that there will be more than my own faith that is equally salvific and truth-giving. The results of my enquiries led me to a pluralist outlook as being more in tune with today's realities. This proved controversial and remains so. But I have been encouraged by the endorsement given to the typology by a colleague and fellow-traveller, Professor Perry Schmidt-Leukel, who has presented, convincingly to my mind, a revised and more systematic triadic schema applicable to all traditions.[11]

The present book defends both the legitimacy of the exercise of theology of religions and the pluralist convictions that I came to embrace.

Part One (Critical Foundations) traces my general approach to theological exploration, much of which has been heavily influenced by the rise of historical consciousness over the last two hundred years in western thought. During this period Christian faith has undergone huge shifts in self-understanding and I portray this as a form of hermeneutical 'inventiveness' in

---

11. Schmidt-Leukel, "Exclusivism, Inclusivism, Pluralism," 13–27.

response to change and subsequent developments. With the end of Christendom, Christian faith needs to discover a more modest form of commitment, open to the possibilities of truth from wherever it beckons. The exchange with a Muslim critic clarifies further the hermeneutic principles underlying the need for a dialogical future embracing interreligious theology. I argue against a notion of "tradition" as a fixed marker of identity and for a more open and provisional outlook which is the result of engagement with secular and other religious experience.

Part Two (Constructive Theory) is the most theologically developed section of the book. It traces the theoretical outline of how a critical consciousness, taking into account the presence, persistence, and impressiveness of many religious traditions, might apply in a Christian theology of religions. It asks whether the dialogue of religions signals a new "providential opportunity," to use that traditional language. The roots of a Christian case for Pluralism are explored with reference to scripture, tradition, and contemporary interreligious experiences. Most importantly, and perhaps unsettlingly for those wedded to orthodoxy, I confront the Christological question head-on: what affirmation of Jesus as a revelation of God is convincing today, and how might that make its impact on both interreligious dialogue and theology of religions? Recent affirmations of Jesus as a "symbolic representation of God" or "parable of God" will be more capable of admitting the relevance of other parables in a wider reflection on religious plurality.

Part Three (Ethics in Dialogue) reflects on several key areas in ethical debate that have a global reach and that therefore demand an interreligious approach. These include so-called religiously-motivated violence, debates on religion in the public square, ecology and spirituality, and hope in the light of global need. If hope is to inspire cooperation there is also the need to tackle issues of religious difference in the light of modernity's theoretical and practical challenges to religious belief and action. I argue for the continuing relevance of global ethic thinking and for deepening the opening provided by the popular ethical theme of "hospitality" in the face of difference.

Part Four (Epilogue) concludes the book, first, with a reflection on why theology of religions remains a pressing concern, despite the naysayers who would rather the topic was superannuated. And finally, in the belief that theology of religions ought not to be confined to the seminar room, I include a sermon, which was first preached at Great St. Mary's Church, Cambridge, as an example of how Christian reflection on interreligious themes might be presented in a liturgical setting.

Diversity, contextuality, interpreted awareness, and dialogical interrogations of one another have all made significant demands on how Christian faith ought to think of itself in a world of multiple religious convictions. Faced with such demands, a nuanced and carefully crafted theology of religions is required now more than ever.

Although some of the chapters in this book may have been devised for other initial destinations, I have taken the liberty of making slight improvements in them where I deemed this to be necessary, but I am clear that nothing of the original thrust of each piece has been diverted from its original intention. Each chapter is prefaced with a brief note of introduction that clarifies its purpose and place in the book as a whole.

Towards the end of *Christians and Religious Pluralism* I wrote: "Pluralism in the Christian theology of religions seeks to draw the faiths of the world's religious past into a mutual recognition of one another's truths and values, in order for truth itself to come into proper focus."[12] Since writing that, I see no reason to dissent from it; indeed, it strikes me as becoming daily more obviously and necessarily the case.

---

12. Race, *Christians and Religious Pluralism*, 148.

PART ONE

Critical Foundations

1

Christianity

2000 Years of Inventiveness

THIS CHAPTER PRESENTS A *history of Christian faith, highlighting change and development as an hermeneutical pattern of inventiveness. It argues that, with the end of Christendom, Christian faith needs to discover a more modest form, one that is open to the possibilities of truth from wherever it beckons. The exchange with a trenchant Muslim critic clarifies further the hermeneutic principles underlying the need for a dialogical future embracing interreligious theology.*

"Jesus proclaimed the kingdom, and what came was the church."[1] In the European Catholic Church of 1902, that was a dangerous distinction to make. As a result of it, the French theologian, Alfred Loisy (1857–1940), was condemned and the Archbishop of Paris, Cardinal Richard, forbade people to read his book, *The Gospel and the Church*. Loisy had spotted a lacuna at the heart of Christian understanding: what Jesus had promised was different from what history had delivered. But there was more. Loisy continued his infamous sentence above: "It came by broadening the form of the gospel, which it was impossible to keep as it was . . ."[2] And in the same passage Loisy also declared the unnerving impact of nineteenth century historical consciousness when he noted that "a considerable change in the state of science (i.e., 'the general state of knowledge in the time and place where they were formed') can necessitate a new interpretation of ancient formulae which, conceived as they were in another intellectual atmosphere, can no longer say all that they need to, or do not say it as they should."[3] It was all too much for the hierarchy of the church. Loisy responded to his condemnation by writing another book.

1. Loisy, *The Gospel and the Church*, 166.
2. Loisy, *The Gospel and the Church*, 166.
3. Loisy, *The Gospel and the Church*, 166.

Loisy's theological dilemma was not an isolated occurrence. Other intellectuals were also noticing that centuries-old assumptions did not necessarily stand up to historical scrutiny. For example, Albert Schweitzer, who was born in 1875, and acquired doctorates in philosophy, theology, and music before the age of thirty, and later a doctorate in medicine, published in 1906 a disturbing book, *Von Reimarus zu Wrede*, which later became a classic in English translation as *The Quest of the Historical Jesus*. In this book, Schweitzer concluded that Jesus remains "a stranger and an enigma to our time . . . who will not allow himself to be modernized as an historical figure."[4] It is easy to imagine how unsettling such remarks might be for a religion centred primarily on a figure of history and not on a holy book. Later in his life, Schweitzer himself turned towards the formulation of what he called "reverence for life" as his religious philosophy, and he exemplified it splendidly pursuing medical missionary work through the hospital he founded in Lambaréné, in French Equatorial Africa.

From a century's distance, this modernist crisis, as it is called, at the beginning of the twentieth century could seem rather exaggerated. For what is controversial in pointing out that Christianity has worn different masks at different times and in different places? Geographically, French Christianity is bound to exhibit different contours from Chinese Christianity, or from Quaker Christianity in American Pennsylvania, or from Christianity in the Outer Hebrides. And in the perspective of history, Christianity in Rome in the late fifties of the first Christian century, when Paul was writing his epistle to the small band of Jewish and Gentile Christian believers there, was light years away from the kind of Christianity alive in the same city in the first decade of the sixteenth century, when the renaissance genius, Michelangelo, was splashing paint on the Cardinals below him while he was painting the Vatican's Sistine Chapel ceiling. Faced with the need to make sense of such teeming diversity and cultural differences in the expressions of Christian faith, the modernist crisis was not exaggerated. Indeed, it is still with us, essentially because the last century of Christianity's two millennia history has witnessed an even greater diversification of Christian thought and life, with new lines of division and argument opening up as Christianity finally reaches its status as a *world* faith.

The problem of integrating historical change into Christian consciousness still comes as a massive shock to the Christian system, which many have thought is not meant to change.

Theology, however, is one thing, history is another; and history is virtually synonymous with change. Even a cursory glance down the tunnel of

---

4. Schweitzer, *Quest*, 397.

2000 years demonstrates the power of Christian faith for change, for survival and transmutation into numerous forms. Whether by conscious adaptation arising from within the dynamism of its own spiritual momentum, or by forced response to external circumstances inherent in the flux of historical change itself, or, more accurately, by a fusion of both factors, Christian history has *per force* been inventive. In terms of cultural forms, habits of cultic and ethical practice, patterns of believing and community organisation, to be a Christian in the year 50 CE, or in the year 750, or 1550, or 1950, has been as different as the different historical periods that shaped Christian life have allowed Christianity to be.

I am tempted to argue even more boldly and press the case that inventiveness implies that Christianity has been, and continues to be, a faith restlessly in search of itself. Some may object at this seeming boldness and complain of hubris. Surely a faith in search of itself is almost an oxymoron: how can a historical movement which readily exists and has achieved its status as a world faith, be in *search* of itself? I believe that that objection raises profound issues, but it is one which reveals essentially a *theological* anxiety. I shall return to theology later in order to defend my notion of "a faith in search of itself" and its implications for future Christian identity. Although anxiety about change continues to dog Christian theological consciousness, I shall argue that it does so mostly for the wrong reasons. For the moment, let me stick to history and my claim that inventiveness is simply what a historian observes: the twists and turns, the shaping and re-shaping of a historical movement in time.

My central thesis, therefore, is utterly simple to state: the history of 2000 years of Christianity is a history of continuous inventiveness.

Let me give you one obvious—you might think it even playful—illustration of that inventiveness. It has been mentioned quite a lot in Christian literature designed for the celebrations marking the second Millennium of Christianity and relates to how we think of the passage of time itself. I am thinking of the adoption of the *Anno Domini* (the year of the Lord) method of dating, which through western expansion has become a near-universal convention. At the beginning of the sixth century in the western European church, Pope Gelasius appointed a certain monk named Dionysius Exiguus (Denys the Short, to his friends) to be his archivist in the Vatican. Dionysius could read Greek and so he was employed as a translator. He also chanced his hand at a new way of calculating the correct date of Easter, which had always been a deeply controversial matter in the church. By assuming that he knew the date of the birth of Jesus, Dionysius literally invented what has become known as the Christian era. That was about the year 525 AD. (Today we would use the notation CE, meaning Common Era, deriving from and intending to signify a new rapprochement between Christians and Jews after the holocaust; but more about that later). The fact that no-one bothered much about Dionysius's calculations at the time didn't matter, because 200 years later the English monk, the Venerable Bede, read the archivist's manuscript and popularized the dating scheme through his highly influential book, *The Ecclesiastical History of the English People*. The method of dating caught on. Hence the Christian, and, by extension—having adopted it or having had it thrust upon them—the whole world's indebtedness to Denys the Short and Bede the Venerable!

After 2000 years, from being a small insignificant band of converts, initially lodged uneasily within another religion, Christianity has become proportionately the largest religious grouping in the world—roughly 2,400,000,000 Christians—and spread to every corner of the world. I mention this not in order to boast, but simply to acknowledge that the fact of it alone is historically and geographically mesmerizing. For good or ill, and the effect has been for both, Christianity can be counted as a cultural success story that cries out for explanation.

Part of an explanation that Christian philosophers and others sometimes offer is the spiritually sensitive one that Christianity has been able to meet human needs at profound spiritual levels. As these needs and levels are bound to vary for different people, it is a virtue that Christian faith has been able to generate a wide spectrum of religious types. These types, moreover, may even be portrayed as opposites. For example, Christianity has supported belief both in what transcendentalist theologians have called "the infinite qualitative distance between God and the world" and also what mystics have considered as the "sharp dart of longing love" that pierces "the cloud of unknowing," leaving the impression not of infinite distance but of a deep unity at the heart of all reality. Or again, Christianity has fostered both the strong articulation of love as the defining quality of our very humanity and simultaneously held out for justice in all our personal and social relationships.

We could set in contrast other human needs that Christian faith has sought to meet. So, it has catered for quietists as well as activists; it has appealed to the intellect as well as the emotions; it has raised up Mother Julian-type optimism that, in her celebrated phrase—"all shall be well, all manner of things shall be well"—as well as deep despair exemplified most severely by the doctrinal threat of eternal damnation in the flames of hell for those who are unrepentant of their wrong-doing. Perhaps through it all, the appeal of Christianity's central belief in the incarnation of the love of God embodied in human form has given human beings a sense of living within the presence of God who knows from the inside our deepest human needs, pains, and desires. In the person of Jesus, the claim goes, the greatest chasm that separates earth from heaven has been bridged. There is a bigger story of our being human after all: the material has been sanctified as a bearer of the divine, and that must be Good News.

Some have even wondered whether the *via media* positioning of the Christian incarnational outlook—half-way on the scale between the Semitic suspicion about divine embodiment and the Asiatic preponderance of it in many forms—is also a point in its favour: a kind of Hegelian synthesis of a prophetic thesis and a mystical antithesis, the two dominant currents of religious life covering all time and space, so far as we know them. This may be a juicy thought but of course it is highly speculative. As it is, we know that prophetic religions generate their mystical *alter ego*, and mystical religions their prophetic shadow.

Yet, no matter how inclusively Christianity has displayed its different types of religious expression, these appeals to its power for meeting human needs does not explain everything. Historically speaking, the rise and spread of Christianity has as much to do with its embroilment in political power as it has with its own inherent spiritual worth. In this sense, the American Christian feminist theologian, Rosemary Radford Ruether, has captured a grittier explanation of Christian cultural success. "The history of Christianity," she writes, "is a history of continual tension and conflict between two models of church: church as spirit-filled community and church as historical institution."[5] This is certainly a striking perspective: Christianity has not only generated phenomenologically different religious types, but also a dialectical struggle. So, it has inspired whole pacifist churches and also sanctioned state violence. It has been ruthlessly convinced of its own exclusive possession of the truth while, in some phases, accepted other witnesses to the truth beyond the church door. It has upheld the bourgeois capitalist ideal whilst also undermining it by championing the liberationist slogan of the gospel "bias to the poor." Between the transcendent aspiration of the spirit and the cautious drag of the institution's preservative instincts, there is bound to be tension. Christianity's cultural destiny has obviously been dependent on how that tension has been negotiated.

But there is more. The negotiation of historical tensions inevitably trails a shadow. There is every reason to think that Christianity's shameful shadow has been the Christian treatment of Judaism and the Jewish people. Historical connections can be traced between the Christian rejection of its ancestor-faith, the rise of theological anti-Judaism, cultural anti-Semitism, and the Jewish holocaust of the second world war. Christianity has been a

---

5. Ruether, *Women-Church*, 11.

major part of forging those connections. In other words, Christianity bears some relationship to, even a measure of responsibility for, the horrors of the holocaust. I shall return to this theme later in my lecture.

So far, I have outlined two kinds of contrasts: *phenomenological* contrasts between different types of religious expression and *historical* contrasts embedded in the struggles between institutional defensiveness and spirit-filled aspiration. They could both be expanded on at length. But all that I wish to note here is the obvious, but reluctantly acknowledged, point that Christian faith has been manifest in multifarious ways, even sometimes in seemingly irreconcilable ways. It has been impressive—producing heroes, such as the writer of John's Gospel, the pioneer hermit John Cassian, the author and illustrator of the Book of Kells, the spiritually versatile Hildegard of Bingen, the scholastic genius Thomas Aquinas, the painter Giotto, the musician Johan Sebastian Bach, the tough nun Mother Teresa, the martyr Martin Luther King. (You could make up your own list of heroes). It has also been hateful: burning witches and heretics, inspiring the Crusades, blessing battleships. But it is the sheer diversity in cultural expression that strikes the historian. In light of it, the celebrated historian of Christianity, Adrian Hastings, has asked the provocative question: "How does one portray the history of such a many-faced monster?"[6] Hastings does not intend his reference to a monster as an insult to Christianity, but more as a provocation to facing the central problem of Christian identity precipitated by 2000 years of history. His answer, perhaps not surprisingly, is that the central figure of Jesus, accompanied by the witness to him in the scriptures, is what holds Christianity together. This is an attractive minimalist answer and it can scarcely be gainsaid. We should remember, however, that this figure of Jesus is one who never wrote a word, and who, at least in Schweitzer's estimate, remains a stranger and enigma outside of first century eschatological times. Could we conjecture that, in spite of Schweitzer, it is precisely this enigmatic quality which has kept Christianity dynamic, and has been a spur to Christian inventiveness and to the search for its own soul?

FOUR KINDS OF INVENTIVENESS

I want now to illustrate the inventive quality of Christianity in four brief examples drawn from Christianity's 2000 years. I shall highlight: first, the creativity at the heart of the gospel tradition, involving therefore the core documents of Christian faith; second, the effect of the merger between Greek metaphysical thought and Hebrew ethical monotheism, the twin

---

6. Hastings, *World History*, 2.

pillars of classical Christianity; third, Christianity's characterization of itself as a historical religion; and finally, the greatest shift of all that has taken place in Christian consciousness, under the conditions known as modernity in western Enlightenment culture.

Gospel traditions

First then, the example of the New Testament gospel tradition. The gospels are second generation documents, written 40–70 years after the death of Jesus and the experience of what his first followers called his resurrection or exaltation by God. As the promise of Jesus's return to earth did not materialize in the lifetime of these first congregations, and in order that the memory of his impact was not lost, the gospels were written to carry his message into the future. They were not biographies of the saviour, but religious texts designed to meet the religious and survival needs of small fledgling churches. Therefore, a variety of layers of influences have fed into the making of these documents—oral reminiscences, pressures resulting from liturgical and pastoral practices in local churches, and finally the theological biases of the Gospel writers themselves.

It is probably with regard to the reshaping of the gospel traditions by the four evangelists that inventiveness is most readily observed. Take, for example, their four different portraits of Jesus. Mark's figure is a mysterious, angular, confrontational preacher of the Kingdom of God, who embraces his tragic suffering as a "ransom for many" and, as the doorway into this kingdom, invites his followers to share the same destiny. Matthew's portrayal is of a teacher of a "greater righteousness," a new Moses of the messianic end times, who makes impossible demands such as the outrageous challenge that nothing less than the love of one's enemy will be acceptable to God. Luke's Jesus is seemingly a more humane figure, a man who attracts by his power for telling a good tale and for modelling the very heroic compassion he advocates, especially towards the poor, and becoming himself the quintessential symbol of ideal humanity. Finally, John's portrait, long recognized as quite different in texture from the other three, is of a paradoxical Jesus, existing before time and identified with God's all-encompassing Word or Wisdom, whose enfleshment provides the clue to the very meaning of creation itself.

These declarations of Christian inventiveness in the gospel traditions can be illustrated further. If we accept the near universal scholarly consensus that Mark's gospel was written first, we can see that Matthew and Luke who copied him made their own alterations to his text. For example, they made additions: prefacing the opening of Mark's Gospel account with stories about the birth of Jesus, symbolic curtain-raisers containing all the major spiritual themes that were to follow in their lives of Jesus proper. They made deliberate alterations, such as the famous reversal of Mark's malleable words attributed to Jesus, "The one who is not against us is on our side," to Matthew's definite either-or version, "the one who is not with me is against me." It represents a defensive firming up of the Christian community's institutional boundaries by Matthew. (Incidentally, these two attitudes—having or not having partners for the sake of the Kingdom outside of the Christian group—represents an early argument that has a bearing on Christian relationships with other faith-communities in our own day. Suffice it to say that once Matthew made the reversal, Mark's potential openness became a lost cause, and Christian exclusivity on many levels was bound to ensue). Mark was added to, altered, and also enlarged upon. For example, at the end of Mark's Gospel the women who go to the tomb, wrongly expecting to anoint the body of Jesus, discover a young man who tells them that if they go to Galilee they will see him, as Jesus himself had promised them when he was alive. But the women do not do this, and they leave the scene in terror. This was all too much for Matthew and Luke: for how could the message of Jesus' resurrection have established itself if no-one told of it in the first instance? So Matthew and Luke took out the terror scene of Mark and enlarged their gospel endings by adding theological stories of their own, stories of visual encounter with the resurrected Jesus. The success of these alterations has been such that to this day discussion of the resurrection of Jesus is generally conducted in terms of the visual encounter with a risen body.

Why did Matthew and Luke make these changes of addition, alteration, and enlargement? Did they suppose they were correcting Mark, and thereby superseding his account? Did they think they were bringing out the truth of the gospel message as they saw it for their own circumstances? Whatever their motives, their changes were deliberate and not simply a matter of adding further information about their hero that was, as it were, lying around at the time. My point is that they were inventive. In many respects, of course, these moves were not out of the ordinary given the biblical style of truth-telling, a religious form more interested in the *meaning* of events than in what we would term strictly the *happening* of them. What we have are four versions of the gospel message, side by side, but also in some respects in tension with one another.

Ethical Monotheism and Rational Metaphysics

My second illustration of inventiveness takes us into the heartland of Christian cultural success and runs as follows: the twin pillars of Christian identity, combining Jewish ethical monotheism with a Jesus-twist, on the one hand, and Greek rational metaphysics, on the other, created a distinct religious configuration that has been the driving force of Christianity's expansive universalism for 2000 years.

It may be easy to see why this combination became so potent. On the one hand, ethical monotheism believes in one God who is providentially active for the whole world. On the other hand, speculative metaphysics believes in the power of the human mind for transcendent truth which, by definition, must apply throughout the whole world. Put the two together and a potency or creativity for ever-expanding religious explanations of human experience is launched. Once the Romans had destroyed Jerusalem and its Jewish Temple in 70 CE, and the "parting of the ways" between Jewish and Christian messianisms became inevitable by the end of the first century, the door was opened for Christianity to express its biblical heritage through a dominantly Greek intellectual matrix. In terms of Christian thought, Augustine of Hippo, in north Africa, was the first major Christian theologian to systematise more fully than any of his predecessors the ways of God with the world, from the dawn of creation to the final eschaton. This was Christian universalism with definite theological teeth.

Historians, however, also know that this theological universalism was enlisted in the service of cultural-imperial universalism, when Christianity was gradually adopted as the religion of the Greco-Roman empire through the fourth and fifth centuries. Greek culture thought of itself as universal and therefore superior; Christianity thought of itself as universal and therefore superior. It was a perfect match. The merger of the two superiorities created Christendom, with a sense of its own powerful universal destiny. The emperor Constantine's court-theologian, Eusebius of Caesarea, sums up the ideology of the Christendom mentality in the happy coincidence he conjectured between the time of Christian origins and the providential arrangement of Roman government:

> No one who reflects upon the matter can fail to be convinced that it was no mere accident that the majority of the nations of the world never came under the unifying rule of Rome until the time of Jesus. For his wonderful visitation of humankind coincided with Rome's attainment of the acme of power ... And no one can deny that it was not without God's help that this should have happened at the very same time that the teaching about

our Saviour took its rise. Consider the difficulties involved in the disciples' journeying, had the nations been under separate governments and therefore not having any dealings with one another. But with those separate governments abolished, the disciples could accomplish their projects in safety. The supreme God had smoothed the way before them, controlling the animosities of those hostile to true religion through fear of a strong central government.[7]

If it was not for the fascist overtones of Eusebius's appeal to strong government we might treat this extract as a piece of theological fun. It reads like a definite post-facto rationalisation reflecting the change in fortune which Eusebius experienced as the church changed from being a persecuted minority to being a group destined to become the favoured majority. Yet Eusebius's theological inventiveness justified the terms of reference for Christendom for centuries to come. Among other matters, it issued in the notion of the Holy Roman Empire. This Empire lasted in Western Europe from its revival with the coronation of Charlemagne, Charles the Great, on Christmas Day in 800 CE, to the time when Napoleon took the alternative title Emperor of the French in 1804, and when Francis II two years later relinquished the title altogether and became Emperor of Austria. In Eastern Europe, it took another century, until 1917 and the Communist Revolution, for the notion of Christendom finally to give up the ghost. Christian universalism, then—one faith for the whole world—both legitimated political authority as well as received the latter's protection, in a very distinctive Christian theocratic rule.

The notion of Christian universalism has had other effects, not least in providing the inspiration and drive for the missionary endeavours of the churches. The reasons for Christian mission are complex and have changed over twenty centuries. In the early days it was the eschatological horizon—the coming of God's Kingdom—that provided the motivation. In the pre-Constantine centuries the blood of the martyrs played a part. Since Constantine, and on through the Middle Ages, it was the theocratic ideology of Christendom that supplied the *raison d'être*. Christian divisions which forced some to flee centres of power have also played a not inconsiderable role in mission—for example, the establishment of Nestorian Christianity outside of Byzantium, eventually ending up in China, because of help from the so-called Silk Road, in the seventh century. The spread of monastic communities, beginning with the hermits of the Egyptian desert in the third century and later with the religious orders of the Middle Ages, have played

---

7. Eusebius, *Demonstratio*, 30–3.

their part, as have pilgrimage routes and the Crusades. In its most recent phase, over the last 500 years, the tie-up between Christian missionary universalism and colonial expansion from the West around the globe has left its indelible mark. Christian mission has been bombastic, insensitive, aggressive, and triumphalist. It has also displayed great sensitivity, as for example, when the Jesuit Fr. Matteo Ricci adopted the dress of the men of letters in sixteenth century China, in a bid to relate the Gospel to Chinese customs and traditions; or in the example of the Dominican, Fr. Bartolomé de Las Casas, who came to take the side of the indigenous Indians and protested against the brutalities of the Spanish colonising the West Indies early in the sixteenth century.

With the end of western colonial rule in the twentieth century, churches in former colonial territories have turned to developing their own indigenous forms of Christian faith. The current fashionable missionary notion of inculturation is intended to create the theological space for the development of a truly authentic Indian or African or south American Christianity, while simultaneously seeking to exorcise the demon of colonial domination. Inculturation gives permission for the evolution, even mutation, of universal Christian faith in many forms. It also creates the conditions for the notion of mutual mission between many emergent forms of Christianity, and for the end of western hegemony in determining Christian identity. Christianity is now said to be growing most rapidly in the two-thirds developing world, though this must be as much to do with population explosion as with conversion.

Authority of the past

I turn now to my third area of Christian inventiveness. Again, it derives from the early centuries, but it has coloured every subsequent period. I refer to the way in which Christian identity established orthodoxy (right belief) in contrast to orthopraxy (right behaviour) as the theological nervous system of a whole faith-tradition.

Let me explain further. As Christianity survived into its second century inevitably questions would arise over what was different about this faith. Jews had their own story, their ancestors, prophets, and heroes, as did other religious groupings in the empire. What was the Christian story and how was it different? The Church had to have one, not only for its own spiritual benefit, but also because venerability supplied the passport for religious acceptance in the Roman empire. Differentiation came to centre largely on belief. But how was one to decide correct belief? The scriptures did not speak with one voice, theologians said different things, churches had adopted local colourings in their attitudes and customs. Part of the answer lay in an appeal to the authority of the past, and it is this style of decision-making about belief which I take to be the greatest legacy of Christianity's classical period. We are talking of the ancient Greek world, and that world was besotted with the past. Thus Plato: "The ancients are better than we, for they dwelled nearer to the gods."[8] And "nearer to the gods" in the Christian view was the period of the Apostles. Therefore, that which is in agreement with the apostles must be real Christian truth. It is this fixation on the past that has determined the shape of Christian truth down the ages. When in later years the Church would split into its three main branches of Orthodox, Catholic, and Protestant, all three made appeal to the past in order to legitimate their particular claims. The Catholics looked to the western Fathers, and later created the church's teaching office as a guarantor of the apostles teaching; the Orthodox looked to the eastern Fathers and supplemented this with addiction to an unchanging Liturgy as the embodiment of Christian truth in doxological (worship) form; the Protestants gave birth to Biblical Theology, a species of theology which holds that the Bible somehow supplies its own controls for true Christian believing in every generation. Each of Christianity's three main branches is quite different in style and content, but all share the platonic ideal of the past being nearer to the gods.

There is more to the platonic ideal. Not only the past, but the past as *unchanging* was the further important point. Theologians therefore battled to find the unchanging Christian truth. As this was hard to come by, church councils had to be called from time to time to settle disputes. From these arrangements the place of Creeds assumed importance in Christian identity. Signing on the dotted line of belief is what counted and continues to demarcate Christian affiliation. Unchanging essence, purity of form, single truth, all this was held in God's eternal store, and in Jesus and the apostles it was given to earth. The first versions of Christian history were written to reassure believers and sceptics alike that this eternal truth had indeed been preserved. Henceforth history would be written as a contest between the orthodox good guys and the heretical bad guys, the true believers versus the enemies of pristine truth. For a long time, the history of Christianity was written as the history of doctrinal truth. One consequence of this has been the condemnation of Christianity to a lifetime of quarrelling, and this is surely one of the least attractive features of its history.

---

8. Cited by Wilken, *Myth*, 50.

The notable historian of Christianity, Robert Wilken, has summed up this symbiotic entanglement between the idealization of the past and the Christian search for identity extremely well. He writes:

> To serve the needs of their age, Christians in the second and third centuries constructed a historical portrait of Christianity whose outstanding characteristics were antiquity, tradition, continuity, and unity. In their construction, they shunned change and innovation, diversity, and discontinuity...[9]

The interesting point throughout this whole early period is that both sides of the argument accused the other of novelty. With hindsight we can now see how everyone was involved in novelty of a sort: the past in need of interpretation cannot avoid it. Historically speaking, we look back and see "change and innovation, diversity and discontinuity" at every turn, the very problematics that the ancients could never integrate into their intellectual styles of comprehension. Wilken adds that this construction of what he calls "the myth of Christian beginnings" was undertaken "for good reasons." In other words, they could do no other. But it does leave open the question for us of how best to characterise the Christian past, given twenty centuries of hindsight.

Impact of Enlightenment

I come now to my fourth area illustrating Christian inventiveness. This brings us to the modern period, by which I mean that period in European history which begins with the Enlightenment of the late seventeenth century and which is now beginning to receive severe criticism from philosophers and others. Some might have expected me to point to the Protestant Reformation as the start of the modern period in Christian history. Certainly, the Reformation and its aftermath unleashed an abundance of Christian inventiveness. It centred chiefly on the Bible, as witnessed by the famous words of the Anglican divine, scholar and fellow of Trinity College, Oxford, William Chillingworth (1602–1644): "The Bible, I say, the Bible only is the religion of Protestants."[10] Then the divisive effects of the Reformation altered the map of Christian adherence permanently. Of the one billion Christians in the world, roughly 575,000,000 are said to be Roman Catholic, 300,000,000 Protestant, and 125,000,000 Orthodox. And Protestant splinter groups continue to sprout up in all corners of the globe. Despite these

9. Wilken, *Myth*, 51.
10. Chillingworth, *Religion of Protestants* (1638).

massive inventive effects, however, I consider the Reformation really to be a bridge period between late European medievalism and the beginnings of modernity. The paradigm shift initiated by the Enlightenment has had a far greater impact on Christian inventiveness than the Reformation.

I am tempted to say that the modern world has been so successful in its permeation of western Christian culture that Christianity has virtually been remade in the latter's image. Consider the following two instances of this transformation of Christian faith in modern times: first, from the field of social ethics, and second, from the Christian attitude towards other religions, and in particular its half-parent religion, Judaism, and first-cousin, Islam.

First, then, from the field of social ethics. Along with everyone else in modern democratic societies, the Christian churches have come to take the language of human rights for granted. Yet this has not always been the case. In the middle of the nineteenth century the language of human rights was too bound up with theories of revolution, or with anti-church currents, for human rights to be acceptable to the Christian mind. Human rights felt like human grasping and pride, and supporting them seemed also to undermine religious authority, which was perhaps more to the point. By the end of the twentieth century, however, no-one has been more vigorous than Pope John-Paul II in his defence of human rights all over the globe. After a full survey across the Christian ecumenical spectrum, the American theologian, Robert Traer, concludes: "For many Christians today, human rights are as clear as God's creative and redemptive presence and as compelling as life itself. Human rights are at the heart of what they believe and affirm to be their common faith."[11] Human rights is a thoroughly modern notion, but now it occupies the heart of Christian common faith! Similar sentiments could be expressed over the Christian support for the related vision of democracy. Apart from the support given to democracy by some of the Protestant Dissenters from the radical wing of the early Reformation, the democratic vision was largely held suspect by the Church. Today it is embraced fairly unreservedly by all the churches as the best possible option among all political systems of human governance which are said to reflect the values of the kingdom of God.

Christian inventiveness in the modern world entails that many of the values which Christian faith once approached with great caution come finally to be embraced by it. A major historical landmark for this whole development was of course the second Vatican Council of the Roman Catholic Church in the early 1960s.

---

11. Traer, *Faith in Human Rights*, 92.

My second instance of reversal in Christian thought in the modern period comes from the attitude of the churches towards other faith-traditions, and in particular towards Jews and Muslims as kindred spirits in sharing the monotheistic ethos. It is worth considering the case of each relationship separately, for the history of the two relationships is quite different.

Once castigated as a pariah people, the Jewish people are now being restored in Christian eyes, as a people whose covenant with God remains irrevocable (to use the technical theological term). So, the Jewish religion has not been superseded theologically by Christianity, as 2000 years of Christian teaching has always insisted. This is now the position of all the major denominations, through their official pronouncements. What we have are two different religious trajectories, each dependent upon and developing from the Hebrew scriptures: rabbinic Judaism and Hellenistic Christianity.

It is worth recalling the depth of Christian antipathy towards Judaism in order to realise the extent of this reversal. The history of rejection regarding Judaism and the Jews has, of course, been appalling. Initially, Christians were cast out from the synagogues, but with the alliance between Christian faith and state power after Constantine, eventually the tables were turned. In Christendom, Christian theological anti-Judaism, attested already in the New Testament, was eventually transformed into Christian anti-Semitism. The accusation of the Jews as Christ-killers and God-killers, a crime that clearly warranted punishment, gave permission for Christian rulers to arrange for the Jewish people to be treated as a subjugated race. Only after the terrible events of the Jewish Holocaust in the second world war and the founding of the state of Israel was the church made to face up to the Christian "teaching of contempt" against the Jews, as the Jewish writer, Jules Isaac, poignantly named it as the title of his book.[12] In general terms, it is now accepted that this teaching had some, albeit elusive, but nonetheless real part to play in preparing the cultural ground for the Holocaust. The Christian reversal of its view of its Jewish heritage, therefore, has its motivation in horror.

This has not been the case in respect of Christian relations with Islam and Muslims. Unlike Jews, Muslims have wielded power and have sought to spread a civilisation. This brought them into confrontation with the Christian empire directly. Christianity and Islam each harbors its separate history of militaristic advance over the other. Christians can point, firstly, to the rapid conquests of Christian lands in the mid-seventh to mid-eighth Christian centuries by a new religion which posed a major threat to the integrity of Christendom as such; and second, to the Ottoman bid for world

---

12. Isaac, *Teaching of Contempt*, (1964).

supremacy in the fifteenth to seventeenth centuries. In their turn, Muslims remind Christians of the medieval crusades and of the Christian entanglement in western imperialism over Muslim lands in more recent centuries. It is not long, in serious conversation with Muslims, before the ghostly and ghastly subjects of suspicion, rivalry and war between two religiously based civilisations come to haunt the dialogue table. Yet the history of Christian-Muslim relations is infinitely more complex than the broad stereotyping associated with the history of warfare would lead us to believe, and therefore it is important to keep a sense of perspective. For example, it may be that the crusades loom larger in contemporary debate than perhaps their impact historically warrants. As Jeremy Johns has written: "The crusades did not amount to a military threat to Islam, nor did the Muslim counter-attack threaten Christianity."[13] If that is so, then reckoning with the crusades should not be made the major stumbling-block for relations between Muslims and Christians today.

Theologically speaking, in relation to Islam Christian faith found itself placed as a kind of preparation or forerunner to the greater Islamic truth, a similar move made earlier by Christianity in its theological down-grading of Judaism. Jews and Christians could be called "people of the book" in Islam, but it was clear that the Hebrew and Christian bibles were nevertheless inferior witnesses to the final purity of Qur'anic truth. Like Jews before them, Christians did not like to be so upstaged. Therefore, Christian hostile polemic against Islam at the theological level made its mark early in the Christian encounter with Islam. The historian, Vivian Green, has summed up this aspect of the Christian response to Islam: "Yet by and large, the Church regarded Islam as a creation of Satan and a threat to the integrity of the Christian faith which had to be destroyed, by force if necessary."[14] Muslims have a legitimate grievance that there is nothing in historic Christianity which is equivalent to the Islamic notion of the "people of the book."

However, it is also important to note that the Christian response to Islam has not always been so negatively circumscribed: there are some alternative views, albeit of minority status in Christian history. In the Church of the eastern empire, for example, the ridicule of Islam's claim to be descended from Abraham promulgated by John of Damascus (c.675–c.750) was off-set by the more conciliatory tone of the Nestorian patriarch, Timothy I (780–823), author of the *Parable of the Pearl*, which was a Syriac apology for Christian faith set out as a debate with the Abbasid caliph al-Mahdi (775–85). Timothy compares Muhammad to Moses favourably, because

13. Johns, "Christianity and Islam," 166.
14. Green, *New History of Christianity*, 90.

of their agreed prophetic contempt for idolaters. Then in the high Middle Ages of the western Church, the Islamic writings of, for example, Avempace, Averroes, and Avicenna made a substantial impression on thinkers, such as the thirteenth century Christian philosopher figures of Roger Bacon (Franciscan) and Thomas Aquinas (Dominican). Admittedly, the motivation for this hospitality to Islamic systems of thought was mixed, yet it still remains the case that the historical legacy is not all negative. More research of this kind of historical interaction between these two communities of religious commitment remains to be done. It will be a welcome antidote to the antagonistic picture that colours all Christian-Muslim relations.

As Islam assumed proportions as a civilisation, in the way that Judaism did not espouse such aspirations, Christianity's relationship to Islam has undoubtedly been different from that with Judaism. If the holocaust has been a major factor in the Christian re-assessment of relations with Judaism, an equivalent historical occurrence cannot be so easily found propelling a change in direction for relations with Islam. However, among other factors, one could point to the following: the need to stamp out the damaging and disfiguring stereotypical images that many have of Islam; the ending of Christendom allowing, simultaneously, a theological space for a positive re-assessment of the meaning of Islam as a universal religion; the rise in Islamic confidence, in some parts of the world, as an alternative to secularist models of political life.

In general terms, however, the movement for change in Christianity's response to Judaism and Islam now affects Christian relations with all the world religions. From being positioned either as beyond the providential pale or as a preparation for the greater light of the Gospel, people of other major world religions are slowly coming to be viewed as partners in a dialogue which is marked by the search for both mutual understanding and active co-operation, for the sake of improving that most elusive of goals—the "common good." Certainly, the mainstream Christian traditions have now given themselves theological permission to enter such swirling waters. But while dialogue has become a portmanteau term for all kinds of activities and shared endeavours between the faiths, cautious voices still sound off about its wisdom. Dialogue has about it the whiff of what one theologian has called parity between traditions, and it is this that rings alarm bells for some. It suggests an unprivileged level playing field in our perceptions of religious meaning and truth. However, if the Global Dialogue Institute at Temple University in Philadelphia is correct in believing that the dialogical principle not only represents a "whole new way of thinking" but also forms "the very basis of *all* reality,"[15] then obviously we are at the beginnings of a sea-change in our perception of religious truth itself. During the last twenty years the Christian theological library of reflection on religious pluralism has expanded exponentially. The same is beginning to happen with other faith-communities. What has yet to be harnessed are the fruits of dialogue, and it is these that I believe will propel Christianity even further towards inventiveness in its relationship with other faith-communities and faith-visions, and hence with the other two-thirds of the world's population. The globalising forces affecting all dimensions of life render its advance unstoppable.

NEEDED: A MORE MODEST FUTURE

It is time to draw my thoughts to a provisional conclusion. 2000 years is a long time, though still a relatively short time as historic religions go, and in the eyes of the Divine Life a mere twinkle. I have spoken of that time as one of inventiveness in four areas of Christian existence, and each area has of course its own implications. First, I have pointed to the inventiveness of the gospel tradition as one which demonstrates Christian faith as a dynamic and open movement already in its basic scriptural texts. As part of the meaning of faith itself, such inventiveness was a spiritual move of genius that provided Christianity with a kind of built-in permission to adapt itself according to new needs and demands that would unfold in the future. Second, I have highlighted the intellectual power that stems from the twin strands of Christian thought in biblical ethical monotheism and Greek metaphysics. This interweaving of two strands provided Christianity with its basic theological language and universalist vision, thereby underpinning its expansionist missionary interests. The remarkable consequence of this marriage has been that Christian faith is now a world religion in every sense of that word. Third, I have spoken of the dominant Christian theological view of its own history as an inventive vehicle that secured the past-centred focus for assessing Christian truth. It promoted a faith that was strong on continuity but weak on dealing effectively with historical change. Moreover, it condemned Christianity to a history of quarrelling as it divided people and movements into orthodox and heretical categories. The consequence of this development has been that Christian vision lost its perspective on the future as a realm of promise, new truth, and vitality. Finally, I have held up the modern period as the period of greatest inventiveness. From having been suspicious of the humanistic and democratic spirit that developed at

15. Swidler and Gangadean, "Technology of Deep-Dialogue," 1–6.

the beginning of modernity, Christianity has learned to embrace a different ethos, more accepting of human achievement and more open to truth from different quarters. In particular, it is learning to undo a painful track-record in relation to Judaism and to create a new partnership with Islam and people of other faith-communities through dialogue.

The combination of biblical monotheism and Greek metaphysics has certainly produced some elegant systems of Christian thought, some daring treatises of mystical intuition, and a whole raft of spiritualities in ever-expanding multiple forms. The sum of Christian thought and experience has been considerable. Yet how do we receive this Christian universalism today? Given the idealisation of the pull of the past, it is easy to think of the sum of Christian thought and experience as an answer to the problems of today. In some respects, the same kinds of problems do crop up again and again through Christian history—problems such as faith versus works, or mysticism versus rationality, or history versus myth. But a better historical perspective realizes that the sum of Christian thought and experience to date is the product of arguments and reflections of particular times and places. What we argue about now may on the surface seem similar—the great themes of love, suffering, human worth, sex, the meaning of life, are perennially familiar—but the truth is that we experience these matters in quite different terms from the past. So we are left to find our own solutions. It will surely be necessary to escape the idealization of the past if Christianity is to flourish in the future. God speaks to every age equally, so a historian avers, and so a theologian might believe.

At the end of the first century, sophisticated intellectuals ridiculed Christianity for being atheistic (they did not have the right view of the gods), for indulging in cannibalism (they consumed body and blood in a sacred meal), and for being rather unvirile (they worshipped a figure on a cross and generally were absent from the army). At the end of the twentieth century, sophisticated intellectuals dismiss Christianity for different reasons: for being too theistic and presenting an untenable set of propositions about the world and its alleged Creator; for enacting meaningless rituals; and for having been too virile in its blessings on the weapons of war. In between these eras—early survival and present anxiety—Christianity has flourished and offered the world hope through its distinctive symbol of the dying and rising of a saviour. It has also exercised power, and power corrupts. Therefore, the loss of power might help Christianity discover its soul afresh, as a summons from the future rather than a repetition of the past.

In some respects, one could make a case for saying that Christianity survived against the odds: its first dreams of the return of its Lord came to naught; its unlikely central symbol was an instrument of brutal torture and death; it was born under dictatorship. But survive it did, and then it flourished. Perhaps in our own age and culture which is radically secular, plural, dialogical, and critically aware, Christianity is having to learn a second lesson in survival after two millennia, or at least a greater modesty about itself. Surely that is no bad thing.

Speaking theologically, some might judge that my category of inventiveness does not do proper justice to what has taken place in the history of Christianity. It seems too neutral, even free-floating. But I believe it does describe what has happened. I could also appeal to the philosophic recognition that knowledge is not, as it were, a carbon copy of reality, but an *interpretation* of reality which is conditioned by all kinds of historical and cultural processes, and that this challenges many of the assumptions that yearn for stable patterns of Christian thought. No matter how hard Christian theologians have tried to turn the truths of the past into timeless truths, they are bound to be defeated. Of course, I accept that viewing the past in this way brings us to the brink of historical relativism, always a boo-word for those whose faith relies on well-established foundations. But the historian knows that the past bequeaths a set of arguments: often good arguments, interesting arguments, sometimes pointless arguments, but arguments nonetheless. Christianity, as the philosophers might say, has become a contested site. In these circumstances we cannot help but become inventive. Inventiveness in this sense is a category useful not only to historians but also to theologians. All that is required is for theologians and the churches to see it so.

Christianity has shown remarkable agility in negotiating intellectual challenges and institutional change. The task now I believe is for Christianity to declare itself intellectually, institutionally, and ethically in more modest terms. The contemporary struggle in Christian faith and life is between, on the one hand, those who want to reinstate what they perceive to be Christian truth, declared and defined in the past, but which has since been sullied by secularism and unbelief, and those, on the other hand, who want the church to be more provisional about its sense of what is possible for the future. Both groups will be inventive. The most strait-jacketed approach to the reinstating of the past is so-called Christian Fundamentalism. But Christian Fundamentalism, like any Fundamentalism, is a new religion, invented during a time of perceived decline. Historically, Christianity has just never existed in that form before now. More sophisticated conservative theologians might complain that a line of approach which relies on inventiveness as a guiding principle pretends to be escaping tradition, and that in reality there is no alternative to placing oneself under the umbrella of tradition, even if not all of tradition needs repeating for the future. The problem with this approach, it seems to me, is that while it is true to say that we cannot escape the past, it is also true to say that we are not bound by it. Moreover, the past is too various for "tradition" to be able to do the theological work that traditionalists want it to do. Therefore, it seems better for the church to reorientate itself on the future and not the past, looking to many quarters for the truth of our world and our humanity. Dialogue across many boundaries really will become the name of the theological game. Expressed differently, we could urge that the past be viewed as a spur and not a dictator for theological inventiveness in the future.

Christianity is a faith that is continually in search of its own identity.

'CHRISTIANITY: 2,000 YEARS OF INVENTIVENESS'—A MUSLIM CRITIQUE

Maryam Jameelah[16]

All the major historic religions of the world, regardless of differences in doctrines, creeds, and rituals, have always been committed to the concept of objective Truth which remains the Truth regardless of man's belief or unbelief. All are characterized by supreme reverence for sacred and absolute transcendental theological and moral values. All have inspired complete civilizations affecting every aspect of private and public life including great artistic and other cultural endeavors. In their explanation of the meaning and purpose of life and man's place in the universe, all concentrate on the Absolute, the eternal and timeless and man's direct responsibility to the Divine for giving his accountability for his life on earth. This has always been true especially of Christianity and Islam. Both the Christian and Muslim of medieval days could have understood each other very well had they only allowed themselves to do so. Tragically, they did not!

It is only recently that dialogue across religious boundaries is being promoted for inter-faith understanding and cooperation. The only valid purpose of dialogue should be to forge a united front of all the world religions against the forces of atheism, materialism, secularism, and modernism that equally threaten them all. Otherwise, dialogue has no justification and at best should be approached with extreme caution.

At least medieval Christian hostility to Islam was honest, frank, and open. The Muslim must, however, beware of present Christian underhand and very subtle tactics expressed in deceptively mild language luring him

---

16. Maryam Jameelah was an American-Pakistani author of over thirty books on Islamic culture and history, and a prominent female voice for conservative Islam. She was born 1934 in New York and died 2012 in Lahore, Pakistan.

during the process of dialogue to the modern heresies of evolutionism, historicism, relativism, and subjectivism. All are wholeheartedly adopted by the Anglican parish priest whose faith is much more in Darwinian evolution than in Christianity. Only an out-and-out modernist could describe his religious faith in terms of innovation and change or what this priest terms as future-oriented constant inventiveness. In fact, this is no religion at all, not even Christianity as it had always been understood, at least before Vatican II.

The priest now declares his task is to formulate Christianity in more humble and modest terms when all that should count for him is whether Christianity is the Truth or not—there is no alternative. The modernism of this priest is dangerously akin to agnostic humanism, like Felix Adler's Ethical Culture Movement, the Unitarians or the Bahá'í. Lack of faith in their own beliefs characterizes the malaise of Western churches. The irreverence of this priest for his own historic past, particularly the medieval Roman Church, is eloquent testimony to that. The reader must note the absence of reference to the Divinity where mention of God is conspicuously absent.

This Anglican priest embraces the heresies of evolutionism and progressivism—a future bliss on earth made possible by science and technology replacing Paradise in heaven. He is eager to trace his faith from its "primitive" and "backward" forms in medieval times to the advanced enlightenment of today. In other words, he is convinced that religion automatically improves with the passage of time so that the newest version must always be superior to the old and obsolete. This is diametrically opposed to Tradition in all the world religions which teach that mankind was best at his origin after which he degenerated. Degenerate humans can be redeemed by correct faith and practice known through Divine revelation. Humankind achieves salvation not by changing with the times but by embracing timeless absolute Truth.

For a long time, the Roman Church fought religious modernism with all its strength. Every Catholic priest was compelled to denounce verbally all the tenets of modernism before ordination. The Roman Church was likened to a solid rock which never changes. All that was drastically reversed by Vatican II.

The priest feels proud to declare his inventive faith as a great success story throughout the entire world. An inventive faith prizing, above all, constant change, innovation, and newness, must be by definition purely human-made. As for his parish church, he will find it nearly empty. Since Vatican II, he must admit to an unprecedented mass exodus from the church, from the priesthood and nuns from the convents as the new innovative faith fails to inspire conviction or commitment. Irreligion in Europe has become so strong that even priests hesitate to mention the Name of God, much less his reward or punishment in the Hereafter, for fear of unpopularity.

Over the destruction of Christian Tradition, Muslims have no cause for rejoicing because the disintegration of one religion leads to the destruction of others and the prevailing irreligion in the West cannot but deeply affect the East, not least, the whole of *Dar al-Islam*.

Let the downfall of Christendom be a lesson and a warning for all Muslims!

A RESPONSE TO MARYAM JAMEELAH

I am grateful to Maryam Jameelah for her response to my article "Christianity: 2000 Years of Inventiveness." My title was chosen carefully, if also mischievously. All of us write from particular perspectives, and my intention was to elicit the sense in which human beings are not only receivers of religious truth but also makers of it. That is a significant divide, and Maryam Jameelah is on one side and I am on the other. She raises a fear, shared by many across the boundaries of separated traditions, that once traditional forms of expressing religious truth are placed under critical scrutiny, this is but the first step on the road to religions oblivion. Talk of inventiveness seems simply to sum up this whole way of thinking. I believe that while her reaction is understandable, it is also regrettable morally, and probably untenable intellectually.

Maryam draws attention to two styles of religious believing. On the one side are those who think that being faithful entails adherence to a set of unchanging truths, givenness in revelation, idealism in ethics, and repetition in spiritual praxis. Unchanging truth is to be found by looking backwards to an imagined time of perfection and clarity. The Divine (God, Allah) is outside of time, but our role is to shape our humanity and the world according to perceived timeless values. On the other side are those who think that faithfulness consists is responding to the Divine as this is glimpsed on the inside of life's circumstances and is shaped by the mundane forces of culture, time, and place. This view thinks of the historical flow of time itself as the locus for religious truth, which thereby becomes a matter of interpreting religious experience in relation to the best of flawed human knowledge at any one time. The origins of a tradition have an intrinsic place in this scheme of understanding but have no privileged access to the nature of the Divine.

My own leaning is towards the latter approach, mainly because I do not see how I can ignore the effects of historical change as an intellectual challenge. Christianity just has been different in different ages. There have been views that supposed it has always been the same, and this was an attitude that set in at an early moment in Christian history. However, there were reasons for thinking like this and I discussed some of them in my article. But these reasons were involved in significant distortions of the past, such as the view that all the Christian gospel writers spoke with one voice. They did not; and I am therefore left incorporating that evidence into my understanding. Christianity is really a series of Christianities. If I may venture to suggest it, historical observation demonstrates also that Islam has been internally diverse and continues to be so.

How may both Muslims and Christians absorb the observations about historical change into their understandings—for themselves first, and then about and for each other?

It is important not to misunderstand my position. I was writing mainly as an historian. If I had written mainly as a theologian, I would have involved myself more in the doctrine of God, as Maryam would have liked. However, the issue would have been the same: how to interpret change in relation to the notion of God? Classical Christianity and classical Islam both have a difficult task here. How does the providence of God relate to the notion of human freedom? Does God command or does God invite? How we answer will depend not just on our received views of the Divine, but on how we experience the circumstances of life in the present.

It is a pity that Maryam polarizes the choice before us as one between obedience to received truths or reliance on materialism and secularism. This is a caricature and like all caricatures tells us more about the one believing the caricature than the real position of the one being critiqued. Genuinely thought-out criticism is always welcome, caricature is not. I did not say that modern reliance on technological progress substitutes for Paradise in heaven, or that religion improves with the passage of time. I hold no myth of progress, and indeed hold that progress is always ambivalent. My use of the term "inventiveness" was designed playfully to draw attention to the observation that it is human beings who shape culture, knowledge, and spiritual understanding. As I understand it, Islam has a high view of human responsibility, so why should "inventiveness" be problematic?

Yet there *is* progress from time to time. I am glad that the churches have given up thinking of torture as an instrument of God's punishment for wrongdoing. I am glad to support human rights, so long as they balanced by community and social rights. I am glad that we have repented of anti-Semitism. I am glad that serious Christian theologians no longer think that Islam is a terrible mistake. I am pleased that I do not have to compromise my intellect by believing that the world was literally made in six days. I am pleased to think that the insights of literary criticism can help me enlarge my understanding of Christian scriptures.

I do not have irreverence for the past. The past was simply different. We learn from it. But we are not bound by it: we have to discern. St. Augustine said some wonderful things about love. He also said some terrible things—about hell, for example—and who was destined for it. All of us discriminate in relation to the past, whether or not we own up to it. The past hands us a set of arguments about the nature of God and human community and many other matters. That is reason enough for learning from the past. It is also an invitation to find our own answers afresh for our own time. Some of those answers, of course, may be the same as have been given in the past. But some will not be.

I would like to make one final remark in relation to the dialogue between religions. I do not think that it would be good to enter dialogue on the basis that religious people join forces to combat the secular world. That sounds too belligerent and the world suffers enough belligerence, from religious as well as secular quarters. It seems to me like falling into the trap of splitting—imagining all the good to rest with those who are religiously committed and all the bad with everyone else. The religions have scarcely been innocent when it comes to propagating violence in the world. The dialogue could start with dispelling the caricatures we have of one another. After that, we could ask a similar question of one another. Muslims could ask themselves: "Why are there so many Christians in the world?"; and Christians could ask: "Why are there so many Muslims?" If we believe in the providence of God, what is God up to by allowing different traditions, *each impressive in their own ways*, to motivate so many people on their spiritual paths? All traditions hold that the transcendence of God (or ultimate reality/truth) far exceeds our human grasp of God's purposes. That too would provide a humble and *faithful* enough reason for dialogue. I invite Maryam Jameelah to the new world of dialogue.

2

Quarrying Tradition

THIS CHAPTER OUTLINES FURTHER the trajectory of the hermeneutical principles deriving from historical research into Christian faith as a phenomenological reality. It argues against a notion of tradition as a fixed marker of identity and for a philosophically more open and provisional outlook as a result of engagement with secular and other-religious experience.

We are heirs to tradition, yet to live out of tradition alone is not enough. More accurately, if more clumsily: in a pluralistic society we are heirs to a number of traditions—Christian, other religious and secular—but they do not wholly define who we are. This is the paradox I wish to explore, and I begin by drawing out the problem with a journalistic analogy.

I was once told that, in the days before *perestroika*, in order to spot any new thing that was being said in a Soviet newspaper, it was necessary to look at least three quarters of the way down the article. As a way of reinforcing the predetermined structure of the whole, the newness was said to be hidden within a lengthy rehearsal of Party ideology. Whether or not the accusation was true, the point being made was clear. Many a Christian theology textbook, it seems to me, could be examined along similar lines. There is a given shape to a problem, and following the historical rehearsal of its track record, we finally arrive at the modern discussion as the latest involvement in a continuous narrative.

Now, while it has been entirely possible to analyze tradition in that way, my suspicion is that it has become increasingly difficult to do so. This is the result of a number of factors: the recognition that the Christian faith has been an immensely varied phenomenon *historically*; the breakdown in critical thought of the role and notion of authority, itself so much bound up with the concept of tradition; the historical observation that tradition has functioned ideologically; and the realization of how much individual factors are present as a dimension of a theologian's craft. In this light, the concept of tradition seems in need of its own *perestroika*.

Tradition is now regaining a central place as a major factor in Christian theology, though mainly, I suggest, for reactive reasons. Both the impact of a period of deconstruction through the application of the critical method, and the prospects of pluralism in religion and culture, have precipitated a sense of disorientation in the life of faith. In these circumstances, the bid to recapture tradition is an understandable reaction. At one extreme, Fundamentalism's popularity is one manifestation of this mood; at the other is the sophisticated re-appropriation of tradition as a *sine qua non* of theological enquiry proper.[1] But the difficulties are more deep-seated than either reaction might be prepared to admit.

The cluster of problems involved in "tradition" (the inverted commas implying both a category for discussion and a sense of awkwardness about thinking we know what we mean when we use the term) includes at least the following: (a) the history of diversity, (b) the concept of the "dynamic of tradition," and (c) the ideological use that is often made of it.

I wish to comment on each of these three aspects of the total problem, before suggesting how a more relaxed view might bring some benefits for the life of faith and theological enquiry.

HISTORY OF DIVERSITY

On the institutional level it is usual to conceive of Christian diversity as three-fold: Orthodox, Catholic, and Protestant. But diversity in Christian faith predates this division and has given rise to numerous attempts to characterize it in the main as a problem of identity. Famous was the attempt of Bishop Vincent from the Mediterranean island of Lérins in the fifth century CE. His hypothesis that the true faith is "that which has been believed everywhere, always, and by all"[2] pointed to what all Christians held in common, a kind of highest common factor approach. There are samenesses

---

1. For a sophisticated view, see Lindbeck, *Nature of Doctrine*, 1984.
2. Vincent of Lérins, *Commonitorium*, Ch. 2.

and differences in the diverse teachings, but it is the samenesses that count. Not many would subscribe to that manner of handling the problem now, though versions of it are prone to reappearing today in Christian ecumenical discussions. Then, in the twelfth century, there was Pierre Abélard (1079–1142), who collected a list of quotations from the Church Fathers on 158 questions and placed them side by side. The divergence was inevitably immense: hence the title of his book, Sic et Non (Yes and No). Abélard used many devices to explain differences in what most assumed was an identifiable tradition of teachings. But in the face of genuine contradictions, he said that "the one that is more powerfully attested and has been more fully substantiated is to be preferred."[3] This might sound reasonable and eirenic enough. But the problem, as Abélard conceived it, ran essentially along the lines of eternal truth and its contradiction in history, rather than how best to characterize comprehensively the change and movement that are actually found in history.

It is possible therefore to solve the problem of tradition by appealing to unchanging platonic substance and changing historical embodiment. But historical consciousness really does undo this line of approach. No matter how loudly theologians proclaim that Christian traditions are (in some sense) the result of divine inspiration, they cannot do so in a manner which relegates their roots in culture and history to a position of secondary significance. Being a Christian in the first century is different from being a Christian in the fourth century, in the thirteenth century, and so on. It seems an obvious point to make now, but many theologians are still reluctant to acknowledge the consequences. Pressing historical consciousness and cultural diversity even further, one could say that "tradition" yields an even more various face: there are black, white, yellow, and brown traditions, sophisticated and folk ones, men's and women's variations and so on, all cutting across the inherited boundary lines. In other words, we have historically in Christian tradition not so much a fugue with a strong recurring theme as a medley of variations, perhaps even enigma variations. It is small wonder many now feel that tradition has become an unstable concept.[4]

TRADITION AS DYNAMIC DEVELOPMENT

At this point a critic might argue that I have drawn the net of tradition far too tightly, and assumed that it implies unchangingness, or mere repetition. Within identifiable continuities, tradition could be conceived not as

3. Cited in Wilken, *Myth*, 101.
4. Houlden, *Connections*, 111–22.

static repetition but as dynamic development. Newness and change should be welcomed, the critic claims, for that is what keeps an organism alive. I myself warm to this understanding: it is potentially more honest about historical change and it opens the door for creativity in the present. In principle it commands strong support in the theological community.

Principle, however, is one thing and practice often another. Under the covers of the dynamic concept of tradition the full impact of historical dependency and change is easily muted. For example, the Catholic ecclesiologist, Avery Dulles, celebrates the opening up of the concept of tradition with Vatican II, and he sees the need for reinterpreting the experience of faith in succeeding generations. Seeking a *via media* between what he sees (wrongly, in my view) as Alfred Loisy's historical relativism and Adolf von Harnack's inclination towards the earliest layers of the New Testament as a golden age from which all else has been decline, Dulles opts for patristic criteria in the interests of preserving theological truth:

> No subsequent age will be required to do again what the Fathers accomplished. But in building on the work of the Fathers we are not obliged to repeat mechanically what they did and said. Their venerated formulations have to be reinterpreted through modern patterns of thought, probed with the help of contemporary investigative techniques, and restated in terms intelligible to present-day believers.[5]

In one sense this leaves the door wide open, for who is to set limits to the task of reinterpretation? But despite his stress on "modern patterns of thought," Dulles's real intention is a definitely cautious hermeneutic: "It must be renewal rather than innovation."[6]

What is missing in Dulles's account is any acknowledgement that theological construction in the patristic period is its own innovation, deeply enmeshed with the intellectual and political pressures of the times. The Fathers might have been horrified to be thought of as innovators, indeed their competing claims to truth were based on precisely the opposite notion. But with hindsight we are able to see how those claims and the actual history of the period are two dissonant aspects of a fictional tradition that we inherit.

The hidden danger, then, in the "dynamic of tradition" school is that it masks the real nature and extent of theological innovation and diversification that has gone on through history. It shares the aspirations of Newman's model of development as organic growth: from seed to flower, the plant of Christian truth blossoms through continuous unfolding, all guaranteed by

5. Dulles, *Catholicity*, 102.
6. Dulles, *Catholicity*, 105.

the presence of the Holy Spirit. But tradition, we can now aver, has been more a matter of fits and starts than Newman's essentially aesthetic appreciation allowed. In other words, theologians have been more innovative than they have cared, mostly, to imagine.

IDEOLOGICAL APPEAL

The suspicion of innovation in Christian theology introduces my third aspect of tradition: the ideological appeal to the past as a validation of present beliefs. It is easy to see how the appeal to the past established itself quickly and necessarily with the birth of Christian faith. All the New Testament writers indulge in it in one form or another, searching the Hebrew scriptures for clues and hints to connect the new thing as they experienced it from Jesus with their inheritance of the Jewish past. This was necessary not only because Jesus had initiated what Larry Hurtado has called a "Christian mutation" within the Jewish pattern of monotheism (so that there was an issue about continuity), but also because life in the Roman empire demanded a hallowed pedigree for survival in religion.[7] Once Christianity had passed fully into gentile hands, the assumption of the appeal to the past for validation, plus an assumption of essentially unchanging faith, became twin filters for sorting out answers to new questions in later generations. By the time we reach the Middle Ages the impression is given that Christian faith is such and such because it has always been so—and will continue to be so—for ever and ever, Amen. That is to say, the assumptions take on the status of an ideology.

The investment in tradition, as a symbol of continuity, achieved the status of ideological authority, and it is this which is proving so troublesome in the present. To live in succession with the past is one thing: we can hardly do any other. But to elevate the past as *normative* for us is a second step in the process of making tradition. And the fact that this process has a history implies that it is not necessarily an automatic step to be taking now. New Testament scholar, Dennis Nineham, pointed out the difficulty in the consecration sermon for Bishop David Jenkins: "It is quite unrealistic to try to bypass or short-circuit our disagreements by appealing to statements and formulas of the past, because the question at issue is precisely what we are to make of those formulas."[8]

Concern for identity and the human need to be, in some sense "in a tradition" can, I accept, hardly be gainsaid. But to establish the concern in

7. Hurtado, *One God*, 93–124.
8. Nineham, "Ye Have Not Passed," 361.

the inherited terms now looks overly restrictive. In order to rescue ourselves from the trap, it is worth pondering a little more on the sense in which tradition has been a matter of imaginative innovation.

TRADITION AS INNOVATION

This can be amply illustrated from the New Testament. In his gospel, Matthew devoted much of his attention to tidying up the enigmatic impressions and ragged edges of the Marcan story he inherited. Where Mark was elusive and suggestive, Matthew formalized. For Mark, Jesus was a man of puzzling riddles; for Matthew, he was a man of lucid teaching, even rather ecclesiasticized teaching. Now it is quite respectable, from one point of view in scholarship, to see Matthew as the author of much of the material not found in Mark. The Lord's Prayer, the Sermon on the Mount, the Great Commission—favourite material in the church—all emanating from the creativity of Matthew's theological outlook and style as he drew upon hints in Mark.[9] In any case, he certainly endorsed these changes: they represented his beliefs. How, then, is Matthew in the *tradition* of Mark?

He wrote a gospel, to be sure, but what he thought he was doing we can only speculate. If he was "bringing out the truth as he saw it" from Mark, then he belongs to the "dynamic of tradition" school. Yet it is just as easy to read him as making his own variation of the gospel, under different circumstances and pressures, without always having to look over his shoulder for permission to think and write what he wanted. His respect for Mark was obviously strong enough for him to follow in his footsteps. All the same, he changed Mark's narrative and added his own material as he saw fit. In short, he was an innovator.

So where does this deconstruction of "tradition" leave us? Am I being over-pusillanimous about the problems? There is continuity in Christian faith surely, otherwise how could I even deconstruct it? Nor is it the case that in the light of the critique we are now tradition-less, though some will feel that that is in effect the end result. No, I have lived in the Christian flow of things and have been nourished; and I continue to be so. No-one starts each day wholly afresh. The problems of the human drama reoccur; it would be folly to begin reflection on suffering or love or God, as though no-one had pondered them deeply before today. Human beings cannot but help live in traditions of some kind. Traditions may be products of the human imagination, but they go before us.

---

9. See Goulder, *Midrash and Lection*, 1974; and Houlden, *Backward Into Light*, 1988.

Nevertheless, reflection takes place within a setting, and settings change. Even the acknowledgement that human beings cannot live without traditions does not mean that tradition as a problem is merely a speculation of the academic or theological mind. How best to characterize tradition remains problematic. The pipeline of succession is plainly false; the model of development omits too many of history's disjunctions and remains platonic at root; the idea of "the dynamic of tradition" is better, but this too is in danger of playing down innovations. And tradition, when used ideologically, has so often stifled creativity, not to say wreaked too much havoc in history when used as a tool of oppression, for the concept to be sanctioned as such. To reach a second innocence in relation to tradition seems scarcely manageable.

If a second innocence remains elusive, that does not mean that theological enquiry takes only a negative form. It is still incumbent on the critic to offer some suggestions for the task of reconstruction. What form might these take? I suggest that we view tradition now as a quarry. It is a model more relaxed even than seeing oneself in the flow of the dynamic of tradition. What has been done and thought previously in Christian history is a stimulus to fresh work in the present. It is a *stimulus* because innovation is a mark of theological creativity. And it is *fresh* because the range of data that theology is required to bring within its purview has mushroomed in the modern period. Let me give three illustrations of how "tradition as a quarry" might be a stimulus for us, and so point to the freshness that critical thought could yield in the future.

First, it allows me to treat Christians and theologians from the past with the utmost respect yet without having to bend my purposes to theirs, nor theirs to mine. I read Augustine (say) on love and feel attracted and repelled at the same time. On any model other than the quarry I would not know how to knit my response to him into theological reflection. Best leave him in his time and be stimulated to love God afresh in my own time, thankful for some of his intensely suggestive insights, but pleased not to have to stand on his shoulders. Or take a current controversy: the ordination of women to the priesthood in the Anglican church. Both the "traditional" and the "dynamic of tradition" school seek justification in the past: the one for the absence of women priests, the other for the thrust of inherited incarnational faith which claims to embrace change in ministerial practice without altering fundamental theological substance. But the debate cannot be solved in these terms. The first is doggedly ideological; the second has the appearance of artificiality. Neither allow for criteria from the present fully to be heard.

Secondly, accepting tradition as a quarry enables a different perspective on the place of belief in Christian faith to emerge. Part of the problem with tradition stems from its reliance on beliefs as *the* defining characteristic of Christianity. There is much to be said for Christians now letting go of this criterion as the principal one. More stress could be laid on membership of the community of the church as being important. Here there is a context of worship and action for sustaining identity, and theology functions as a means of stimulus, encouragement, and self-criticism. What commends itself in belief and practice will answer to the needs of the community's mission as a whole: quarries are mined by teams of workers not isolated individuals. The theological enterprise will be less anxious about maintaining such-and-such a belief or tradition as essential, while there will still be a need for rigorous reflection, given the explosion of knowledge. It will be necessary to discern some continuities, though these may be pursued in a less familiar mode. Perhaps continuity could be sought in the power of the past to provoke and ask questions of the present, rather than in the supply of answers to present-day questions which the past anyway was never designed to meet. Overall, theologians should be less anxious about straying beyond their own boundaries in search of knowledge and illumination elsewhere, thus benefiting from a relaxation of the scope of their discipline's usual remit.

My third example comes from the field of interfaith encounter. With "tradition as a quarry" we can abandon that exclusivism which treats one's own tradition as stemming from God, while others remain merely human productions. We all live with various human productions, generated certainly from the perception of the activity of God with human history, but human productions, nonetheless. Jettisoned also will be the tendency to embrace other faiths according to the degree to which they approach our own conceptions. "Tradition as quarry" enables a more open kind of interfaith encounter to occur, better tailored to the actual pluralism we find in the world. While no doubt it is extremely difficult to imagine such a prospect, from a Christian base, I once put it like this:

> We have a foot in two camps. We celebrate and share what we know of God through the impact of Jesus in our world. We also wait to hear, learn, and be judged by others who tell of a different experience, without defining their experience by virtue of our criterion of the Christ. We participate according to the Christian norm, yet with other norms which are also universally binding.[10]

To be fully human in the future will involve living out of more than Christian resources alone.

10. Race, "Truth is Many-Eyed," 187.

Perhaps some will espy a degree of apostasy in my analysis of tradition. That would be a criticism wide of the mark because it arises from within a view of tradition which I believe is no longer sustainable. I have suggested some features of a different model as a means of looking towards more positive prospects. Our commitment is to God, not tradition. Ultimately that distinction, made from within prophetic religion, allows for a greater degree of boldness in theological *perestroika* than we are usually prepared to risk.

PART TWO

Constructive Theory

3

Truth is Many-Eyed

THIS CHAPTER DEVELOPS HOW *a critical consciousness might apply to a Christian theology of religions. It explores as a test case the theology of the Anglican liberal theologian John A. T. Robinson, who developed a model which was affirmative of the experience of the religious other but which retained the eventual superiority of Christian faith, essentially for Christological reasons. The chapter explains why Robinson's nervousness about pluralism was unnecessary.*

One sign of vitality within a religious community is its ability to adapt, critically, to changing circumstances and new experiences. When this does not happen, a community is likely either to atrophy and become irrelevant to the lives of its people, or to assume an arrogant triumphalism and dominate them.

John Robinson's *Honest to God*[11] was supremely an experiment in presenting Christian faith in the context of a culture which was unable to live with ready-made answers from the past. The crisis related chiefly to how Christians could reappraise their tradition so that it cohered at the deepest level with a range of human experience in the present. The new accounts of reality describing that experience, especially prominent in the fields of

---

11. Robinson, *Honest to God*, 1963.

existentialist philosophy, historical science, and psychology, all seemed to require the revision of faith if it was to continue to command respect.

There is every reason for pressing ahead with this critical method in theology which *Honest to God* embraced. If the issue of the nature of God is the central question of theology, then the context in which it arises is no less important. Today this must include the realization that the world is ineradicably plural. That is to say, in the context of world religious pluralism, being "honest to God" from now on must include the recognition that for many people their "salvation" takes place within other equally powerful and vibrant religious settings. When the *dharma* travels West, and when the Christian missions in the traditional cultures of the East have met with only minor success, Christian faith can no longer assume a monopoly of religious truth or think of itself as rightfully supreme.

CHANGED CONTEXT

We have been made aware of the new context for theology by various means. Through travel, we are confronted by whole civilizations where religions have fostered the transformation of human beings by spiritual practice without any reference to Christianity. Through the historical and phenomenological study of the world religions, we are inspired by literature and reflections of deep wisdom, comparable to much that the Christian tradition has produced. Through personal friendships, we are impressed by the strong faith of human beings who espouse a religious pathway which for them is noble and life-giving, and which remains sufficient for their aspirations. As a result of new experiences, we are forced to recognize the degree to which religious truth is also a function of birthplace. A satisfactory account of Christian faith cannot now be given without simultaneously showing how it relates to the vast range of religious experience outside the Christian framework.

John Robinson began to face this frontier in his book, *Truth is Two-Eyed*, given first as the Teape lectures in India in 1977.[12] The title itself contains an explicit repudiation of the attitude which has characterized much of Christian thinking in the past, namely, the exclusivist view which holds that the knowledge of God has been confined to one stream of cultural religious history alone.

In retrospect, one could be forgiven for thinking that the problems surrounding *Honest to God* were fairly parochial, compared with those that arise when pluralism is placed on the Christian agenda. Given the new

---

12. Robinson, *Truth is Two-Eyed*, 1979.

awareness of religious pluralism, the one-eyed view of religious truth seems more and more moribund. Sheer experience tells against it. Moreover, the foundations on which the most recent forms of exclusivism were built, in the middle years of the present century, now seem untenable. The shape of both the biblical and dogmatic arguments have changed. Developments in biblical studies, for example, have shown us the problematic nature of deriving answers to modern questions, such as the Christian response to a religiously plural world, from literature which was not designed to answer them, at least in the form in which they now present themselves. So, a recent study of the theology of mission, facing the question of the missionary relationship with the other world religions, concludes that "No comprehensive solution to this issue can be found in the Bible, but it does offer some leads."[13] Interestingly, however, the leads the authors of this book suggest we follow speak positively of discovering the love of God beyond the boundaries of Israel and the church. Second, developments in systematic dogmatic theology point out the role of the human religious imagination in describing religious experience. The distinction between "religion" and "revelation," a device which enabled exclusivists to promote Christianity as *sui genesis* among the world's religions, now appears as an attempt to circumnavigate the human element in interpreting Christian faith. It seems dangerously anachronistic and might even be a form of religious imperialism.

Rejecting exclusivism closes off one avenue of approach; it does not in itself solve the problem of the Christian response to religious pluralism. It is worth setting out the position of *Truth is Two-Eyed* in a little more detail, both as a window on to the issues involved, and in order to demonstrate alternative avenues of exploration.

TWO-EYED TRUTH

Experience, combined with the thrust of the universalist strand within Christian belief, compelled Robinson to recognize the unity of the divine life lying behind the world's religions:

> The God who discloses himself in Jesus and the God who discloses himself in Krishna must be the same God, or he is no God—and there is no revelation at all. *Ultimately* for both sides there are not "gods many and lords many" but one God, under whatever name . . .[14]

---

13. Senior and Stuhlmueller, *Biblical Foundations*, 345.
14. Robinson, *Truth*, 98.

But within this all-encompassing affirmation there was room for distinctions. The model Robinson used to clarify this was that of an ellipse. Here two centres (eyes) of religious truth, each representing a dominant, though not uniform, religious cluster, characterized roughly as prophetic (West/Semitic/Christian) and mystical (East/Indian/Hindu), could co-exist in a creative tension. The worth of the model lay in the fact that it overcomes the isolation between religions yet also respects their differences. Moreover, it could claim some validity in actual reality. The dividing line between the two religious types ran not only between, but also within East and West. In a twofold observation, Robinson showed first how each religious eye in practice had developed elements of its opposite mode in the ellipse, e.g., prophetic religion harbored mystics and mystical religion made space for prophetic voices; and second, how when each eye on truth was treated in isolation it led to a distortion, e.g., the West has often expressed itself myopically in a "historical positivism or fundamentalism of an all-or-nothing kind," and the East at its worst has been tempted by a "dangerous historical absenteeism, making for a quietist indifference and fatalistic irresponsibility."[15] Overall, the model countenanced religions as complementary witnesses to the one divine reality which animated the heart of all religions, and yet it was also alert to the remaining unease in the tension that exists between the different philosophical and theological affirmations stemming from those witnesses. It would not appeal to everyone as a viable way forward in an age of comparative religious studies, but it was an extremely imaginative proposal, and could take its place as a serious contender among a number of experiments emerging at the time.

Robinson stopped short of affirming a full pluralist theory, which is the view that the different world religions represent different religious paths of normative value for those who follow them, none being reducible to another, each bringing salvation/liberation/enlightenment, according to its historical and cultural setting. It accepts the person of Jesus as one norm among other norms, one uniqueness among other uniquenesses, in a world context where the fullness of religious truth is pursued in a spirit of mutual respect and shared criticism. The clue to why Robinson shied away from this conclusion lay in his Christology. He was fond of using the description "decisive" (borrowing from the process theologians) to explain the impact and importance of Jesus, both for Christians and for the world. In other words, Jesus was not the exception to humanity but its true representative. In him the intended goal of creation in the relationship between God and human beings came to fruition. This way of expressing belief in the incarnation was

---

15. Robinson, *Truth*, 54, 56.

in line with a certain fruit of New Testament studies, which reports Jesus as the eschatological agent of God's kingdom, and not as the God-Man of subsequent doctrinal development. In philosophical terms, this means that in Jesus the self-expressive activity of God in creation reached a climax.

Now this may be an improvement on the older apologetic which talked of two natures in one person, but in the context of a positive approach to interfaith relations it created an ambiguity. For the implication of this shift (and Robinson was not alone in this move), in the direction of what can be called the historicizing of the incarnation, is that the way is opened up for there to be other saviors and revealers, other incarnations in other times and places, other normative representations of the meaning of human life under God. Yet Robinson did not quite follow through these implications. He admitted that his Christology did not confine God to Jesus, and that whatever was glimpsed of God in Jesus was always open to "completion, clarification and correction" in dialogue with others, thus maintaining the complementarity between religions in line with the belief that "truth is two-eyed." But he also maintained, as a matter of confession, that in Jesus the love of God was present to the highest degree, the "profoundest clue to all the rest."[16] Thus he maintained a hold on the uniqueness of Jesus, albeit in an untraditional form.

Robinson's discussion highlights the ambiguity of the term "decisiveness" as this is applied to Jesus in the light of the positive impact of living in a religiously plural world. On the one hand, as a function of dogmatic theology, decisiveness means that Jesus remains *a priori* the ultimate norm for all humanity and all other potential revealers. This gives the impression of pursuing the Christian judgmental attitude in a milder form. If the concept of incarnation includes other religious representations than that in Jesus, who by definition is the "completion" of God-with-humanity, then this merely repeats the pattern of Christian superiority. At this point exclusivism and inclusivism look like two versions of the same approach. On the other hand, as a function of experience, "decisiveness" points to Jesus as the "profoundest clue," on the basis of at least implicit historical comparisons. This gives the impression of being sensitive to historical enquiry as a means of demonstrating the value of the term, in relation to different religions, but it is likely to claim too much. In this respect, Robinson contended that Christianity has the potential to incorporate, more satisfactorily than other religions, those factors which are inimical to religion, which he named as evil, the impersonal, and the feminine. This was a bold act of faith, but it requires much more prolonged and careful enquiry than Robinson ever

---

16. Robinson, *Truth*, 129.

gave it before it could command widespread support. Many would contend that it could never prove anything worthwhile in any case. If this is correct, then Robinson was open to embracing a full pluralist position without too much adjustment in his overall model, though he remained reluctant to do so. It may be that the ambiguity of the term "decisive" is less helpful than at first it looks.[17]

HISTORICAL CONSCIOUSNESS

At this juncture, before we spell out the pluralist case, it is worth enquiring further into the meaning and consequences of living in an age of historical consciousness. For much of the argument for a shift in the Christian response to a multi-religious world depends upon accepting certain premises in relation to it. Two implications of the rise of the modern historical consciousness strike me as pertinent to our discussion.

First, historical reality, as in Ernst Troeltsch's phrase "a continuous connection of becoming,"[18] contravenes the older view of religious truth which was grounded in an interventionist supernatural account of its origins. We have come to see that religious truths are more humanly constructed truths than we once thought. It is from within historical time and space that women and men have constructed the means for interpreting and acting upon their experience. Patterns of meaning and understanding have developed, directly related to the needs, institutions, perceptions and religious ideas of a society at any one particular period in history. Religions have provided frameworks within which human life and struggle can have meaning and orientation. If we accept that this process describes the history of all religious communities, including the Christian—and we have no reason to think otherwise—then we must find a way of incorporating this knowledge into our own Christian self-understanding. The implications of this historicist picture for the sense of absoluteness which has traditionally been attached to Christian faith have been summed up by Gordon Kaufman:

> We now see the great theologians of Christian history, for example, not simply as setting out the truth that is ultimately salvific for all humanity (as they have often been understood

---

17. Robinson's position here is not dissimilar to that of Hans Küng in *On Being a Christian* and *Christianity and the World Religions*. See my discussion of Küng in "Christianity and Other Religions: Is Inclusivism Enough?" 178–186.

18. Troeltsch, "Historiography," 716–723.

in the past), but rather as essentially engaged in discerning and articulating one particular perspective on life among others.[19]

A historicist perspective which values religious truths as radically human constructs begs the question of the role of divine revelation in religious life. Yet it need not necessarily undermine the concept of revelation altogether, as point up the need for its reinterpretation in the light of new knowledge. What is seriously called into question, however, is the sense of exclusive absoluteness that religions have traditionally accrued to themselves.

The second effect of historical consciousness relates to its bearing on change in the identity of Christian faith and concerns the distinction between faith and its interpretation in limited, partial, and culturally conditioned forms, each circumscribed by its own reference points and assumptions about reality. In Christian discussion at present the search for a coherent understanding of the person of Jesus, one not bound by the philosophical categories of the ancient world, is one example of how this impact has been felt. But historical consciousness presses further than the need to find some comparable restatement of the two-natures doctrine. It looks behind that doctrine at the concept of finality, a concept which the doctrine of incarnation was designed to embody from within the different philosophical assumptions of the subsequent early centuries. This oldest view of the finality of Jesus derives from both the impact of the figure of Jesus himself and the background Jewish apocalyptic view of history, with its attendant expectations of the final messianic figure, which was the matrix for Christian belief at this earliest time. Deep as the hold of that view of history has been on Christian consciousness, so that the modern clamour for "decisiveness" is a latter-day instance of it, it nevertheless sits oddly with modern perceptions of history as the "continuous connection of becoming." Given a different setting for Christian faith in the present, there is no reason why attachment to the way of Jesus should express itself in a framework involving that same sense of finality. In an age when religious pluralism is accorded positive value for so many reasons, Christians can feel freed from that ancient finality to work out their commitment to Jesus alongside and in dialogue with other religious commitments, and not against them. Nor is this a matter of adjusting Christian faith simply in order to accommodate other religious ways, as it is sometimes said. It is a recognition that changes in Christian self-understanding, as a result of the developing historical consciousness, make possible a positive global recognition of the place of many

---

19. Kaufman, "Religious Diversity," 9.

religions in the purposes of God. Coupled with the first effect of historical consciousness, outlined above, it could be even said to demand it.

My contention then is that, under the pressure of historical consciousness, with both internal changes in Christianity's perception of its own identity and the positive valuation of a vital pluriform religious world, Christian theologians (and the same will be true for theologians from other traditions) are required to construct a new theology to fit the new experiences. What shape might such a theology take?

PLURALIST MODEL

A number of theological models in this vein have been advanced now, and there is no need to repeat them here in detail.[20] My own view has the features of what has been called "unitive pluralism."[21] This recognizes that the world religions reflect genuine experiences of the divine life at their roots, and that these experiences have generated differing philosophical patterns of belief and community life. It accepts Wilfred Cantwell Smith's observation that "faith is a global human quality,"[22] and that "God has participated more richly in human affairs, man *(sic)* has participated more diversely in God, than we once knew."[23] It holds that "salvation," or its various cognate terms such as "liberation" and "enlightenment," is taking place within the various world religious patterns of thought and practice, to varying degrees which are virtually impossible to grade. It retains the uniqueness of each tradition, but not their unrelatedness, and the elliptical model of John Robinson's proposal is most helpful in picturing this aspect for us. It is more at home with metaphor, symbol and parable as the chief vehicles of religious truth, each bearing the linguistic quality of both representation and instrumentality, than with purely metaphysical descriptions. It believes that the person of Jesus is both a parable of God's love and care for the world and a door of human response to the divine mystery. He is of universal importance, thus providing Christianity with a foundation for mission, which in relation to the other world religions, assumes a dialogical character. Equally, it holds the Buddha's enlightenment, for example, as indispensable for human well-being, and as universally binding, to be learned from and celebrated. Such a shift is now possible if Christian faith is to take full cognizance of the

---

20. Hick and Knitter, *Myth*, 1987.

21. Race, *Christians and Religious Pluralism*, 70–105; Knitter, "Catholic Theology of Religions," *Concilium* 183, 99–107; Thompson, *Jesus Debate*, Chapter 13.

22. Smith, *Towards*, 171.

23. Smith, *Towards*, 172.

dominant historical consciousness of our time. It is also necessary if we are to do justice to the new data made available as a result of growing contacts and dialogue between people of faith.

The pluralist model is constructed inductively and is not without difficulties of its own. Some have said that it represents a move to a supposed Olympian point, a kind of meta-position beyond the positions of any of the world religious traditions themselves—in effect, a new religion! The argument continues that the pluralist case is incoherent because religious traditions speak out of particular and unique centres, which, theologically, are simply part of what is given in those traditions. So, Christianity relates to the world by virtue of its concept of "the Christ," Islam through "the Qur'an," and so on. I think this objection overstates its case, and it is dependent on too static a view of religious tradition. What the pluralist model asks of us is that we engage in the new world of religious dialogue with, as it were, one foot in the Christian circle and the other in a circle which encompasses an unknown quantity. It is an engagement which experientially we know to be valid (true) even though it remains, for the time being, still something of an analytical puzzle. Some have attempted to provide epistemological backing for the enterprise. Perhaps the most well-known of these schemes is that of John Hick, who makes use of a Kantian distinction between noumenal and the phenomenal worlds. The former applies to Reality (God) in his (her, its) inner being and therefore strictly speaking unknowable, and the latter applies to God as imaged from within particular historical and cultural settings and therefore known diversely in human response.[24] Paul Knitter speaks more loosely when he says that "in the new model of religious truth, absoluteness is defined and established not by the ability of a religion to exclude or include others, but by its ability to relate to others, to speak to and listen to others in genuine dialogue."[25] Cantwell Smith prefers not to speculate about epistemology, believing most Western epistemology to be orientated on things rather than persons.[26] It must be said that these suggestions have not found common acceptance. That does not invalidate them *tout court,* so much as sound a note of warning. As an alternative route, others are exploring a liberation perspective for an ethical foundation for affirming a pluralist position.

Those who are sympathetic to viewing religious pluralism, and therefore interreligious dialogue, in a positive light but who refuse to espouse a full pluralist theory, because of the fear of a meta-position, are exercising a

---

24. Hick, "Religious Pluralism," 147–64.
25. Knitter, *No Other Name?*, 220.
26. Smith, *Towards,* 81–103, 189.

rightful caution.[27] But caution need not become an unnecessary obstacle. For pursuing some kind of dialogical relationship between religions does seem to harbor an expectancy which implies some provisional relationship between the different traditions, some relationship between transcendence and varied global religious life. Being open to receive truth from whatever quarter it comes has its own virtues but being open to another religious perspective surely carries a different expectation about what can be learned from dialogue and openness. Otherwise, why should there be anything special in inter*religious* encounter as such? The pluralist model, therefore, does not propose that Christians participate in a meta-position, but perhaps suggests something like a meta-tradition. We have a foot in two camps. We celebrate and share what we know of God through the impact of Jeṣus in our world. We also wait to hear, learn, and be judged by others who tell of a different experience, without defining their experience by virtue of our criteria of the Christ. We participate according to the Christian norm, yet with other norms which are also universally binding.

A related criticism of the pluralist model could be aimed like this. The problem is that it solves the question of conflicting truth-claims between religions too easily. It seems to ignore the very real diversity of the language and symbol systems of the different traditions. It looks as though what is being proposed is a view which holds that all religions are the same thing underneath, all equal, so that what a person believes is of no real significance. Despite the caricature in the latter part of that argument, it does hold some force. But pushing this criticism all the way would mean living with an unsatisfactory relativism, such that religions must remain for ever locked in their own language boxes. This is untrue to history, where religions have often borrowed from one another and absorbed different insights from other traditions. It is also untrue to experience, where the practice of "passing over" to another tradition has enabled a richer faith to emerge, an enlargement and exchange that implies a deeper grasp on religious life and truth. More theologically, the criticism ignores the radical relativity of religious symbols, themselves pointers to divine reality rather than replicas of it in contingent form.

The stress on religious belief and practice as relative to the divine Absolute enables the uniqueness of the different religions to be affirmed, while also allowing the possibility of their complementarity. As William Thompson says: "It is the commonality of the one God which finally undergirds the complementarity of the religions."[28] He also adds a further

---

27. Cobb Jr., *Beyond Dialogue*, 1982.
28. Thompson, *Jesus Debate*, 388.

function in the model, which is an insistence on mutual *criticism* between the traditions, as a means of keeping the bad aspects of relativism at the door. So, for example, he adds that Judaism's stress on covenant ought to criticize and correct Christianity's lapses into individualism, while in turn Judaism can ponder Christianity's insistence on a Messiah who suffers and empties himself. Similarly, we could add that Christianity could learn from Buddhism's insistence on the human heart as the locus of the solution to the human predicament, correcting Christianity's tendency to opt out and leave everything to divine intervention. Simultaneously, Buddhism could be made to ask itself about the reality of the world as a place of real process, where things go wrong, where evil does pervade. A critical dialogue would quicken the unique centers of the world's religious traditions, while teaching them to shed the vestiges of exclusiveness and intolerance. In short, the dialogue would show how each needs the other to be itself. To that extent the question of whether there is salvation in the church is not answerable independently of the question of whether there is salvation outside the world! To be fully Christian in the future will, paradoxically, involve living out of more than Christian resources alone.

I admit that the proposal for a pluralist approach in the Christian response to a multireligious world is a new venture for Christian faith, and Christians have generally been trained to see newness as a threat. But an alternative reading of Christian history is possible, one which sees it as marked by radical newness and change more than we have cared to recognize. Christian terms and expressions, including even central doctrines such as the belief in God as Trinity, which have been thought to body forth the essence of Christian truth in a claim to continue the line of authentic tradition, can easily be read as innovations in their time. That of course does not necessarily discredit them. But it does leave a sense of relativism, where hitherto theologians have thought of themselves as handling stable tradition.

Such a reading of history can induce vertigo. It can also release us from the restrictions of the past and enable faith to find its appropriate expression with reference to the dominant realities which inform our world in our own time. These are irrevocably multireligious. Being "honest to God" now implies being "honest to Gods." Affirming religious pluralism as "God's" manner of dealing with our world, in all its exuberant variety, can be a valid Christian option and, for the reasons given above, becomes a necessary one. Radical novelty, given a certain perspective on history, is not sufficient reason for being wholly mistrustful. The vulnerability of the pluralist theory, and the intellectual pitfalls surrounding it, are only too obvious, not to say overwhelming.[29] For Christians, the life of vulnerability Jesus himself lived and the universalism he achieved can be our guide on the way.

The pluralistic theology of religions is, I repeat, constructed inductively. If it is problematic for some, it is also provisional and open to revision. Part of the test of its adequacy is whether it will turn out to be valid in practice, whether it will hinder, pre-empt, or enable the dialogue to proceed. Whatever the intellectual reasons for being cautious, they should not be sufficient to stand in the way of embracing the positive good of partnership between religions as the next phase of Christian involvement in history, now begun. The many threats to a sustainable life on planet earth are reasons enough for religions to cooperate, learn mutually, and act.

---

29. Driver, *Myth*, 203–18.

4

The Dialogue of Religions

Pragmatic Necessity or Providential Opportunity?

This chapter introduces the impact of interreligious dialogue into the theology of religions debates. If critical thinking opens up the tradition then interreligious dialogue extends the challenges to traditional faith even further. The twin tracks of theology and dialogue are explored and in the process invest the future with a new providential opportunity.

In Christian terms, I take it that the notion of providence, at least at a minimal level, concerns the availability of the reality of God, glimpsed in and through the texture of the world's processes, for the sake of the transformation of the world. On the whole, Christian theology has explored this promised reality of transformation accompanied by a sense of its own self-sufficiency and cosmic confidence as a universal religion. However, in modern times, providence has had to come to terms with the rise of critical thought and a deepening sense of radical human freedom in the face of and responsibility for the way the world works. As the world metaphorically shrinks, it is having now to come to terms also with the vibrancy of other religious ways of imaginatively interpreting human experience. This means that the question of providence receives a further twist: what does it mean that we are confronted with other religious ways which equally embody a universal spirit and a cosmic confidence? Does providence intend the religions to be in competition? Or does the contemporary encounter between religions serve a different purpose?

Certainly, for most of its history, though by no means all of it, Christianity has fallen in with the competitive spirit, and in many respects encouraged it. There are reasons for this, and they stem both from the internal theological dynamic of monotheism as well as Christianity's role within the politics of Christendom. But an alternative non-competitive strand in Christian thinking has always been present and could be said to have been guaranteed simply by virtue of the basic Christian doctrine of creation and related ideas of providence. It is echoed in the biblical provision that "God has not left himself without witnesses" (Acts 14.7), and in the ancient doctrine of the *logos* of God, the divine reason and purpose that is at work everywhere for goodness, truth, and justice. Perhaps there is a legitimate reason for imagining that the religions of the world can be said to provide concrete evidence of these universalist principles ringing true.

The mainstream Christian world has gradually been moving from a competitive spirit to a different *modus vivendi* in relation to other religious traditions. In broad terms we can call this dialogue, so long as this includes encounters of all kinds—theological exchange, sharing spiritual experiences, and people across traditions seeking common cause for the sake of a better world. The context for these new dialogical encounters is being shaped materially by the social, economic and political factors inherent in a shrinking planet and intellectually by the rise of critical thinking.

Theologically, dialogue has relied on an alternative strand in Christian history. If God has not been without witnesses, then let us find out what those witnesses have been and said. It is difficult to date this new non-competitive spirit, but Vatican II in the 1960s was a major milestone in the Catholic world, as was the World Council of Churches' development of *Guidelines for Dialogue* in the Protestant world in the 1970s. Moreover, in the 1980s, scholarly publications in this whole area increased exponentially. In 1991 the Vatican went further and averred that the world religions play "a providential role in the divine economy of salvation."[1]

If we ask what providence is up to now, part of the answer must include the unleashing of this dialogical endeavour, not just because religious plurality is a given fact but because of the religious expectations inherent in our globally interwoven context. But this developing history of dialogue and encounter has in turn generated its own momentum, its own rules of the game. This means that we have now what I call the twin tracks of

---

1. Pontifical Council, *Dialogue and Proclamation*, 17. https://www.vatican.va/roman_curia/pontifical_councils/interelg/documents/rc_pc_interelg_doc_19051991_dialogue-and-proclamatio_en.html.

interfaith encounter—one concentrating on the theology of religions, that is, on interpreting the fact of our multiple religious world, and the other on honing the assumptions, processes, expectations and skills of dialogue as such. These tracks each have their own integrity, it is often said, and there is reasonable agreement about that. Where the agreement breaks down is in how the two endeavours might be related. For what has happened during the intervening period, since we gave ourselves permission for dialogue, is that a significant gap between theological theory and dialogical practice has opened up. It is a gap which can be characterized as follows: the theological permission that the Christian world gave itself for the purposes of engaging in interreligious dialogue and for developing positive relationships with people of other religious traditions has been overtaken by all that has been unleashed under the umbrella of dialogue itself—new information, positive impressions, different experiences, blossoming friendships, shared practice in spirituality and social responsibility. In short, the whole impact of plurality, felt under the existential conditions of encounter, requires to be matched by a suitable theology.

I want now to explore a little further the twin tracks of dialogical practice and theology of religions, and the gap between them, and suggest a possible way forward.

DIALOGUE TRACK

Let me begin with dialogue and illustrate it with two examples. The first comes from the witness of Fr. Ignatius Hirudayam, who founded the Christian ashram, Aikiya Alayam, in Chennai (Madras) in the early 1970s in the wake of Vatican II, precisely for the purposes of dialogue. Writing 12 years ago, and making reference to the late 1940s, Fr. Hirudayam said that already in this pre-dialogue era he had noted, after twenty-five years of study on Indian soil, that "there was nothing deep, profound or soul stirring in the writings of the Christian church which could not find a parallel somewhere or other in the vast Tamil literature." He continued this recollection with the comment:

> Forty years later and after nearly twenty years of in-depth interreligious dialogue experience, I am absolutely convinced of this fact. Give the most striking verse from any of the vast Christian literature of the past twenty centuries and right away comes our dialogue partners' rejoinder and confirmation in a quotation

which parallels it in content and often excels it in a poetic form and rhythm that penetrates our mind and heart.[2]

What to make of this kind of observation and reflection? Perhaps it is simply the sheer impressiveness of the religious other, at their best, that makes a difference. Our permission-giving theology from the 1960s and 1970s led us to expect something of God at work elsewhere, but perhaps we did not expect appreciation for that work to be so fulsomely celebrated as at Aikiya Alayam. Of course, for those for whom experience counts for little in the theological enterprise, it cuts no ice. But then these theologians presumably live only a single-tracked life.

My second example illustrates a different point. It comes from a Jewish account of the experience of dialogue, but it could equally have been written by a Christian. Rabbi Rami Mark Shapiro recalls encountering a Jain monk in 1985:

> A Jain monk was explaining that in his tradition the soul is fundamentally independent and on its own; there is no union with God or connection with other beings. Those of us in attendance did our best to rework what the monk was saying so that it more closely matched our own teachings about unity and unification. But try as we might the integrity of our dialogue refused to permit us to pretend to some agreement that was not in fact there. As this point dawned on me I began to laugh . . . I laughed as an expression of "something awakening." I laughed as the idol of a false unity was toppled and the wonder of diversity was affirmed. I laughed with joy at our different paths and the fundamental pathlessness of Truth.[3]

Two points emerge for me from this account.

The first is that the desire to interpret the other in terms of one's own theological framework, to somehow squeeze the experience of a very different world into the familiar mold of one's own theological parameters is natural but usually forlorn. It is a strategy that generally ends up with the placing of others as lesser versions of oneself—for example, prophethood as a lesser version of incarnation; non-dual mysticism as a less developed instance of Christian personal mysticism; and so on. But we have come to see now that the religions are just different, and sometimes radically so.

The second point that interested me from that quotation was the intriguing phrase "pathlessness of Truth." It is not intended to be as non-realist

---

2. Hirudayam, "My Spiritual Journey," 57.
3. Shapiro, "Moving the Fence," 36.

as it sounds. It is not saying that there is no transcendent reference in religion. It is affirming that dialogue creates a situation where religious truth does not lie at the end of one particular path, but lies, in a sense, in the developing relationship between traditions. Shapiro is echoing here one of the great architects of the dialogical approach to truth, his fellow Jewish philosopher, Martin Buber. "When people act authentically," wrote Buber, "when they move beyond themselves to discover the other person as an equal, they discover a basic reality, a 'sphere of between' that links humanity in some greater wholeness."[4] If this is correct, then dialogue really does represent a different approach to religious truth; not a new religion but most surely a new religious consciousness.

Dialogue is not debate, not a contest to see who can trump the other; nor is it simply exchange of information. The value of dialogue can be glimpsed in its dynamic process, a movement that progresses through learning *about* the other (discovery), *with* the other (acceptance), and eventually *through* the other (transformation). I say progresses, but it is always a matter of uneven steps.

Looking back over a dialogue process, manifest in its most recent phase, it is not unfair to observe that dialogue does seem to have generated a life of its own. Of course, the word itself has come to take on numerous meanings and can be a source of confusion rather than enlightenment. But all are agreed that dialogue at its best involves at least the following three strands:

- expectations of mutual enrichment
- relationships that assume a standing of equal rights for participants to be respectfully heard
- an invitation to stand inside the shoes of the other, at least so far as this is possible, before making judgements.

There is talk in dialogue even of one's need of the other as an intrinsic component of coming to terms with one's own identity. In other words, we do not know truly who we are apart from our dialogical relationships. Actually, this has probably always been true of theology in so far as historical and cultural contexts have shaped theological life; only now we adopt dialogue self-consciously as an intrinsic component of our theological methodology.

Some of these elements emphasizing mutuality in respect and parity of esteem in dialogue have been reflected in the various recommended so-called "Guidelines for Dialogue," the production of which has become

---

4. Shapiro, "Moving the Fence," 33.

something of an industry. For example, consider two of the guidelines produced by Paul Mojzes, first published in 1989 and formulated after many years of interreligious involvement, many of them in conflict situations:

> Soul-searching and mutual enrichment should be part of dialogue. Neither truth is absolute. Each partner needs the other in order to get a more complete picture of truth. Monopoly in thought leads to sluggishness in thinking and to perversion of truth.
> Dialogue is impossible if either partner claims to have already solved the problem for all time to come.[5]

At one level, dialogue is a process of mutual critical encounter between traditions for the purpose of change. For the most part, it can be described in a neutral vein, that is, anyone can dialogue with anyone else, provided that they are open to receive as well as to give. Yet it has to be admitted that most Guidelines for Dialogue, or at least those produced outside of ecclesiastical control, do harbor an emphasis on the de-absolutizing of religious truth—"Neither truth is absolute," says Mojzes. For how else is mutuality possible? There should be no reserving of a corner of the mind for the eventual superiority of one's own tradition. The problem is of course that this is exactly what religious tradition does.

Therefore, at this juncture a divide opens up between two perspectives on dialogue. On the one hand, there are those who hold that no conceptual presuppositions are necessary in dialogue, and certainly no necessity to specify any common ground prior to dialogue. One can engage in dialogue robustly, seeking an enlargement of one's own understanding of the other and subsequently of oneself, and do that even with an assumption of Christian finality. The minimal requirement is respect for the human person, non-aggression, and a willingness to listen. "It is not the case," says Karl-Josef Kuschel, "that my confession of Christ prevents respect for other confessions of faith, even if I am of the opinion that other faith witnesses do not reveal the same encompassing depth of truth as does the Christian."[6]

Part of the problem here, it seems to me, is that we have to ask how one knows that Christian faith or any other faith-stance encompasses depths of truth missing from other faith-stances. The witness of Fr. Hirudayam that I remarked on earlier suggests otherwise. Moreover, all of the world traditions seem to be such mixtures of wonderful insights combined with mistaken cul-de-sacs, that any comparative judgement in this area seems virtually impossible to make. Alternatively, one could start out with an *a*

---

5. Mojzes, "The What and the How," 205. Paul Mojzes was Provost and Professor of Religious Studies at Rosemont College, Pennsylvania, USA.

6. Kuschel, "Faithful," 92.

priori doctrinal conviction of finality. In these circumstances, it seems to me that dialogue is bound to remain severely limited in scope, in spite of assurances from its advocates that the opposite is the case.

On the other side of the debate is a stance such as that of the theologian Paul Knitter, who finds it hard to imagine any dialogue, which is based on parity of respect, to be authentic unless participants surrender that corner of the mind which is reserving a space for the eventual superiority of one's own tradition. In his own words:

> Only if Christians are truly open to the possibility . . . that there *are* many true, saving religions and that Christianity is one among the ways in which God has touched and transformed our world, only then can authentic dialogue take place.[7]

It does seem to me that authentic dialogue relies on a sense of mutuality that is missing from the reserving-a-corner-of-the-mind-for-finality type of approach. This is perhaps the real challenge from dialogue to theology. Recall Paul Mojzes again: "Dialogue is impossible if either partner claims to have already solved the problem for all time to come." Yet claims to finality suggest just that.

This was the conclusion to which Shapiro was led in his dialogue that I cited earlier. The other refuses to be folded into the scheme of a single tradition: dialogue discovers and relies on difference. Yet that is not all. Following his remarks about the "pathlessness of truth," Shapiro continued:

> . . . regardless of Jainism and Judaism, regardless of sutras and scriptures, regardless of all the words spent on explaining our differences—there was in fact common ground: the here and now dialogue and sharing that we were involved in made a greater statement of Truth than any doctrine we might take up and examine. There was something in the act of listening, of speaking, of taking the other to heart that opened my heart to ineffable wonder.[8]

The key term here is ineffable.

There is a meeting point which of necessity cannot be precisely formulated, for that would be hubris on our human part. But that ineffability is the ground of meeting itself. We might say that the paradox of dialogue is that the unity it uncovers depends upon the diversity on which it thrives.

It seems, therefore, that there is a difference between those who sally forth from time to time in dialogue, and who may also admit positively to

7. Knitter, *One Earth, Many Religions*, 30.
8. Shapiro, "Moving the Fence," 36.

having been enriched by the experience, and to having had their perceptions challenged and corrected, and perhaps even judged, and those committed to the dialogue as such, as "a whole new way of thinking." For this latter group, dialogue itself has become the defining matrix of truth and not simply the name for a process of encounter—in terms of my title for this chapter, a providential opportunity and not simply a pragmatic necessity.

Before leaving the dialogue track, I want to point out that the new matrix of dialogue can seem threatening, particularly for ecclesiastical authorities. The point is a simple one: dialogue undermines the self-sufficiency of a single tradition understanding of the world. Dialogue insists that it is not enough to live, exegetically as it were, from tradition alone. By way of illustration of this point, let me ask a question: why did the Vatican's Congregation for the Doctrine of the Faith produce the document *Dominus Iesus*?[9] This document contained the line that other world religions are "gravely deficient" for the purposes of salvation, and it sent shock waves through many theological establishments around the world. "Gravely deficient"—many commented that they had not heard those pre-Vatican II-sounding words for a long time, and it was certainly a step back from the thrust of Vatican II's *Nostra Aetate*. Of course, if by salvation we mean the transformation that the Christian world knows through its participation in Christian life then the document's words are tautologous. But more than that was intended.

The ostensible reason for *Dominus Iesus* was the noise emanating from Christian theologians in East and South Asia. These theologians were saying that dialogue is not an optional extra but defines their everyday context. It seemed as though theologians, particularly Jacques Dupuis, were advocating pluralism not simply as a *de facto* part of the existential realities of life but were stressing pluralism as *de iure*, i.e., part of God's divine plan. So Dupuis:

> The task ahead consists in showing how the affirmation of Christian identity is compatible with a genuine recognition of the identity of other faith-communities as representing in their own right distinct facets of the self-disclosure of the Absolute Mystery in a single, unitary, but complex and articulated divine economy.[10]

That looks like a pluralist theology in the making. However, it was not intended in that way by Dupuis, who remained committed to the orthodox constitutive nature of Jesus Christ and not simply to a representative view.

---

9. Congregation for the Doctrine of the Faith Declaration, *"Dominus Iesus."*
10. Dupuis, *Toward*, 210.

Some of his language was ambiguous and spread nervousness among ecclesiastical authorities. The result?: *Dominus Iesus*.

THEOLOGY OF RELIGIONS TRACK

The question now, after many years of dialogue, exchange and working together, is: what kind of theological development reflects our new circumstances? This leads me to my second track, the theology of religions.

I begin by recalling a forceful challenge to the Christian reluctance to grant Judaism full status as an authentic spirituality and salvific religion. The challenge was directed by Rabbi Tony Bayfield in response to Marcus Braybrooke's engaging account of issues in Jewish-Christian relations:

> We are fed up to the teeth with Christian triumphalism and imperialism. We are not prepared to hear any more that the covenant with the synagogue and with the Jewish people has been broken. We need to know that you acknowledge that ours is a valid, independent faith, a living tradition, a source of revelation and just as good a religion as Christianity.[11]

Bayfield further calls for Christians to let go of their claim on Jewish souls: "There is salvation outside the church. Kindly lay off and state unequivocally and once and for all that you do not need or want Jews to convert to Christianity."[12] No punches pulled there!

Now, given that Jewish-Christian relations have shaped much of the Christian approaches to other religions, perhaps representatives from other traditions could plead the same cause as Bayfield. If so, this is a major challenge to Christian thought which had always expected other traditions to yield to the one true and universal Christian faith.

Interestingly, most responsible (and official) Christian reflection on Judaism has swung away from older notions of supersessionism and fulfilment, and away from the stereotyped polarized oppositions of Judaism being a religion of law and Christianity a religion of grace. This move has been made partly for moral reasons, as a way of seeking to reverse the historic effects of the Christian demonizing of the other that accompanied claims of fulfilment. It is easy to see this pattern of demonizing at work in Christian tradition. In relation to the Jews, as the Church claimed supersession over Judaism, it simultaneously accused them *in toto* of the unforgivable crime of deicide; or in relation to Islam, it accused Muhammad of being a cheat and

---

11. Bayfield, "Response," 115.
12. Bayfield, "Response," 116.

a womaniser. Examples of demonizing could be multiplied in relation to all religions. But as the demonizing is dismantled so the theology of fulfilment is having to be abandoned.

Theologically, the move away from Christian supersessionism recovers a simple logic: when God makes a promise, God keeps it. Therefore the "old" Jewish covenant is now renamed the "first" covenant which remains, to use the jargon, "irrevocable." Now while it is not right to apply the *details* of Jewish-Christian debate to debates with other traditions, the revolution, even reversal, it represents in the overall picture is symptomatic of the general thrust of Christian approaches to plurality.

What now can be said theologically, applied not only to Jewish-Christian relations but also to the Christian theology of religions more broadly? It is here in the theology of religions that the most heated debate has been conducted in recent times. Where have we got to? Let me list a number of observations for convenience of painting a broad picture and offer some comments on them as we proceed.

- The shift from viewing multiplicity and plurality in religion with deep suspicion to accepting it as a positive feature of a growing global outlook has more or less been accepted in principle by most theologians, apart, that is, from those committed to a fundamentalist stance. This has been picked up by Edward Schillebeeckx as follows:

> Logically and practically, multiplicity now takes priority over unity . . . the multiplicity of religions is not an evil which needs to be removed, but rather a wealth which is to be welcomed and enjoyed by all."[13]

The consequence of this appraisal is that Christian exclusivism—the view that only Christians have a chance of transcendent vision and human transformation—has few supporters among the mainstream of Christian theological life. To be sure, exclusivism hovers over formulations such as that expressed in the Vatican document *Dominus Iesus*, which described other traditions as "gravely deficient" in terms of their saving potential, but most commentators have distanced themselves from this kind of formulation.[14]

It is this persistence of the great world religions that calls for explanation beyond exclusivism. In relation to the notion of providence,

---

13. Schillebeeckx, *The Church*, 163, 167.

14. https://www.vatican.va/roman_curia/congregations/cfaith/documents/rc_con_cfaith_doc_20000806_dominus-iesus_en.html, 22.

the Indian Christian theologian, Stanley Samartha, once asked the question: "Can it be that it is the will of God that many religions should continue in the world?"[15] If the answer is No, then we are thrown back on to solutions that view religious plurality as a function of either error or evil, or both. These have been the favourite strategies of the exclusivists, but the problem about these solutions is that they simply do not fit the facts. It was the sheer spiritual impressiveness of the Tamil literature that affected Fr. Hirudayam; and it was the strength of the personal witness of the Jain monk that convinced Shapiro of the value of multiplicity. Presumably, therefore, it would be theologically and morally perverse to be impressed positively by something which was at root a function of either error or evil.

- Most theologians have adopted an inclusivist stance whereby other religions are accepted as vehicles in some sense of God's salvific purposes. This is a view that takes seriously the facts of historical consciousness, which avers that all our knowing, intuiting and struggling are mediated realities. Any knowledge of the divine therefore arises in the context of cultural formations. However, ever since Karl Rahner's assertion that people of other traditions are "anonymous Christians" (he never used the phrase "anonymous Christianity") inclusivist theologians have felt the potential imperialism of even this view and have striven to present inclusivism with a kinder face. Most often this is being done in the name of the Trinity, thus emphasizing a division of labour, as it were, between the work of Jesus Christ and that of the Spirit. To let the Spirit roam free, liberates other traditions from the Christological responsibilities of the Christian church, and accords a certain validity to the faith-traditions of the religious other. However, my own view is that there is still no escape in this framework from a certain theological priority being awarded to Christ and the church. In orthodox terms, the Spirit is the Spirit of Christ, and so even in the trinitarian framework the Christological measure cannot be circumvented. It is the Christological measure in the orthodox framework that returns the argument to Christian absolutism, however kindly intended.

Interestingly, what has happened is that there is now more emphasis on an eschatological resolution of the relation between the theological normativity of Christ and the facts of spirituality elsewhere. In other words, it will be after death when people of other religions will encounter Christ. This was the view of the Church of England's

---

15. Samartha, *One Christ*, 79.

Doctrine Commission's report *The Mystery of Salvation* (1995) and was the conclusion of Jacques Dupuis's encyclopedic book *Toward a Theology of Religious Pluralism* (1997). After celebrating complementarity and convergence between traditions, Dupuis then states: "An eschatological 're-heading' (*anekephalaiosis*, Ephesians 1:10) in Christ of the religious traditions will also attain its goal in the fullness of the Reign of God."[16] Apart from knowing what meaning can actually lie behind these words, it feels like a last-ditch effort to retain the eventual superiority of the Christian tradition.

Some might respond that the priority of Christ is just a given with the theological enterprise: Christian theology looks out on the world in terms of the symbol of Christ, who is bound to remain as the author and measure of what God might be up to, by virtue of the universal presence of the Spirit. But in that case, there seems no escape from the eventual imperialism of the inclusivist stance which the positive appreciation of multiplicity calls into question. Moreover, under the conditions of historical consciousness, it would be philosophically tortuous in the extreme to explain how it is that the historical Jesus can be the author of universal salvation in the years before his birth.

- Noticing the deficiencies in inclusivism, there is now a move to abandon this whole way of thinking in favour of an outlook dubbed the "tradition-specific" approach. This approach is keen to preserve the incommensurability between traditions, at least in terms of their different religious aims. Encouraged by certain developments in postmodernist writings, particularly those which emphasize the limitations of all language, the tradition-specific approach abandons the issue about the extent of "salvation" present in other faith-traditions, for "salvation" is a Christian word and applying it to other faith-communities they suppose is probably a category mistake. Furthermore, given that there is no neutral space between traditions, no outside vantage point from which to make judgements, tradition-specific approaches abandon any attempt to interpret other religions as generic structures of "transcendent vision and human transformation" in any sense. We simply have no theological equipment for making those judgements. Thus, the Catholic writer, Joseph DiNoia, says that:

> . . . other religions are to be valued by Christians, not because they are channels of grace or means of salvation for their adherents, but because they play a real but as yet perhaps not fully

16. Dupuis, *Toward*, 389.

specifiable role in the divine plan to which the Christian community bears witness.[17]

I confess that I struggle to comprehend what DiNoia really means by this view that the role for the religions in the divine plan is "real but as yet perhaps not fully specifiable." Interestingly, DiNoia speaks of plurality in terms of "the providential diversity of religions." By this he expects other religions to remain as a fact of global life, and he resorts to what he calls a "prospective" interpretation of plurality. This again retains the supremacy of Christ and relies on the encounter after death between Christ and members of other traditions. From my perspective, this strategy repeats the old preparation-fulfilment schema of classical Christianity precisely at a time when historical consciousness has shown the problematic nature of this manner of thinking. Postponing the final reckoning to a time after death only serves to mystify that is really being proposed.

The hard-edged confinement of a religious tradition to the history of its own language entails the abandonment of the search for any theology of religions that seeks to provide an overview of global religious history. It does not necessarily, however, lead to the abandonment of a dialogue between traditions. Tradition-specific theologians agree that the Christian tradition at its best has always promoted the view that the work of God is not confined to the church. But what this universal presence amounts to can only be known by the application of Christian criteria, for, as I have said, there are no neutral criteria, theological or ethical or even anthropological. Gavin D'Costa for example, in his book *The Meeting of Religions and the Trinity* (2000), speaks of "signs of the kingdom inchoately present"[18] within other religious cultures by virtue of the work of the Spirit. He also agrees that "There is to be no separation of the Spirit's 'universal' and 'his particular activity within the Body of Christ.'"[19] That looks like inclusivism to me, and it suffers the same problems as inclusivist thinking generally.

- My fourth observation covers the debates that are taking place centred on the pluralist hypothesis, the view that the world religions are genuinely and truthfully orientated on transcendent reality, which itself is complex, deeply mysterious, and multi-faceted. For pluralists, on the one hand, no single tradition is the arbiter, however eschatologically

---

17. DiNoia, *Diversity of Religions*, 91.

18. D'Costa, *Meeting of Religions*, 114. D'Costa is here citing the Vatican encyclical *Redemptoris Missio*.

19. D'Costa, *Meeting of Religions*, 115.

nuanced, of finality for all, and, on the other hand, each tradition values the distinction between the deeply mysterious nature of transcendent reality and the apprehension of that reality under conditions of historical life. Pluralism maximizes the cognitive implications of the analysis that understands the traditions to have arisen historically relative to their cultural conditions, which in turn have shaped particular religious outlooks in very distinct forms. This does not lead to relativism in the self-contradictory bad sense, that is, of a kind which says it does not matter what you think, or that all religions are really the same underneath their cultural clothing, or which desires a blended religion for a blended world. Religious particularities are distinctive, but this need not, however, rule out analogous recognition between them. Indeed, pluralists claim that it is precisely the distinctivenesses that are safeguarded in the pluralist hypothesis. Stanley Samartha has pointed this out in the following way:

> Pluralism does not relativize Truth, it relativizes different responses to Truth which are conditioned by history and culture."[20]

If Samartha is correct here it entails that in terms of their basic visions the religions are more likely to be complementary than contradictory, though the sense in which this applies remains one of the unfinished tasks for the work of dialogue to tackle.

The genuineness of the religious apprehensions of the world traditions is partly confirmed by their fruits. I say partly because each has spurned cultural products and religious and moral fruits that exhibit both greatness and depravity. And John Hick in particular has been fond of saying that if one religion claims finality over all others then one would expect that religion to have exhibited over time greater moral and spiritual fruits than the others. But this has not transpired—therefore in the absence of any superior fruit the claim to superiority of any one claim is placed in jeopardy.

This general scenario is now well-known. Part of its intellectual difficulty lies in accusations that it takes to itself a privileged vantage point outside of any one tradition. The pluralist's claim, however, is an inductive one: what is good for the Christian goose is good also for the other-religion gander. Christians trust their religious experience to be genuine, so why can't the same reliance on trust be extended to the experience of others?

Perhaps the real difficulty for pluralist views is that they seem to undercut the vitality of religious commitment. That is to say, if Christian faith lets

---

20. Samartha, *Between Two Cultures*, 190.

go of its hold on finality, then how can discernment in faith be made, and how can a religion endure without norms of judgement? Because of these problems other writers have preferred to couch their pluralism in different language. So Paul Knitter makes liberation his central theme. A religion's response to the suffering world provides the criterion for genuine faith. The fact that the religions interpret suffering differently is grist to the dialogical mill rather a reason against making suffering central to the pluralist outlook.

Another theological contribution has been that of the Jesuit, Roger Haight, in his comprehensive book *Jesus: Symbol of God* (1999). Haight suggests that it is not the impressiveness of spirituality elsewhere which should convince the pluralist of the value of plurality, but the very universal message of Jesus himself. Relying on the representative function of Jesus as bearer of salvation, Haight says that it is because of what Jesus reveals that we can speak positively of our plural world. As he puts it in condensed form: "Jesus reveals something that has been going on from the beginning, before and outside of Jesus's own influence."[21] Jesus retains normative value for both the church and the world, but not in any superior sense. Because of the principles of critical thought and historicity, other religions will have their norms also. But norms function negatively in this whole area of religious plurality. Again, Haight: "Jesus functions negatively for the Christian imagination by implying that God is not diametrically other or different or less than the core truth existentially encountered in what is mediated by Jesus."[22] With that kind of norm there is huge scope for viewing the religions as complementary visions of mysterious ultimate reality.

It is time for me to draw some threads together. Our pluralistic world desperately needs a regime of dialogue. At the pragmatic level, the realities of ignorance about, prejudice against, and antagonism towards the other require firm opposition. The world's sufferings, of people and planet, deserves dialogical patterns of working together for the sake of a sustainable future. But my contention in this chapter has been that beyond pragmatic necessity, the emergence of dialogue represents a providential opportunity in its own right. If this is the case, we are bound to ask what theology of religions can do it justice. There is a gap between dialogical practice and theological theory that requires bridging. Dialogue speaks of mutual accountability before a shared responsibility, whilst theology tends to cling to its absolutist framework.

What is required is a theology which does full justice both to the radical differences between the traditions and to the deep sense of transcendence that unites them. It seems easier right now to acknowledge the differences

21. Haight, SJ, *Jesus*, 422.
22. Haight, SJ, *Jesus*, 409.

than to specify the unity. But that is no reason for not trying. There are ways of drawing the religions into patterns of relationship where the notion of family resemblance between them is neither inept nor inappropriate. Moreover, dialogue itself does require the unity as well as the diversity, otherwise dialogue becomes merely a foil for self-definition and not a genuine locus for new learning and transformation. We could say that without the unity we will have essentially only pragmatic dialogue. Alternatively, dialogue as providential opportunity, is necessarily grounded in unity. The philosopher, Ashok Gangadean, expresses this as follows:

> This to me is one of the greatest lessons of the centuries of interreligious dialogue and interaction—that Logos is so deep in its Unity that multiplicity, plurality, and diversity are the essence of this Unity. And right here we see the deepest seeds of the origin of dialogue and the evolution of dialogical consciousness.[23]

Common ground between religions may be an elusive reality and attempts to define it too closely in phenomenological terms tend to fail. Perhaps the sense of common ground is intuitive. The notion of ineffability or mystery at the heart of all basic religious apprehensions provides further grounding in philosophical epistemology.

The alternatives to grounding dialogue in a principle of unity seem less than satisfactory. Some have suggested the possibility of a plurality of ultimates, but this seems deeply unattractive and even more philosophically uncertain than the transcendental unity of religions approach. The refusal of hard-edged postmodernism to entertain even the possibility of common ground—in either transcendence, or shared humanity, or the suffering world—ignores even the analogous common meanings that people of different traditions might create between them in dialogue. Birth, death, suffering, joy, liberation, community might all be interpreted differently by the traditions, but they present the context for bonds of communication and relationship to be established in tension with the varied substance of each of them.

Without unity we will not overcome our suspicions of one another. Without diversity we destroy the idea of rich dialogical relationships between us. We need to work for critical mutuality and relationality in theology, ethics, and spirituality, with respect for both differences and their unity in mystery. If dialogue is what there is now, then it requires a pluralist framework for its full providential underpinning.

---

23. Gangadean, *Meditations*, 236.

5

Can There be a Christian Pluralism?

THIS CHAPTER STATES MORE *directly the Christian case for Pluralism in theology of religions. The roots of Pluralism are explored with reference to scripture, tradition, and contemporary experiences. A summary of Pluralism in 8 propositions is offered.*

Perhaps unusually, I begin by presenting two forms of my conclusion regarding a pluralist Christian theology of religions—one expressed in a negative form and the other positive. Both emanate from Christian scholars of the last quarter of the twentieth century. The first is from the celebrated Canadian historian of religion, Wilfred Cantwell Smith:

> Those who have heard of these and know something of them [other faiths] must affirm with joy and triumph, and a sense of *Christian* delight, that the fact that God saves through those forms of faith too corroborates our Christian vision of God as active in history, redemptive, reaching out to all men (*sic*) to love and to embrace them. If it had turned out God does not care about other men and women, or was stumped and had thought up no way to save them, then that would have proven our Christian understanding of God to be wrong.[1]

---

1. Smith, *Towards*, 101.

This is a rather clever formulation, for it reverses the usual theological approach to issues of religious pluralism: it enjoins the positive reception of other faiths as a litmus test of Christianity's own truthfulness. The usual methodology has been to assume the truth of the Christian revelation and then enquire into ways by which other dispensations might measure up to it. Here Smith suggests that if there is no indication of "salvation" elsewhere then this would undermine the Christian affirmation of whatever is intended by belief in the experience of salvation itself.

My second formulation comes from the pen of the Indian theologian, Stanley Samartha, the first Director of the Sub-unit on Dialogue at the World Council of Churches. He writes:

> If the great religious traditions of humanity are indeed different responses to the Mystery of God or Sat or the Transcendent or Ultimate Reality, then the distinctiveness of each response, in this instance the Christian, should be stated in such a way that a mutually critical and enriching relationship between different responses becomes naturally possible.[2]

Samartha here echoes a version of the view which could be termed the "mystical unity of religions." We should note, however, that this is neither a monist nor a philosophically perennialist view, but one which entails a dialogical programme of mutual accountability between traditions in real-life terms.

It has to be said that neither formulation has won lasting favour among Christian intellectuals debating theology of religions, yet both are the result of a lifetime habit of historical and theological studies and dialogical interaction with people of different traditions. Both authors also held Christian truth to be a contextual matter and provisional in principle, and these convictions too have not met with every theologian's approval.

Having given you a significant hint of what a Christian support for pluralism in the theology of religions might be, let me now outline four methodological assumptions which underlie my own thinking.

NOT QUITE BEEN HERE BEFORE

First, the theological task is not simply a derivative top-down process. That is to say, we do not necessarily lift from the past direct answers to theological questions as these strike us in the present. Sometimes the Christian tradition is not able to answer particular present-day problems by appeal to

---

2. Samartha, *One Christ*, 86.

the past because these problems had not arisen until the present. In ethics, for example, think of whether or not Christian support should be given to stem-cell research; or consider even more centrally in theology, how the issue of the meaning of the dual identity of Jesus Christ as a God-Man, as in the ancient Chalcedonian formula, has become quite opaque for many. The question of Christianity's theology of religions strikes me as one of those enquiries that has not been faced previously in quite the same manner as it strikes us now. For today we are more knowledgeable about the religions than ever before and we are able to meet one another more authentically than ever before, two factors which must necessarily affect our thinking about the plurality of religions in our own day.

CONTEXTUALITY

The second assumption, which follows from the first, wants to maximize the seriousness with which we should attend to the contextual nature of all our formulations. First-century or fourth-century or sixteenth-century assumptions about what counts for religious truth may all be strikingly different. Four factors, it seems to me, conspire to create what might be termed a paradigm shift in the approach to religious truth today and therefore by implication the assessment religions make of one another. These can be listed as follows: a) knowledge about the history of religious traditions (including the history of interreligious encounters); b) the sense that religious ideas are part and parcel of a wider context of philosophical, social, and political realities; c) the weighing of religious truths in relation to the best of critical understanding at any one time; and d) the rise of modern dialogue with its expectation that we set out to learn from one another. Each of these four aspects in the approach to religious truth are contentious in numerous ways. My own view is that they are unavoidable in an age of critical thinking.

THE MEANING OF RELIGION

My third assumption concerns the definition of the term "religion." For some the term has ceased to be meaningful because it has become misleading. This group is comprised of those who imagine "religion" either to refer only to the intellectual belief-element of a tradition or to think it necessarily has only a theistic connotation. My own approach adopts a family-resemblance model and assumes that all religions, worldviews and spiritual movements incorporate roughly four interrelated dimensions: 1) a diagnosis of what ails the human condition; 2) a particular realization or impact of transcendent meaning (usually in the form of persons, scriptures, nature or mystical awareness) transforming the human condition; 3) a pathway for living in the light of the disclosure and the change it envisages; and 4) a goal which draws the transcendent purpose to completion. In short, I contend that all religions exist for the purposes of "transcendent vision and human transformation." In relation to the project of theology of religions, if there is no family resemblance of this kind, or some equivalent, then theology of religions itself can have no obvious raison d'être.

AXIAL CONSCIOUSNESS

My final assumption derives from the assessment that we live in a new era of axial consciousness. So, the late American historian of religions, Ewert Cousins, building on insights of the German psychiatrist, historian and philosopher, Karl Jaspers, describes the age into which we have now entered as a second axial period. The first axial period was defined by Jaspers as being roughly from 800 to 200 BCE, when the fundamental features that underpin current civilizations took shape. These included the evolutionary emergence of human individual awareness being integral to the rise of the world religions as movements for transformation in the world. Such an emergence encouraged the idea of the subjective spiritual journey, as we have come to know it. The accompanying religious awareness was varied in different parts of the world: think of the seminal figures of prophet, mystic, and sage as a clue to this varied emergence. According to Cousins, we are now facing the dawn of a second axial period, whereby the fragmentation of consciousness through religions and civilizations is being transcended by convergent global consciousness.

The first axial period produced remarkable results with differentiated cultures and religions. With the shift towards convergence, Cousins writes of what this means for the religions:

> Now that the forces of divergence have shifted to convergence, the religions must meet each other in center to center unions, discovering what is most authentic in each other, releasing creative energy toward a more complexified form of religious consciousness.[3]

The tasks and challenges of theology of religions fall within this larger dawning of a second axial period in history. It is to be noted that this global consciousness will not be an undifferentiated, abstract form of life, but a

3. Cousins, "Religions of the World," 15.

more dynamic—because dialogical—form of consciousness. It will be concerned to recover some earlier dimensions of consciousness (such as ecological connectedness) but evolve to embrace a sense of interrelatedness between religions and cultures which hitherto has not been historically possible.

The possibilities within an emerging second axial period arise because of the universal thrust at the heart of first axial religions. The world religions are precisely that—*world*; that is to say, universally applicable beyond the particular conditions of their origins. As such, a universalist thrust expects there to be religious awareness beyond any boundaries of particularity, and it is this expectation which creates the conditions for the second axial period. The universal applicability, embedded in separate religions, invites the mutuality of giving and receiving of insight and truth among the religions.

ROOTS OF PLURALIST VIEWS

Christian support for pluralist approaches in theology of religions has a number of roots which can be explored in turn, under the following headings:

1. Jesus and the New Testament
2. Developing church doctrinal tradition
3. Contemporary experiences and critical thinking.

   Let me now explore some issues further under these headings.

1) Jesus and the New Testament

It is notoriously difficult to make assessments in the area of Jesus research. But what we can say is that whether we look to the impact of the historical Jesus or to the experience of the risen Christ what stems from the Jesus figure is a vision of transformation which reaches beyond the confines of his own Jewish community; in other words, a vision which is universal in scope and liberative in intention. His message was that the "Kingdom of God" or the "Rule of God" was being opened up through his words and deeds, including his confrontation with the Roman powers of domination and their co-opted Jewish temple leadership, an impact summarized through a kind of shorthand formula as his "death and resurrection." The application of Jewish categories of an imagined and envisaged eschaton to his person and activities entailed that he was interpreted as in some sense final—a revelation of God for all time and space. It was this framework which led to the classical belief in his uniqueness and unsurpassability in relation other putative visions of transcendent purpose and goodness.

However, it is by no means clear how we should approach the First and Second Testaments as evidence for theology of religions today. At the historical level, we have Jesus-stories of healings, table commensality, and teachings about servanthood and inclusivity, but an overarching message directed primarily at the oppressive forces of Roman rule, after the manner of Israel's prophetic voices before him. This too would be the assessment of many Jewish scholars of first century Judaism, who place Jesus on a spectrum of protest voices of first century Jewish Palestine. Jesus was not against his inherited religion, Judaism, though he would likely have been against perceived compromised and potentially corrupt religious leadership. What this entails for the theology of religions is that older analyses which built the uniqueness of Jesus and Christianity on a foundation of Jesus's rejection of his inherited Judaism no longer have credibility.

Furthermore, and interestingly, some historical research is beginning to analyze the relationship of Jesus to the Gentile and Samaritan (and therefore outsider) populations of his native Galilean and Palestinian context. Far from imagining that Jesus defended an introverted view of Judaism he can be depicted as one whose mind and heart was open to the presence of spiritual awareness beyond the boundaries of his native tradition. And there are occasions when his own mind appears to have been challenged and changed by outsiders. This is not to say that Jesus approved of the "other religions" (Roman and Greek) of his day, but it does provide a certain kind of hermeneutical backing for openness to others even if it is not yet a theology of religions proper. Nevertheless, there is a recognition by Jesus that the compassion of God knows no boundaries and that "God is able to reveal himself to people outside Israel and to guide them."[4]

At the theological level, it is clear that there is not a consistent view emanating from the biblical text. Commenting on Christianity's relationship to non-Christian religions, Catholic scholars Donald Senior and Carroll Stuhlmueller, observed that "No comprehensive solution to this issue can be found in the Bible."[5] Although much of the New Testament material tends towards theological triumph over Judaism, the majority of texts date from the post-70 CE period when the Christian movement and rabbinic Judaism were vying for the correct interpretation of the ancient Hebrew scriptures. This is the historical background to the biblical Christian polemic against

---

4. Robinson, *Jesus and the Religions*, 259.
5. Senior and Stuhlmueller, *Biblical Foundations*, 345.

Judaism and the historical reasons for it are well known. However, most mainline churches and theologians have now overturned supersessionism, the view that Jesus renders Judaism theologically superfluous. Given this advance in our understanding, it is no longer possible to use the New Testament as clear-cut evidence of how Christians should theologize about other religious traditions. My own view is that we have only an indirect route in our use of scripture for developing our theology of religions today. Most of the cultural assumptions which are embedded in the New Testament material are not shared today and these include assumptions also especially about historical finality. Yet Senior and Stuhlmueller do offer the following encouragement from the New Testament texts in their assessment, for example, that "the God of the Bible sends his people out to reveal and to discover his love in places beyond sectarian borders."[6]

2) Developing church doctrinal tradition

The biblical hints of divine universal presence beyond the bounds of Israel's history receive a more systematic treatment at the hands of the Christian philosophical tradition. Whether employing the language of the divine word (*logos*), divine wisdom (*sophia*), divine spirit (*pneuma*) or the divine Christ (*Christos*), the general profile of Christian responses to other traditions have historically, and in varying degrees, acknowledged that other traditions have participated in God-centred awareness: they comprise what has been called Christian inclusivism. Let the theologian Origen (184/185–253/254 CE) be an example from the third century of the Christian classical period:

> ... there never was a time when God did not want men to be just; he was always concerned about that. Indeed, he has always provided beings endowed with reason with occasions for practising virtue and doing what is right. In every generation the Wisdom of God descended into those souls which he found holy, and made them to be prophets and friends of God.[7]

Not all writers would have expressed themselves in these terms, but that God could be perceived through reason, conscience and "spiritual awareness" was a shared assumption. The well-known Vatican II formulation of *Nostra Aetate* (1965) summarises a long history when it avers that "The Catholic Church rejects nothing of what is true and holy in these religions."[8]

---

6. Senior and Stuhlmueller, *Biblical Foundations*, 345.
7. Origen, *Contra Celsum* 4:7. Cited by Sullivan, *Salvation*, 17.
8. Flannery, *Vatican Council II*, 739.

A later ecumenical statement by Catholic and Protestant theologians in 1990, known as the Baar Statement, would take this further and speak of other religions as not only "seeking" but also "finding" transcendent reality through their different historical matrices:

> We see the plurality of religious traditions as both the result of the manifold ways in which God has related to peoples and nations as well as a manifestation of the richness and diversity of humankind. We affirm that God has been present in their seeking and finding, that where there is truth and wisdom in their teachings, and love and holiness in their living, this like any wisdom, insight, knowledge, understanding, love and holiness that is found among us is the gift of the Holy Spirit.[9]

But is this pluralism? The answer is: not quite. In terms of theology of religions it is certainly the traditions and not simply individuals which are affirmed as vehicles of saving truth. Yet it has often been noted that what the doctrinal tradition gives with one hand is taken away by the other. So the same Baar report continues: "The saving presence of God's activity in all creation and human history comes to its focal point in the event of Christ."[10]

Officially the doctrinal position has not been able to find its way out of what seems to many to be an impossible dilemma. In spite of the affirmation that other traditions are vehicles of saving potential the further belief in the eventual superiority of the Christian Way seems nothing but arbitrary. In particular, it has no basis in the experience of encounter itself.

One of the advances over the last 50 years has been the affirmation of other traditions as necessarily embodying the religious spirit present at the heart of human beings. If others outside of the Christian dispensation know God then it must be "because of" and not "in spite of" their historicised cultural embeddedness. This is the significance of what the Baar theological development asserts. Whatever God gives, offers, and inspires, God does through the usual channels of historicised forms. This leads us the next section and to the thresholds of pluralism proper.

3) Contemporary experiences and critical thinking

Post-axial religions (which include Buddhism and Christianity) exist on the basis that their messages have the purpose of transformation at their heart and therefore necessarily project themselves as universally relevant.

---

9. World Council of Churches, "Theological Perspectives on Plurality." II.
10. World Council of Churches, "Theological Perspectives on Plurality." III.

Therefore, speaking theistically, God as known through the Christian matrix necessarily desires the salvation of the whole world. But the contemporary experience of the persistence of global religious plurality, combined with the unanswered question of what the place and presence of God might mean prior to the appearance of Jesus of Nazareth and since, renders the issue of Christianity's proposal of universally relevant salvation more complex. Might it be that the salvation which Christianity announces is known in other forms and through other cultural and religious matrices? Furthermore, the fact that the concept/reality of God can never be exhaustively encompassed by fallible and finite human minds lends some credence to the possibility that this has been and continues to be the case.

Contemporary encounters, informed by respectful interreligious dialogue, personal knowledge, and cultural analysis, suggest that the practical effects of salvation are shared without bias among the religions, and are known as the spiritual and moral fruits of religious adherence. This means that what Christians name as "the boundless love of God" has not been confined to the Christian tradition either alone or in greater measure than instantiated elsewhere. It would be a contradiction of that boundless love to think otherwise, as Cantwell Smith wrote in my citation at the start of this chapter.

Nevertheless, moral fruits apart, it remains the case that phenomenologically the religions are different in many major respects. Their theologies and worldviews are consistent internally, each to its own outlook. That raises a question about the relation of the salvific effectiveness of many traditions to their phenomenological differences.

OUTLINE OF PLURALIST THEOLOGY

The pluralist model has been proposed in large measure as a solution to this seeming disparity. Let me now sketch the main outlines, as I see them, of a pluralist model, and I shall do this in the form of a series of propositions:

1. The authenticity and truth of the Christian Way is based on the validity of the religious experience it embodies; i.e., the basic Christian affirmation of "transcendent vision and human transformation" is trustworthy as real experience and it has cognitive implications.

2. The Christian experience of trust in God's boundless love, together with the affirmation that God is salvifically present to the whole world, argues for the extension of a similar trustworthiness to others on the basis that other religious contexts too provide a framework

for "transcendent vision and human transformation"; i.e., there is no reason to doubt the validity of the religious apprehension of other religious traditions and every reason to accept their integrity.

3. The spiritual fruits of the many faith-traditions seem comparable: all have inspired saints and holy figures who have been active on either individual or sociopolitical levels (or both), and all have demonstrated their share of complicity in support of different kinds of ills, such as racism, violence, war, sexual prejudice, patriarchy, neglect of the environment, and so on; i.e., the comparability of spiritual fruits provides a *prima facie* case for a common source of inspiration, however this might be portrayed in different traditions.

4. The distinction occurring in all faith-traditions between the hidden unknowability and the knowability through symbolic/iconic forms of Ultimate Reality is the key distinction which allows for the hypothesis of Ultimate Reality to be experienced and conceptualized in different symbolic/iconic forms according to cultural history; i.e., Ultimate Reality as ineffable, beyond categories, is yet the deeper ground of the varied manifestations of ultimacy glimpsed through the varied lenses of the historical and cultural forms of the religions themselves.

5. Theologies and religious philosophies have evolved within particular cultural environments, reflecting the limitations of these environments, but the faith-traditions now need to develop new directions for their theologies and philosophies in order to account for the wider picture encompassed by religious plurality. In Christianity, this entails formulating Christian belief in a manner which respects the integrity of other traditions, desires to learn from them and integrate new perspectives which result from the learning; i.e., the effectiveness of Christian belief need not depend on theological interpretations which are held either as necessarily absolute in themselves or dismissive of others.

6. Criteria for distinguishing between good and bad religion, and between true and false religion need to be developed jointly; i.e., in order to dispel the relativist caricature that "anything goes" pluralists have an ongoing task to specify critically the grounds on which certain manifestations of religion are more and less acceptable. This will involve ethical criteria as well as critical thinking in relation to the best knowledge we have about the world through other disciplines.

7. Each tradition has both an adequate and inadequate grasp of the relationship between particularity and universality; i.e., each particular

vision of the universal availability of Ultimate Reality is an adequate (if also conditioned and partial) view of the whole yet in some sense complementary or analogous to other equally adequate (if also conditioned and partial) perspectives of the whole.

8. Belief systems are practical pathways for achieving the religious ends of transcendent vision and human transformation. While this entails that many metaphysical and other disagreements between traditions will remain it does not invalidate the basic picture of relatedness; i.e., patterns of what constitutes relatedness can be pursued through critical dialogue, in mutual respect and without prejudice.

Critical voices against pluralist approaches have been many, chief among them being the accusation that this view is a perspective claiming an Olympian overview which is simply not available to any human being. But the accusation is misplaced as pluralism is an inductive hypothesis that recognises the necessity of extending the plausibility of trusting one's own religious experience to others. At root is the distinction between the infinite richness of ultimate reality and its apprehension in multiple material forms and pathways. It is also a view that allows for the exploration of phenomenological differences between traditions in line with what we now know through the historical, cultural, material study of the religions as such. Pluralism is not built on phenomenological samenesses between traditions, but it is designed precisely to account for the plurality of different manifestations.

Even so, it remains a vital issue as to how to construe pluralist views of transcendent reality given the phenomenal differences between traditions. In this respect, Leonard Swidler has written how differences could be of three kinds. Such differences may be (1) *complementary*, encompassing, for example, an emphasis on both the prophetic and the mystical in religious experience; (2) *analogous*, as for example, accepting the notion of God in the Semitic religions alongside that of Śūnyatā in *Mahāyāna* Buddhism; or (3) *contradictory* where the acceptance of one entails the rejection of the other, as for example, the opposition between the Judeo-Christian notion of the inviolable dignity of each individual person and the (now largely disappeared) Hindu custom of suttee, widow burning.[11]

Complementarity has long been canvassed by pluralists. "Analogous relationships" is perhaps the more controversial concept but is by no means impossible to hold; and accepting contradictions echoes the need for critical thinking in relation to ethical and theological affirmations generally.

---

11. Swidler, "Interreligious Dialogue," 23.

Returning, finally, to Stanley Samartha's conditional "If" from my citation at the start of this chapter. The "If" is there because Pluralism as an approach in theology of religions is an hypothesis not a certainty. Pluralists are not abandoning Christian faith for some agnostic transcendent vagueness but accept that theological revisions already underway for two hundred years—including stimuli from biblical and doctrinal criticism, contextual analyses, recognition that all our language and formularies are necessarily limited, and insights gained from interfaith dialogue itself—now need to take account of vibrant religious awareness from other traditions which have stood the test of time.

For pluralists, each tradition embodies an experience of the whole. We do not envisage pieces of a jig-saw puzzle where the religions represent different pieces of a greater whole. We each experience the whole, but we do so in distinct and partial ways—and also in misplaced ways. Furthermore, our human capability for empathy and the willingness to stand in the shoes of the other creates the prospect for mutual accountability in the search for truth through dialogue. Why should the facts of phenomenological difference lead us to expect that only incommensurable differences between us can be the real measure of truth? To me, that just seems odd.

6

Christ and the Scandal of Particularities

THIS CHAPTER PROVIDES A *summary of Christian Pluralism in the context of Christological debate. Jesus remains a revelatory figure along with others throughout history. The chapter lays out the main debates in Christological enquiry in the light of critical thinking and explores a view of Christ as a "parable of God," which is capable of admitting other parables in the wider perspective of religious plurality.*

The "scandal of particularity" is a theme running through both ancient and modern Christianity. As an evocation of the absolute uniqueness of Christ, it has functioned as a rallying cry for the Christian faithful, fundamentally safeguarding their identity on theological and political fronts. Theologically, it has protected the *sui generis* nature of Jesus Christ as a savior figure on the stage of world religious history. Politically, it has provided ideological divine sanction, at one extreme, for Christian separatism (e.g., as in Karl Barth's Barmen Declaration against the rise of Nazism), and, at the other, for exploitation, domination, and imperialism (e.g., as in some of the manifestations of the European politico-missionary expansion of the last three or four centuries). The *scandal* of Christian particularity relates therefore to the sense of *exclusiveness* regarding the truth of its religious claims and the political use that has been made of those claims. Yet no matter how pervasive the evocation to the absolute uniqueness of Christ has been, at least three developments during the twentieth century signal the need for its careful scrutiny.

First, new encounters between people of different world faiths are demonstrating how each religious tradition provides a living context for religious aspiration, unswerving faithfulness, and vibrant spirituality outside the Christian circle. Growing positive respect for these world faiths is leading some theologians to re-evaluate the concept of the absolute uniqueness of Christ in relation to other perceived revelatory visions of transcendent reality.

Second, historical and philosophical currents of thought have demonstrated how religious truths are more humanly constructed than we once imaged. Doctrines and patterns of meaning are not inviolable, but have been linked inextricably to the needs, institutions, perceptions and religious assumptions of a society at any one period. Historically, reality as "a continuous connection of becoming" (Ernst Troeltsch), leaves little room for the older view of religious truth which was grounded in a supernatural interventionist account of divine activity. On the philosophical level, religious beliefs now tend to be held less as direct descriptions of transcendent reality than as provisional pointers to truth using symbolic and metaphorical forms. Clearly, the doctrine of Christ is not so readily or easily circumscribed under these conditions.

Third, awareness of the ideological function of the absolute uniqueness of Christ in the missionary exploitation of other cultures and religions has rightly attracted strong criticism on moral grounds. Now, while the religious and political abuse of the uniqueness of Christ does not discredit the concept of Christ's absoluteness as such, there is no necessary connection between the scandal of particularity and the Christian refusal to acquiesce in state power when the latter shows pretensions to politico-divine triumphalism. This was even true of Barth's opposition to Nazism through the Confessing Church. In other words, the act of Christian resistance to state power is not dependent on espousing belief in the Christian scandal of particularity.

If there is an assumption that the scandal of particularity is synonymous with Christian faith, it has become an ambivalent blessing. It might even run the danger of becoming a "scandal of obscurantism."

The scandal of particularity was eventually protected in the history of Christian thought by the doctrine of the Incarnation. In the light of new encounters and developing Christian consciousness, dare we ask if this hallowed term also deserves careful scrutiny? Conceptually, the Incarnation is certainly more elusive than is generally imagined, as the variety of its historical linguistic forms could demonstrate. Yet, no matter what form of words has been employed, the *idea* of the Incarnation has been taken to furnish Christian faith with a clear criterion for evaluating its relationship to the other world religions. Augustine, for example, could rejoice after many years of religious searching that he had not found elsewhere the unique doctrine that "the word became flesh." This was the distinctive message of the Christian faith that separated it from other religious possibilities.

If the concept of the Incarnation both forms the distinctive heart of Christian faith and also provides the central criterion for judging Christianity's relationship to other world religions, then it is small wonder that the Christological issue remains central in the debate about the Christian response to today's religiously plural world. What I wish to do here is first to trace some of the internal criticism being made of the doctrine of the Incarnation by Christian theologians, and second to show how Christology relates to differing stances within the changing Christian response to the world religions. There is a dialectic between these two endeavors. Modifications within Christology allow for a more open approach to the world faiths than has traditionally been assumed; and the growing demand for positive recognition of the world faiths in turn places a strain on inherited assumptions that protect the uniqueness of Christ.

CHRISTOLOGY IN INTERNAL CHRISTIAN DEBATE

The variety of the linguistic forms of the doctrine of the Incarnation is a clue to the complexity of the problem of Christology. In its classical Chalcedonian form (451 CE), the difficulty is usually posed as how to combine the divine and the human natures in the one person of Christ. The legacy of that fifth century Council has been that it set the parameters for future discussion. But today this specification for Christology is too narrow, as a number of factors have arisen to force a shift in perspective. It is worth rehearsing them in order to demonstrate why the critique has proved so far-reaching. While all of the following points remain controversial, by presenting them fairly bluntly (for reasons of brevity) I hope to sharpen up the issues as I see them.

First, the philosophical assumptions and categories of antiquity are no longer current coin and cannot be reinstated. What it means to speak now of "person," "nature," "substance," and so on, is entirely different from the technical thought-patterns of the patristic era. Not many theologians therefore are prepared simply to repeat these early centuries. But more is at stake than this linguistic difficulty: the story of the Chalcedonian definition involves intellectual assumptions and political manoeuvres which disclose its full historical character. The hermeneutical use of scripture, philosophico-theological assumptions about cosmology and divine activity, and the role of political will are just three extensive elements in a story that with hindsight is impossible to endorse as a way of believing today. Historical change has fractured any easy continuity with the ancient formulae: Chalcedon's putative achievement strikes us not so much as a mystery to be adored, but, outside of its own historical setting, as a puzzling *coup de théâtre*, dazzling yet incapable of conveying any real theological meaning. As it is, no satisfactory coherent interpretation of the "Chalcedon problem" has been forthcoming, and suspicion that it was inherently incapable of acknowledging the real humanity of Jesus is well-founded. The later Second Council of Constantinople (553 CE), for example, stated that the personhood of Jesus was exclusively divine in origin. And Christian history supplies abundant evidence of a kind of quiet or implicit Docetism running through the church's Christology since those early councils.

Second, the revolution in New Testament studies, with critical historical and other methods, has brought about a fundamental shift in the manner of our approach to the earliest interpretations of the figure of Jesus. Basically, the New Testament horizon was one of eschatology, not ontology or incarnation. The writers are thoroughly theocentric, in that they view Jesus as the one from God, who fulfils the promises of God after the pattern of preparation-fulfilment through Israel's history. Even the sporadic elements of incarnational language, found particularly in Paul and John (e.g., Col. 1:15–20; Phil. 2:6–11; John 1:1–18), require to be interpreted in the context both of each writer as a whole and of the eschatological horizons of the first-century, and therefore it cannot be assumed that these texts necessarily indicate what later orthodoxy took them to be. Even John's Gospel is far from clear about whether Jesus is seen as God's agent or simply as God. Besides, incarnational imagery is one thing, incarnational doctrine another. The fact that the Church Fathers found John's Gospel a rich resource for incarnational belief should not over-determine us now: anachronism in the reading of biblical texts comes too easily in theology. To be sure, incarnational doctrine may represent a reasonable evolutionary development from the eschatological biblical basis, but it would need some crafty hermeneutics to demonstrate this. Moreover, the Fathers cannot be blamed for treating the biblical text the way they did, for they did not have present-day critical tools available to them.

Third, New Testament study has demonstrated the diversity of the first reactions to the person of Jesus. The titles used of him—Son of God, Son of Man, Messiah, Word, Wisdom etc.—spring from experience and commitment, by whatever route it came to the writers, and not from some wooden arrangements in the purposes of God. That is to say, the titles are not free-floating, carrying the same fixed meaning wherever they are applied. Each writer interprets Jesus according to his own community response, background circumstances and available theological apparatus for "receiving" him, with all the richness and limitations that that imposes. Jesus is transformative of a writer's whole outlook—whether as Mark's enigmatic and disturbing Son of Man, or Matthew's bearer of the new messianic way, or as Paul's Son of God whose death and resurrection ushered in the new era of eschatological hope, and so on—such that the interpretation could not avoid subjectivity. While diversity indicates vitality, one implication of this development is that we ought not to award higher marks to some writers over others. For example, John's "logos" Christology need receive no higher appreciation than Mark's "Son of Man" view. They are different, simply that, and historical and literary criticism can give us a reasonable estimate why it turned out to be so. Constructively speaking, recognizing this early creativity can spur us on to find our own estimate of Jesus appropriate for our own missionary circumstances. As we do so, of course, we will take full cognizance of the New Testament process itself, as a critical partner in the endeavor.

Fourth, it is possible to acknowledge candidly the myth-making tendencies of early Christian doctrine, beginning in the New Testament itself and stretching out from there through the metaphysical assumptions of the first centuries. What seems to have occurred at the earliest period is what has been called a "Christian mutation" of the Jewish approach to God.[1] In the Jewish background there was a role for divine agency which was of broadly three types: divine attributes and powers (e.g., Wisdom, Logos), exalted patriarchs (e.g., Moses, Enoch), and principal angels. Given this background, the Christian devotion to Jesus led implicitly to the assertion of his pre-existence, which itself later became part of a religious story of "God the Son" coming to earth or of a metaphysical theory of two natures in one person. But what we are to make of this myth-making capacity today remains deeply problematic. The following judgement, by the English Anglican theologian John Robinson, captures the heart of what is being affirmed: "To register the conviction that in this man was fulfilled and embodied the meaning of God reaching back to the very beginning, they proclaim him as his Word, his Image, his Son, from all eternity."[2]

Jesus conveyed the power and presence of God through the impact of his whole personality; in this sense he embodied the love of God for the world. Put empirically: the creative impact of Jesus initiated a new style of

1. Hurtado, *One God,* 93–124.
2. Robinson, *Roots,* 65.

relationship to God, one with its own particular parameters of divine offer and human response. Eschewing pre-existence in this manner has at least the advantage of acknowledging the full humanity of Jesus.

Fifth, the doctrine of the Incarnation has acted as a theological mold for the concept of the finality of Jesus, developed outside of the latter's original Jewish framework. But under the influence of critical historical thinking it is precisely the validity of this concept of finality which has come under serious questioning. As this was attached to Jesus, finality has its roots in the Jewish apocalyptic view of history with its expectation of a messianic figure at the end of days. Critical thinking, while not being dogmatic about history as a closed or open system, is none the less more likely to view history as an interwoven process of cause and effect, with little room for the notion of a final age and therefore of a final savior figure. As it is, looking to the end is reminiscent of mythological thinking. Even Christianity's retention of the theme of the "now and the not yet" of the coming Kingdom, given the failure of that kingdom as Jesus preached it to arrive, remains basically untouched by changing perceptions in historical thinking. But if Jesus is no longer final in the strict sense, this need not imply that what he stands for is not decisive in some way. Distinguishing between the creative impact of Jesus on the one hand, and the interpretation of him in terms of finality on the other, opens the way for new interpretations of that impact in the changed climate of a different historical consciousness and positive religious pluralism. It is worth noting, moreover, that even a writer such as Jürgen Moltmann, who leaves metaphysical speculation on one side in favor of a return to biblical categories in Christology, fails to follow through the critical method at this point.[3] What it means to talk of Christology in *messianic* dimensions outside of the New Testament's own assumptions about the nature of messianic expectation remains puzzling.

Sixth, Christology is parasitic on the experience of salvation or liberation. Incarnation was intimately linked with views about salvation that strike us today as deficient. In particular, they depended on a literal interpretation of the story of the Fall of Adam and Eve as the first historical couple. Remove that background, and the necessity for Jesus to be the God-Man reversing the Fall is undermined. What exactly we might mean by salvation varies in Christian experience and theology, but it is likely to have both individual and corporate, this-worldly and after-worldly references. In other words, Christology now begins with questions of human need under God, asks first how the impact of Jesus meets those needs, and second how his, and therefore our, relationship to God is to be envisaged as a result. In these

---

3. Moltmann, *Way of Jesus Christ*, 1990.

circumstances many theologians have turned the Christological question of the Fathers—How can God become man?—upside down. In a historically and humanly conscious world we no longer have "Christology from above," but "Christology from below": what does it mean to speak of the human Jesus as also divine? Value is placed on Jesus's connection with humanity, not on his difference.

These six points could each be expanded at greater length. Yet I believe they reflect a fair account of what is taking place within Christological debate, certainly within a European context. Inevitably I have reflected my Anglo-Saxon bias! Taken together, however, they amount to a substantial dent on received tradition; and they pave the way for a shift in the work of the Christian theology of religions. I wish now to point out some of the issues within those shifts, before drawing an interim conclusion.

CHRISTOLOGY IN THE CHRISTIAN THEOLOGY OF RELIGIONS

The concept of the Incarnation has had an ambivalent history in relation to other world faiths. While its undoubted implication is that God intends all to follow Christ as the absolute savior, and therefore that the Christian Way represents the finally true Way, this has been expressed either as a confrontation with the other faiths or as the fulfilment of the evidence of transcendent life within them. Neither view takes the above critique of Christology with the full seriousness it deserves. But we need to examine the effects of the doctrine in both cases, and in the light of a changed context and new encounters. As we do so, we shall discover that the work the Incarnation has been required to do cannot meet the new circumstances. The new encounters and the new context place a different additional kind of strain on the merits of incarnation doctrine.

Let the early Karl Barth be representative of the confrontational view: "It is because we remember and apply the Christological doctrine of the *assumptio carnis* that we speak of revelation as the abolition of religion."[4] Barth was here taking religion to mean the humanly misguided attempt by sinful creatures to reach God through unaided effort. He was not initially speaking of other faiths as such, but of the abject failure of human beings to rely on the initiative of God's grace. In the background was the liberal outlook of his former teachers who, it seemed to him, had lost hold of the sovereign transcendence of God and had turned to the human sciences for faith's intellectual and religious justification. Nevertheless, he followed through his

4. Barth, *Church Dogmatics I/II*, 297.

position when he said of Christianity that the reality of grace known in the Christian story "differentiates our religion, the Christian, from all others as the true religion."[5] The strong distinction between the concepts of revelation and religion, the former being indicative of grace and the latter of human grasping, enabled Barth to drive a wedge between Christianity and the other faiths, and to promote Christ as the absolute savior of all. In relation to the doctrine of the Incarnation, which encapsulated this absoluteness, the Kierkegaardian fascination with paradox was not far from the surface.

As has often been pointed out, there is majesty in Barth's relentless resolution to "let God be God." There is also an invulnerability, which is less convincing. The crux issue is not the legitimacy or otherwise of paradox in theology, but to what extent theologians are prepared to allow their constructions to be open to criticism. Barth allowed a limited role for criticism in being secondary to biblical assumptions, but a generation later we have come to see the difficulties in sustaining that limitation. Once we have grasped the role that the human imagination plays in theological endeavor it is difficult to set boundaries to the effects of criticism. This means that the strong distinction between revelation and religion was really an attempt to circumnavigate the human element in interpreting Christian faith.

In so far as the Incarnation was intrinsically bound up with this whole scheme, that doctrine too was held to be inviolate. Yet the encounter between Christianity and other faiths shows this inviolability to be simply a hidden form of *arbitrariness*. In other words, the truth of Christ's exclusive uniqueness is so because the Christian theologian says it is so: it requires no grounds other than the decision to claim it so! Some might complain at this point that I have forgotten that Christianity is its own self-evident truth. My response to that rejoinder is to say that there is a distinction between authentic religious truth discovered by living and believing it, and sheer prejudice for the absoluteness of this truth in relation to other religious paths. The gospel's character as *sola fide* need not be jeopardized by recognizing divine truth outside the Church. The distinction between revelation and religion can run just as easily *through* all faiths as between Christian faith and the rest.

The *arbitrariness* of Barth's confrontational exclusivism is further highlighted by his inability to allow that the theme of grace known elsewhere, for example in some strands of Asian-origin religion, could modify his *a priori* approach. So, the Pure Land of School of Amida Buddhism speaks of putting trust in the saving love of Amida, thus echoing the structure of faith remarkably similar to the Reformation Christianity that Barth espoused.

---

5. Barth, *Church Dogmatics* I/II, 327.

Barth's response, that "only in Christ" is salvation forthcoming, further compounds the *arbitrariness* of this view. Again, the Incarnation is unable to sustain what is being asked of it.

If Barth narrowed the Incarnation in an exclusive direction the alternative possibility within the Christian tradition has pursued its universalist trajectory. This is the view that the uniqueness of Christ does not entail a negative judgement on other faiths, but is a fulfilment, gathering up clues, hints, pointers, and responses to the presence of God discerned within them. Expounding the logos language of John's Gospel, the Roman Catholic Federation of Asian Bishops' Conferences, in their seven theses of inter-religious dialogue from 1987, expressed this view thus:

> In presenting Christ as the 'Word' mediating the mysterious reality of God's presence to the world, John is implicitly admitting the presence of God's self-revelation in other religious traditions. The fact that John presents the Christ-event as an experience which is not reduced to the compass of his individual and ecclesial experience, but which transcends any particular form of expression and can be identified in the universe at large, shows that the Johannine Church was prepared to enter into dialogue with the surrounding religious traditions.[6]

Whether in reality John's community was so open to dialogue as this interpretation believes we cannot tell; there are other features of that gospel which suggest otherwise. But the theological point is clear enough: incarnation means that God is so committed to the world that we should not deduce from it that God's presence is precluded from being known elsewhere in the world. Yet it would be wrong to conclude from this that God's universal presence is such that all responses in faith to it are the same or equal in quality. Christ remains the crowning glory.

If Barth's confrontational scheme highlighted the *arbitrariness* of Incarnation, this second fulfilment strategy brings out the *ambiguity* of the Incarnation in relation to other faiths. This ambiguity refers to the double sense of the relationship that the Incarnation sets up in relation to other faiths: with one hand the Incarnation speaks of the solidarity of Christ with other human beings, and therefore other saviors; yet with the other hand it continues to affirm Christ's absolute uniqueness. It is therefore likely to be less helpful than many Christian groups assume. Whether Christian fulfilment is mediated dogmatically (from above) or historically (from below), the ambiguity, which is manifest differently in either mediation, is worth further reflection in order to clarify the point being made.

6. Theological Advisory Commission, "Seven Theses," 1989.

Karl Rahner's theory of Anonymous Christians stands as an example of mediating the supremacy of Christ from above. Although he accepted the thrust of historical consciousness—so that he viewed the Incarnation as the perfect embodiment of God's offer of Godself to the world and the free human response, anywhere and everywhere in the world, he nevertheless, out of loyalty to received tradition, retained belief in the qualitative difference between Jesus and the rest of humanity, including other savior figures. "The truth of a divine humanity would be mythologized," wrote Rahner, "if it were simply a datum of every person always and everywhere."[7] Only with the one man, Jesus, has the eternal Word been identified. The consequence in the theology of religions is that Christ is somehow the origin of salvation anonymously mediated through the world's religiously varied communal life. Thus, what Rahner opened up with one hand, he took away with the other. Positing Christ as the historical goal (fulfilment) of human and religious aspiration creates an ambiguity in Christology, for the determining factor at root is really the dogmatic premise that it is Christ who is defined as the original cause of salvation.

The other route of ambiguity, mediating the supremacy of Christ "from below," can be demonstrated by referring to the theological work of John Robinson.[8] Here, Jesus was presented not as the exception to the human race, but as its true representative: in Jesus the intended goal of creation comes to fruition. But Jesus is so constituted, not because he was the unique cause of salvation in the whole world, as was the case with Rahner, but because he is "decisive" as the true representative. Within an overall model of complementarity between the faiths, God's presence in Jesus remains always open to "completion, clarification, and correction" in dialogue with others. Yet Robinson also went on to confess Jesus as the "profoundest clue to all the rest," thus retaining hold on his uniqueness at least on the basis of implicit historical comparisons. By way of additional support "from below" for his confessional stance, Robinson went even further and claimed that Christian faith had the capacity to deal better with those factors that religions have found to be most inimical, and which he specified as evil, the impersonal, and the feminine. But there is a difficulty in knowing what value to attach to Robinson's suggestions at this point. If such a claim is to be substantiated it will require detailed historical comparisons and unusual hermeneutical skills. Many would think it is not possible to make these claims anyway, for religions are not open to that kind of comparative valuing. Once again, even the method of historical comparison is unable to overcome the yearning for

---

7. Rahner, *Theological Investigations* 4, 112.
8. Robinson, *Truth is Two-Eyed*, 97–129.

Christian supremacy which is revealed at the heart of inclusivist Christology. In the theology of religions, the "dogmatic lag" of the doctrine of Jesus's uniqueness gives way to an unsatisfactory ambiguity.

JESUS AS PARABLE

As a result of this kind of analysis, my contention is this: both the internal shifts within Christian thought about the person of Jesus and the inappropriateness of the belief in final supremacy (expressed either as exclusive-confrontation or inclusive-fulfilment) attached to Jesus in a culture which values religious pluralism positively, point to a profound need for reinterpreting what tradition came to call the "scandal of particularity." *The doctrine of the Incarnation cannot bear the weight which Christian thought has put on it, and nowhere is this more highlighted than from within the whole modern debate around the Christian theology of religions.* Therefore the "scandal" now is the refusal to take the necessary steps in Christian theological reconstruction in the light of changed perceptions. This is not to say that simply because Christians are learning to value the religious experience of their neighbors, therefore Christian thought about Jesus ought to change. It is claiming, however, that the factors of *arbitrariness* and *ambiguity* compound the problematic nature of traditional Christology in modern debate once the relationship between Christianity and other faiths is brought into the open.

Pointing out problems in theology is always easier than constructing solutions. Yet there are some constructive suggestions available. Within a pluralist framework in the Christian theology of religions, basically two broad approaches to the place of Jesus, which are sensitive to the concerns of critical consciousness and religious plurality, have emerged. Both are prepared to use the more relaxed language of the centrality of Jesus as mediating the purposes of God for the world, rather than the specialized language of incarnation which carries so much cultural specificity from the early centuries.

The first view is more metaphysical in tone and accepts Jesus as different "in degree," not "in kind," from the rest of humanity and therefore from all other savior figures. Following a general process-evolutionary-historical outlook, in which creation is seen as the field of the self-expressive activity of God, the intended goal of humanity has come to fruition in Jesus as the climactic moment where God's activity and human response achieved perfect pitch. Incarnational and inspirational language are collapsed into a single form: God as spirit is ever energizing the process of creation from within, ever seeking incarnational embodiment. Thus, the divine-human potential is capable of emerging in differing degrees and forms across many cultures and histories. The Christ-event was one paradigm moment in history where the realization of this potential occurred, but it does not preclude other paradigm moments.

The second view is more metaphorical in tone, and speaks of the impact of Jesus using parable, symbol, and metaphor. It believes that Jesus is both a metaphor of God's love and care for the world and a door of human response to the divine mystery. It is not "mere metaphor," as some commentators might put it, for it recognizes that metaphor bears both instrumental and representational power. The objectivity of its power lies in its ability to evoke the perception that with Jesus a new paradigm account of God's relationship with the world is possible; and its subjectivity honors the fact that it is *our* perception that Jesus's way can be trusted as salvation-bearing. Once again, there are other possibilities, other parables and symbolic occasions which have initiated different patterns of the divine-human relationship throughout the world.

Both accounts here spring from the concern to root Christology in the commitment to Jesus as a historical figure through whom we encounter the power and presence of God. The salvation or transformation of human living which he has opened up has come to us in a particular form, stemming from the mixed culture of middle eastern Palestine of the first century CE. Yet Christian faith views him as no less a universal figure than a particular instance of religious response to the divine summons within life. His saviorhood is not so much unique, final, or absolute, as *intentionally universal*. That is to say, while Christ is obviously the named savior figure for Christians, he is not confined to the Christian communities: his significance is *for* the whole world. This claim provides Christian faith with a foundation for mission, which in relation to other faiths now assumes a dialogical character.

Viewing Jesus in this manner holds together both the reality of God that stems from discipleship of him and the vocation to witness to him in dialogue, without assuming him to be the final truth of God prior to the dialogue itself. Jesus need not be the norm above norms, as other norms also make their own contributions to the dialogical process. The purpose of the dialogue will then be to develop criteria whereby a world ecumenism, which respects differences and yet encourages mutual criticism can be pursued.

Of course, the strangeness of this journey leaves it open to being easily misconstrued. Some might think that it amounts to a judgement on Jesus by a prior conception of God other than that found in the Christian tradition.

But this is to miss the point. Once disentangled from outmoded perceptions, Jesus as savior figure for Christians is freed to allow his impact to be felt afresh at the important level of religious experience. In this way the wider religious life of human communities is also challenged.

The kind of epistemology required to undergird this new venture in dialogue has yet to be fully realized. Meanwhile, the experience of persisting religious pluralism entails that truth in the religious interpretation of reality can no longer remain a function of one tradition alone. Of necessity it must embrace many traditions, as well as what we know from the natural and human sciences. In this process of "dialogue for truth" an appropriate epistemological framework for underpinning such an outlook will be forged as part of the dialogue itself. Whatever form it takes, it will be committed to the belief that the particularities of the world religious traditions are not isolated islands, but territories deeply and necessarily related to one another. The scandal of particularity has been superseded by the scandal of particularities.

Christian theologians have long thought that they were handling stable tradition, but that era has now faded. The alternative reading of Christian history is one marked by change and innovation, according to shifts in cultural and historical sensibilities. Given hindsight, we can see how and why Christian faith has taken various forms at different periods in history. It is therefore open for us to make our own variation at our own time and according to our own partial vision and knowledge. If this is a new venture, the scandal of particularities is bound to show itself as a vulnerable possibility. But for Christians, the life of vulnerability Jesus himself lived and the universalism he achieved can be our guide on the way.

PART THREE

Ethics in Dialogue

7

Hospitality is Good, But How Far Can It Go?

THIS CHAPTER WAS FIRST published as a comment on the statement issued by the World Council of Churches, entitled "Religious Plurality and Christian Self-Understanding."[9] The statement was the result of a unique collaboration among three constituencies, usually kept separate in the WCC—Faith & Order, Conference on World Mission and Evangelism, and the Office on Interreligious Relations and Dialogue. Placing this chapter here provides a bridge from Theology to Ethics in the dialogue between religions.

INTRODUCTION

The statement from the World Council of Churches, entitled "Religious Plurality and Christian Self-Understanding," rightly recognizes that the contextual challenges and opportunities within the fact of global religious plurality continue to deepen and take new forms according to the twists and turns of historical change. Furthermore, by yoking together the three networks of Faith and Order, the Conference on World Mission and Evangelism, and the Office on Interreligious Relations and Dialogue, we can applaud the WCC's

---

9. World Council of Churches, "Religious Plurality," Issue 45.

instinctive honesty in placing religious plurality at the centre of Christian self-reflection.

There is a further, related reason for applauding the decision to yoke together the three networks in this exploration. As the academic world splinters into more and more specialisms—a phenomenon also experienced in theological studies—collaboration borders on a bold counter-cultural move. It is as though internal Christian plurality, as this is organized around separated disciplinary endeavours (as opposed to separated ecclesial denominations), is turning to forge its own unity of purpose and theological common ground. In a sense, this mirrors the very problem presented by religious plurality itself, namely, the problem of "the one and the many," in its current twenty-first century guise.

The separation between theology, mission and interreligious dialogue was always arbitrary anyway. Yet given that theology, mission, and dialogue each come to the table with their own developed shapes, historical trajectories, and assumptions about the centrality of their own place in the Christian scheme of things, the attempt at co-operation between them will not be an easy journey to undertake. Moreover, each discourse in itself is not a settled enterprise and therefore part of the achievement of the consensus in "Religious Plurality and Christian Understanding" is that it represents a considerable advance on a former lamentable state of affairs.

Yet the statement must be counted a work in progress. In my view, it seeks to transcend the traditional struggle between the potentially opposing pulls of mission and dialogue, and, not surprisingly, that struggle is not easily resolved. The focus on the notion of "hospitality" is, at one level, a stroke of genius, for it drags the debate away from the usual battle ground of Christian uniqueness versus worldly plurality. This is the statement's strength. But it may also be that highlighting the concept of hospitality amounts to a strategy of deflection away from the arbitration between mission and dialogue that is now required if we are to face the theological issues squarely. Yet I acknowledge that it is perhaps a necessary deflection, especially for the globally troubled times that we have entered. When international relations are so preoccupied with religiously-motivated violence, valuing hospitality could well act as a necessary antidote to the endemic fears that are the result of the misperception and stereotyping of the so-called other.

HOSPITALITY: ETHICS OR THEOLOGY?

Given the historically agonized tension between mission and dialogue, it is no accident that Religious Plurality and Christian Self-Understanding defers to what is essentially an ethical category in the arbitration between them. Its applicability to both international relations and internal Christian division is telling. But hospitality remains an ethical category and functions essentially to encourage relationships between people of different faith communities. In other words, it belongs most fittingly at the dialogue end of the tension between mission and dialogue. I say this irrespective both of the fact that Christian mission is not these days antagonistic to notions of hospitality and of the incarnational-trinitarian theological underpinning in the Christian belief of the transforming graciousness of God in Christ that the statement celebrates.

I have long thought that the era of seeking theological permission for engaging in dialogue and co-operation with people of different faiths has now passed. The Statement endorses this perspective. Building on a permission that is more than 25 years old (the WCC *Guidelines* were issued in 1979), the category of hospitality leads to expectations that God has more in store for us than we once thought possible. If hospitality extends the hand of friendship to others then it is an extension also to the faith or spirit which moves within them, be that of Muslim or Hindu or Buddhist, and so on. In this sense the Baar (1990) achievement that other religions embody not only a "seeking" but also a "finding" of transcendent reality from within different matrices of human response and religious insight is reinforced by this new Statement. I might add that this theological judgment is borne out by the witness of many in the dialogue movement. The resultant theological question forced into the open by our changed circumstances and mood is whether or not the traditional theology which first motivated that permission for dialogue is sufficient to bear the consequences of it. Dialogue is proving to be a Trojan horse. Might it be that hospitality will turn out similarly to be subversive?

One small indication that it might do so is contained in the following observation: Religious Plurality and Christian Self-Understanding has dropped the language of "one and only," "uniqueness," and "finality." Hospitality is not so hard-edged as these theological concepts might like us to be. It allows us to soft pedal their question mark hovering over the acceptance of others in their seeking and finding. This is clearly an advantage in terms of building relationships. But, as I pointed out above, it is at the expense of making adjustments in our theology of religious plurality which hospitality is bound to invite; otherwise, we remain in the realm of ethical permission-giving and not theological consequence-taking, once we really do accept with full seriousness the religious plurality of our world.

The theological dilemma can be sharpened by recalling a question put by the Vatican's International Theological Commission in 1997: "How can one enter into an interreligious dialogue, respecting all religions and not considering them in advance as imperfect and inferior, if we recognize in Jesus Christ and only in him the unique and universal Saviour of mankind?" That question having been raised, however, the Commission did not proceed to tackle it head-on. Similarly, the WCC Statement has side-stepped the awkward conceptual territory highlighted by the Commission's question. Does this mean that, for the time being, we are content to place the theological anxieties on one side as dialogue, co-operation and hospitality continue the work of encounter into an unknown future? Given the lack of consensus on these matters, this may well be the case, and perhaps there is much about it to commend as a strategy of engagement. My own hunch, however, is that sooner or later the theological questions will return.

What then is the relationship between the three hitherto independently developed arenas of mission, dialogue, and theology, so fruitfully yoked together in the Statement? I suggest, as an alternative model, that the theology of religions acts as arbiter between the pulls of dialogue and mission. As has often been pointed out, both mission and dialogue are not so polar opposites as we previously imagined them to be. They have both expanded conceptually in recent years. On the one hand, the heart of mission is the Missio Dei which is inevitably bigger than the church's own participation in it. How can this not be the case? So, commending the Christian faith is not something that is now shouted from the rooftops but is carried out as part of relationships with others. There is a Christian story to commend but it is best commended within a dialogical framework. On the other hand, dialogue, while it has nurtured its own framework of equal respect, mutual accountability, and critical reasoning, it remains the science of the "in-between": there are convictions to be heard and made sense of in the light of what we know about how the world works. Beyond the caricatures both of mission as imperialism-by-another-name and of dialogue as a we're-all-the-same-really kind of tea-party there is work to do. That work is theological.

THEOLOGY OF RELIGIONS

The theology of religions seeks to interpret the meaning of religious plurality in the light of what we know of other traditions, our experience of their impact (their goodness and their negative effects), and the role of critical reasoning (the recognition of the role of history and culture in formulating religious beliefs, spiritualities and ethical postures, and so on). It notes that a religious account of what I call "transcendent vision and human transformation" is glimpsed through a particular concrete focus. That concrete focus might be a scripture, a person, a part of the natural world. In other words, the religions are rooted in concrete experience (particular) but are expansive in their intention and effects (universal).

The theology of religions interprets this structure of particularity and universal relevance among the religions in different ways. Here are three possibilities:

a. You can export your own particular experience and think that the expansiveness which it glimpses ought to take the shape of your own particular glimpsing, i.e., the universality must be defined by the particularity of your own glimpsing—with the result that everyone should become Christian.

b. You can export your own particular experience and not be surprised to find other experiences of comparable goodness and worth—that's what the universal dimension within your own glimpsing ought to lead you to expect. On this view, the theology constrains you to think that other kinds of particularity or rootedness are necessarily measured by your own tradition's experience. In Christian terms, this is done by saying that what is manifest in Jesus is either the origin or the goal, or both, of the universal presence of God in the world. On this view, the fullness of religious vision lies with the Christian version of it, but others might participate in that fullness according to degrees and according to their different histories and circumstances.

c. You can export your particular experience and say that the glimpse of ultimate reality through your own tradition's lens is necessary for the world and its transformation, but necessary as part of the necessity of others also, others whose histories have demonstrated vitality and transformative power. Each religion has a view of the whole of reality from out of the window of its tradition, but it is a partial viewing.

How do these three positions relate to the tension between mission and dialogue? All three positions here accept a role for mission—all three accept that there is a Christian story to relate and that others should hear it, whether that's for conversion, or for their edification that something greater is available than what they have known thus far, or for the sake of sharing and learning from the differences. But how do they deal with the new information from dialogue and hospitality?

Attitude (a) has difficulties. If your theology leads you to expect very little of transcendent vision and human transformation elsewhere then you are likely to be embroiled in a serious misrepresentation of others. And we know that this has happened all too often in the history of Christian relations with people of many faiths. For example, we might recall Hendrik Kraemer's comment that "Islam in its constitutive elements and apprehensions must be called a superficial religion . . . Islam might be called a religion that has almost no questions and no answers."[10] This is an astonishing statement from a scholar of Islam! It is little wonder that many Muslims (and others) have wondered about the validity of the Christian invitation to dialogue when basic mutual respect is missing.

The most common position in Christian circles is attitude (b): God's presence in our world is everywhere hidden, but our glimpsing of it can only be measured by our inherited Christian theological and conceptual framework. The difficulties with this are well-known. How can Jesus initiate the salvation of the Buddhist or the Hindu, both of whom belong to traditions that are older than the appearance of Jesus on earth? And both have generated equally impressive results in terms of ethics and civilisation. What does it mean for the incarnate Word or the resurrected Christ or the Spirit of God—choose your Christian formulation of words (words readily employed by Religious Plurality and Christian Self-Understanding)—to be operative in the world as the decisive focus for the spiritual vitality of others? Theologians who realise this problem seek to ameliorate the effects of this approach by pushing the problem to the point of a post-mortem encounter with Christ for other believers. However, this does nothing to answer the central problem. The encounter with Christ as necessity is retained; only the manner and moment of encounter is changed.

The third view (c) notes that all traditions make some distinction between ultimate reality as known in concrete, particular ways and ultimate reality as being beyond human comprehension (ineffable). In the final analysis, all traditions are rafts, a means to an end, and they conceptualize these means and ends according to the best lights they have. But all lights are limited—pointers, metaphors and symbolic representations—and this is because religious language depicts but does not reproduce the ultimate truth of our condition and the meaning of life. The infinity of ultimate reality is the deeper ineffable ground of the many phenomenal manifestations of religious insight and truth. An empirical justification for hypothesizing this might be that the traditions show themselves to be comparable at the empirical level, producers of both good and bad in spiritual insight and practice. No one tradition has been greater than another in history. It is important to stress that, on this view, radical differences between the religions are retained, for the religions are historically specific in so many ways, but their mutual belongingness in transcendence is also affirmed.

10. Kraemer, *Christian Message*, 216–17.

Some have objected to this outlook in so far as it seems to arrive at a tidy conclusion too quickly. Religions, they aver, have different aims, different expected outcomes: so Christian love is not the same as Buddhist compassion; and Christian justice is not the same as Muslim justice, and so on. We cannot therefore assume that we are all united, even in the realms of ineffability. There just are differences. We can respect one another, we can encounter without assuming superiority, we might even perceive something in the other that enriches our own outlook and which has emerged more fully in another tradition than our own. But don't assume we all meet somewhere, even if that somewhere is mystical.

My own reaction to this criticism is that it simply misses the mark. View (c) is an inductive view. It notes that Christian faith is based on experience that we believe can be trusted, and this basis can be extended also to others. At this point you then have to make sense of the manyness of religious life theologically. Emphasizing the radical differences is fine. But that does not prevent us making the inductive move that as Christian faith is not a projection but a trust of experience and a cognitive response to what we call the divine reality, and that this is partially confirmed by its spiritual fruits, so we can hypothesize that the same is true for others. This then leaves us with the problem of how to explain the diversity of religious life, assuming that the religious life is a valid life based on a varied sense of transcendence and with equal impressiveness and equal unimpressiveness to Christianity among the religions. How to allow for both radical differences and also the intuition of relatedness that is apprehended in and through dialogical encounters? How to honor the assumptions, impacts, and discoveries implicit in hospitality itself? Simply to say we are all different and that's that seems insufficient in the face of the evidence and the practice. Theology has to catch up with the practice.

CONCLUSION

My thesis has been that both mission and dialogue have had their suspicions of one another, but that time has passed. However, the overtures that the one makes to the other require grounding in a theology of religions that enables a new relationship to flourish. Mission is required to surrender the corner of the mind that assumes that one religion alone is eventually superior in terms of experience, insight, and praxis. Dialogue must renounce residual notions that all religions are variations on the same theme. The thrust of mission is to supply religious identity on which dialogue thrives; dialogue and hospitality, in turn, become the new context within which mission learns to practise the mutuality of respect and the mystery of ineffability.

A citation from the late Stanley Samartha captures the mood I am seeking:

> If the great religious traditions of humanity are indeed different responses to the Mystery of God or Sat or the Transcendent or Ultimate Reality, then the distinctiveness of each response, in this instance the Christian, should be stated in such a way that a mutually critical and enriching relationship between different responses becomes naturally possible.[11]

The ethics of hospitality takes us to the threshold of this vision. A theology of religious plurality, affirming the full validity of the great religious traditions, yet held as "mutually critical and enriching," keeps the theology of hospitality honest.

---

11. Samartha, *One Christ*, 86.

8

9/11 and Choices for Dialogue

> THIS CHAPTER PLACES RELIGIOUSLY-MOTIVATED *violence at the center of interreligious dialogue and analyzes why the instrumentalizing of dialogue for the sake of peace is not enough. Questions of acceptance and rejection of the religious other in theology of religions cannot be set aside for the sake of an ethics-only dialogue.*

FRAMING THE QUESTION OF DIALOGUE

"Where were you when JFK was assassinated?" For some years following the killing of the USA President John F. Kennedy (JFK) in 1963 that was a common question. The question itself was indicative of how the killing was being situated in a nation's psyche: JFK was the first Catholic president of the USA, and therefore an embodiment of the American Dream that anyone could rise to be the nation's Commander in Chief irrespective of background and religious affiliation. Some said that he represented hope at the dawn of the social revolutions of the 1960s. In other words, here was a significant cultural moment in a nation's history, one which was being held up as revelatory in some sense: a turning-point when national fortunes were dashed on the rock of shocking violence.

Now ask yourself an updated version of the same question: "Where were you on 9/11?"—when the world allegedly changed, as a result of terrorist attacks on American institutions of finance and power. Has 9/11 assumed a revelatory status comparable with the killing of JFK? Was this also a painful reminder that the American Dream—now in its post-Cold War phase—remains a fragile myth? Or was it revelatory of what the Italian-American novelist, Don DeLillo, chillingly estimated, that "only the lethal believer, the person who kills and dies for faith, is taken seriously in modern society."[1] Even if this exaggerates what is the case, it is sufficiently shocking for most believers' ears, that its possibility has triggered a fundamental reassessment of the place and truth of religious commitment itself.

Certainly 9/11 has become the occasion for an outpouring of many texts, seeking to explain the link between religion and violence. There has also been an exponential increase in texts dealing with the dialogue between religions, many of which seem predicated on the belief that such dialogue will help to renew the credibility of religious commitment *per se* post-9/11.

All of this raises a question for the dialogical enthusiast who may have been building bridges of mutual understanding between religions and worldviews for many years. The question is this: should the dialogue between religions be reframed as a response to what is now called religiously-motivated violence? There is pressure to do just this—from governments, civil society, the academy, and religious institutions themselves—and it is understandable. However, I believe that the answer needs to be more nuanced than this. My own provisional answer is this: yes, the dialogue must face head-on the ugliness of religion's seeming enslavement to violence, yet there are many dimensions to the dialogue and it may be that, in the long run, the answer to religiously-motivated violence lies in the renewal of the religions themselves through dialogical encounter at levels which ask hard questions about religious claims to truth in relation both to one another and to what we know from human enquiry through the sciences and humanities more generally.

HISTORICAL BACKGROUND

9/11 injected a massive shock into the US psyche and into the psyche of all western-style democracies. The Cold War had ended but now a different war seemed to have been declared. Some of us wondered if politicised Islam was becoming a substitute enemy to take the place of the USSR. If this was the case, then it made 9/11 look like an opening salvo in the new confrontation. The

---

[1] DeLillo, *Mao II*, 157.

problem is that the salvo worked. The West would react and confirm the suspicions of those elements in the Muslim world which accused the West of a new kind of colonialism, now pursued under the cloak of economic globalization.

If the international political community was disturbed deeply by 9/11, then the same was true of the international interreligious dialogue community. To date, that dialogue endeavour had expended its energy mainly on the philosophical problems of how to interpret a growing sense of a global religious plurality in the light of specific religious claims. One might say that this was the classical problem of the "One and the Many" in a new key. Is plurality what the religions should expect from their perceptions of God—how does Christianity, Islam, Hinduism, Judaism, and so on, understand themselves now in relation to a diversity which the globalising world has brought into sharp relief? This is a discussion, moreover, which had been generating some sophisticated exchanges over roughly the last forty years.

Then came the cataclysmic rupture. On the surface the attack seemed senseless, but those who knew what was stirring in the corridors of religious fundamentalism were surprised only by the monstrous audacity of the act. Of course, there had been examples of atrocity before in the name of religious anger—documented graphically and analyzed sharply in most recent times by Mark Juergensmeyer in his book, *Terror in the Mind of God* (2000), which cited Muslim, Sikh, Christian, Buddhist, and Jewish examples.[2] These were all instances of what he termed "performative violence," actions designed to draw attention to a cause rather than win a war. 9/11, which occurred after the book's publication, has become the most dramatic, even iconic, performative violent act to date. In this sense, 9/11 has changed everything.

Therefore, for those of us promoting the dialogue between religions, 9/11 was a summons to come out of the ivory tower. For dialogue to be useful it would need to address this under-belly of religiously-motivated violence. Mahatma Gandhi had already said that non-violence was part of the truthfulness of a religion, part of its core affirmation. Any view of life which claimed a spiritual origin, he believed, was, by definition, seeking the supreme good for the world and therefore violence could not be a part of such a view. Since 9/11 there has been much agonizing about how religions can be enlisted as instruments of violence.

TWO APPROACHES TO DIALOGUE

If Gandhi proposed that we cannot solve the truthfulness problem in religion without sorting out religious pretensions to violence, then my thesis

2. Juergensmeyer, *Terror in the Mind of God* (2000).

is that the opposite might also be the case: we cannot solve problems of peace without attending also to the philosophical problems of how religions interpret the world and their relations with one another.

These two views of the dialogical task for today are reflected in two well-known formulations from two seasoned scholars in the field:

The philosophical/epistemological framing:

Dialogue, especially dialogue in the religious, and ideological, area, is not simply a series of conversations. It is a whole new way of thinking, a way of seeing and reflecting on the world, and its meaning.[3]

The ethical framing:

No survival without a world ethic.
No world peace without peace among the religions.
No peace between the religions without dialogue between the religions.[4]

These two approaches articulate almost competing directions for scholars of interfaith relations today. And it is this competition, if that is what it amounts to, that I believe we need to examine more closely if we are to gain a better perspective on the clamour to claim 9/11 as a moment of revelatory impact.

WIDER CONTEXT

Let me now set out two features of the wider context in this struggle between competing claims for our dialogical attention. The first is the naming of our historical period as post-colonial, one characteristic of which is the reassertion of religious identity as grounds for forging political identity. This is true for many ideologies and places—for example, Hindu Nationalism for India, Sikh Separatism for Punjab, Jewish Settlers for Israel, Christian Supremacists for the USA, or Al-Quaeda for Muslim rule across the Muslim world.

The post-Colonial context has been especially significant in relation to the struggle of political Islam against the West. The 9/11 attacks were directed against the essential instruments of American power—the World Trade Centre as economic power, the Pentagon as military power, and the White House as political power (if this was indeed the target of the third

3. Swidler and Mojzes, *Study of Religion*, 146.
4. Küng, *Global Responsibility*, xv.

plane whose mission was foiled when passengers fought back, causing the plane to crash land in Pennsylvania before it could strike). The attacks were highly planned and were not about killing individuals but about striking at the structures of power. If we ask about the intentions of the attacks the answer is not entirely clear. Was it to de-stabilise the perceived superior power of the USA? Or disturb the complacency of Western victory in the Cold War? Was it to rally other Muslims in the cosmic battle between the "House of Peace" (Islam) and "House of War" (the rest of us) and establish a renewed caliphate? We do not fully know.

The second context is the revitalised discussion about the secularization thesis in the western study of religion. The secularization thesis assumed the demise of religious affiliation in the wake of modernity, but 9/11 literally seems to blow that thesis apart. Religion, it might be said, has blasted its way back into public debate. This is obviously not a happy state of affairs. Even if the democratic state continues to promote the principle of separation between politics and religion, it seems it has at least to take account of the fact that there are citizens out there for whom "God" represents a higher authority than democratic institutions and the voting public. In a democracy the rulers are meant to be held to account for their policies and activities, and some people will rely on their religious compass for discerning how to render our political masters accountable. Therefore, religion matters, at least in this minimal sense, for the political process. But because weariness over 16th century religious wars in Europe was a major factor in the desire to abandon the theocratic state there is bound to be nervousness about welcoming religious voices back into public debate. 9/11 is the worst nightmare for those wary of questioning the social contract of modernity and the general acceptance that religion should remain a private affair.

Those two contexts have fed into the default position in many minds that religion is responsible for all violence in the world. Hence this well-known accusation from the philosopher and neuroscientist, Sam Harris:

> Non-believers like myself stand beside you dumbstruck by the
> Muslim hordes who chant death to whole nations of the living.
> But we stand dumbstruck by you as well:
> by your denial of tangible reality,
> by the suffering you create in service of your religious myths, and
> by your attachment to an imaginary God.[5]

Notice how Harris yokes together three anti-religious motives:

- Psychological flaws of religion—it prevents us from facing up to reality

5. Harris, *Letter*, 2006.

- Immoral outcomes of religion—it is a source of harm
- Philosophical groundlessness of religion—it is irrational.

All three accusations identified by Harris have been well-rehearsed since the Enlightenment. But in actuality all three accusations are not necessarily so well founded as Harris's polemic imagines.

First, there is evidence that religious people are no less well-adjusted psychologically when compared to others: the mechanisms which help them to deal with life's transitoriness and anxieties simply lie in spiritual practice. And the science of human happiness places priority on "spiritual well-being" as an indicator of all-round human health. Second, the accusation that religion is the source of all harm, violence, and warfare ignores the fact that it is also the source of much altruism and compassion in the world. Third, the fact that religious commitment stretches beyond the narrowly rational does not render it irrational. In fact, there are fascinating debates now stemming from quantum mechanics and cosmology which argue for a priority of consciousness over materialism, and this raises again the possibility of the reality of Transcendence without accusations of irrationality.

In other words, Harris's accusations spring from his atheist philosophical materialism and not from an examination of all the evidence. The debate between believers and unbelievers is obviously an important debate in its own right, but this is not the same as determining questions of where violence-allied-to-religion springs from and what its perpetrators think religion is for. Moreover, it is worth remembering that the worst atrocities of the twentieth century were set in train by non-religious ideologies—examples include: Communist gulags, Nazi National Socialist holocaust, Mao Zedong's Cultural Revolution in China, the killing fields of Pol Pot's Cambodia.

RELIGION AND VIOLENCE

Turning now to the reasons for violent conflict: there are many of them, but here are three commonly cited ones:

1. Grievances—about land, resources, or a perceived injustice
2. Seeking revenge for unresolved historic antagonism
3. Ideological conviction or empire expansionism

We know that religion is often enlisted to bless other motives based on grievance, historic mistrust, or empire expansionism. To claim transcendent backing lends an almost unlimited force to personal and group agency and cloaks action in a supposed moral authority. However, it is far from clear that religion itself is the culprit behind religiously-motivated violence. In this vein, the British philosopher of religion, Keith Ward, contends: "What makes beliefs evil is not religion, but hatred, ignorance, the will to power, and indifference to others.[6] If this is the case, the most one can say is that religion has been powerless to prevent conflict. Blessing conflict, it turns out, is really a form of powerlessness to prevent it!

Nevertheless, enlisting religion for blessing evil intentions, which have been formulated in relation to other factors, cannot be the sole explanation for religiously-motivated violence. Ward's separation of the evils of intention from direct causation in religious systems and beliefs is reasonable up to a point. But the abuse-of-religion argument is not sufficient to explain religiously-motivated violence fully. There is a category of religious commitment which issues in violence more directly; in other words, there are some religious roots to violent conflict. Needless to say, for the vast majority of religious people religious violence represents a perversion of faith. But this does not mean that there is not some more direct link which needs addressing.

The clue as to the marriage of religion and violence can be discerned from the discovery in a left luggage locker at Boston's Logan Airport following 9/11:

> Tame your soul, purify it, convince it, make it understand, and incite it ... Bless your body with some verses of the Qur'an—this is done by reading verses into one's hands, and then rubbing the hands over whatever is to be blessed—the luggage, clothes, the knife, your personal effects, your ID, your passport ... The rest is left to God, the best one to depend on ... We will all meet in the highest heaven, God willing.[7]

This was instruction for the terrorist hijackers, and it tells of more than simply enlisting divine help for violence based on other causes. Note how the intimacy between the Qur'an and instruments of attack seems almost sexual. The religious blessing sought here is not simply an external aid to a pre-planned malevolent deed; there are specific religious motivations at work.

Unfortunately, we know what these factors are:

- a Manichaeist worldview of Good vs. Evil, where Evil is always the possession of the other who can therefore be labelled "enemy"

---

6. Ward, *Is Religion Dangerous?*, 38.
7. McTernan, *Violence*, 22.

- an egoism which poses oneself as God's instrument of salvation
- literalism about chosen texts which claim "God on my side"
- an exclusivist absolutism about religious truth.

I believe that these factors can be applied across the religious board. At this point, Sam Harris is correct: this is a combination of irrationality, immorality, and psychological malfunction. But Harris ignores how this is also anathema to the vast majority of religiously committed people, institutions, and scholars.

Given this history, how might the religions help? Often "dialogue" is proposed as a greater part of the solution. Here, then, is a provisional definition of dialogue, similar to the one I proposed in the Introduction, from a long-time practitioner, Paul Mojzes:

> Dialogue is a way by which persons or groups of different persuasions respectfully and responsibly relate to one another in order to bring about mutual enrichment without removing essential differences between them.[8]

Although this is not going to solve every problem, balancing the discovery of universality in the depths of particularities is the kind of approach which has propelled a great deal of momentum for dialogue internationally and regionally.

There are many fruits of dialogue emerging in many troubled places across the world. For example, here is a statement that echoes exactly Mojzes sentiments:

> *A Multi-Religious Statement Condemning Violence Targeting a Jerusalem Yeshiva,*
> *8 March 2008*
> We—Muslim, Jewish, and Christian—decry the violent attack targeting the Mercaz Harav Yeshiva in Jerusalem this week. The murder of eight students is a tragedy for all people of faith. The way to advance peace in the region is for religious communities to cooperate, forging an alliance grounded in the moral principles shared by every faith tradition. As Muslim, Jew, and Christian, we are all bound by a common heritage of spiritual struggle under one God. Our collective voice and moral authority are greater than each of us standing alone. Together, we can help calm the rising hostilities and soothe the wounded and the grieving. Each of us is responsible for the well-being and safety

---

8. Mojzes, "The What and the How," 203.

of the other. This is a notion of "shared security" that Religions for Peace has helped advance in the international community.

Making statements does not bring about world peace. Nonetheless, they can be part of the background noise for developing a culture of peace.

What dialogue does is to clear away stereotypes, forge openings for reconciliation following historical grievances, help participants learn to value the other as they value themselves, develop criteria for spotting perversity in religious interpretation, and accept some measure of mutuality in discerning what believing in today's critical thinking world really amounts to.

A further shared statement, arising from the experience of dialogue, reflects this view of dialogue, especially in the desire to "accept some measure of mutuality" in discerning the challenges facing interreligious thought and relations. In 2005, a UK scholarly group of Jews, Christians, and Muslims issued what they called their "Platform Statement" containing Unwelcome and Welcome Truths, as they envisaged them:

A STATEMENT FROM A DIALOGUE GROUP OF JEWS, CHRISTIANS, AND MUSLIMS

Unwelcome Truths

While rejecting the widespread notion that religion is always and necessarily divisive, we believe that Jews, Christians, and Muslims should acknowledge some unwelcome truths:

1. At various times in history relations between the three communities have been marred by discrimination and violence, and within each community religion has also been a source of sectarian strife.

2. In Jewish, Christian, and Muslim scriptures and traditions one can find passages that have often been interpreted to support exclusive truth claims and a sense of superiority.

3. In practice, each faith has been notably self-centred and lacking in self-criticism, claiming for itself a superior position and a unique authority. Humility has often been notably lacking, and in its place arrogance and triumphalism have been all too evident.

The Danger

There is a real danger now that these Unwelcome Truths, combined with political injustice, human rights abuses, poverty, hatred, fear, ignorance, globalization, war as an instrument of imperial policy, and the failure to respect international legal or ethical principles, will aggravate conflicts, intolerance, and even anarchy around the world.

The Remedy

Jews, Christians, and Muslims must not allow their religion to be abused in this way by exclusivist ideologues. We must make a stand together for peace, understanding, compassion and justice. We must welcome religious diversity and concede that no single religion can claim a monopoly of Truth. We must each put our own house in order, recognizing what we have in common, accepting that our scriptures and histories are interconnected, and acknowledging our interdependence. Each faith has its contribution to make both separately and together: indeed, at this era in history we need each other far more than in the past, and the future of our world demands that we teach to our communities the value and benefits of dialogue, cooperation, and interdependence.

Welcome Truths

Jews, Christians, and Muslims can be inspired to change their mind-sets for the better by considering the following welcome truths:

1. We worship and serve the God who created and sustains the universe, the One God of Abraham, Moses, Jesus, and Muhammad. Behind our differences lies the unity of the One.

2. We share the same general code of ethics, which condemns murder, theft, and adultery, and demands that we secure the rights of those who have been denied their rights, to care for those in need, the sick, the suffering, the widow, and the orphan, to welcome the stranger, the outcast and the persecuted, and to offer shelter and refuge to the homeless and the dispossessed.

3. Each of us inherits a broad and rich religious tradition within which many different views can coexist.[9]

---

9. Bayfield et al., "Platform Statement," 270–72.

"We must welcome religious diversity and concede that no single religion can claim a monopoly of Truth." "Behind our differences lies the unity of the One." These beliefs propel the overall Statement beyond an ethics-only stance in dialogue and take us to the threshold of an overall pluralist theology. Such a theology would need to tackle remaining epistemological issues concerning the relationship between the varied and valued truths witnessed to by different traditions.

DISMANTLING ABSOLUTISM

Interreligious dialogue is more than the work of conflict resolution. It involves us in the dismantling of absolutisms. Modesty about our truth claims seems needed more and more. But of course, it is this thrust within dialogue which remains one of its most controversial aspects. However, critical thinking can also help us: for critical thinking has involved us in recognising the perspectival partiality of what we affirm—something which is as true for secularist beliefs as for religious ones. We each have a partial perspective on the whole. In this sense religion is not an add-on to a firmly grounded secularist baseline. Most of us need to absorb more humility both in our forms of knowing and in the dialogue that beckons.

Why do we need this approach especially in religion? We need it because it is the exclusivity of religious worldviews that renders other worldviews threatening and therefore worthy of extermination. Medieval theologians used to talk of heresy as a poison threatening the life of a city. If someone was going to poison the water supply and the only way it could be halted was by killing that person, then you would have to do it. You might regret it; you might wish life were arranged differently, but you would have to do it. More than poisoning the water, the "enemy" nearly brought the whole system of American governance down on 9/11. Similarly, if your total good—salvation—was threatened, then whoever was leading the threatening would have to be stopped, by killing if necessary. Hence you had religious permission to kill heretics—those who threaten the orthodox system—as a moral act. When western powers claim that today's religious militants hate our freedoms and are threatening our freedoms, they are arguing in a manner comparable to their medieval forebears. "Our freedoms" functions in this case as another form of the human good or (secular) "salvation." One commentator expressed it like this, that the use of violence "is employed in order to defend and protect the saving truth and thus the ultimate well-being of the people against the perceived threat coming from the religious other."[10]

The search for peace, therefore, is linked to philosophical/epistemological questions after all. Hans Küng is right that there can be no peace in the world without peace between religions, and that this in turn demands dialogue between religions and critical understanding between them. The atrocity of 9/11 made this abundantly clear. But for that dialogue to succeed it needs to tackle issues in religious epistemology and this has always been an intrinsic dimension of the deeper purpose of interreligious dialogue. In this sense, 9/11 should not be instrumentalized as the sole reason for interreligious dialogue.

Let me bring my concerns together with a quotation from John Hick, one which might claim to fold together the twin emphases of Swidler/Mojzes and Küng cited above. In addition to Küng's affirmation that peace between the religions holds the key to world peace, Hick adds that:

> There will no true peace among the world religions without the recognition by each that the others are different but equally valid responses to the ultimate divine Reality that we call God.[11]

In this light, those who imagine that theology of religions has no real bearing on practical arrangements for a better world could not be further from the truth.

---

10. Schmidt-Leukel, "Struggle for Peace," 23.
11. Hick, *Disputed Questions*, 162.

9

Religious Absolutism, Violence, and the Public Square

THIS CHAPTER EXPLORES WHY only by moving beyond an inherited sense of absolutism through dialogue will any religious engagement with society be beneficial. The conclusion is that interreligious dialogue is both what the religions can offer the world and what the world needs from the religions. The initial setting for this chapter was dialogue between Jews, Christians, and Muslims, but the issues under discussion are applicable ore broadly.

A PARABLE

I once invited a rabbi from the reform tradition of Judaism to address a group of students who were training for Christian ministry. The rabbi informed the group that he had scrapped his synagogue sermon for the previous Friday evening and asked the congregation what they would like him to say to the Christian seminarians. He reported that overwhelmingly they had said, quite simply: "Tell them, we're alright!" There was a quizzical silence among the seminarians.

What could such a message mean? Surely Christians didn't feel that Jews were not alright? Further discussion revealed the following. The Jewish congregation wanted to convey that they did not feel "unfulfilled" or "deficient" in their Judaism; there was no need for any "Christian extra." God had called the Jewish people into being and this congregation were part of a long line of tradition, existing in the present no doubt with its own mix of proud achievements and lamentable failings, but in this respect they were no different from devout believers of any other tradition. "Please hear us," they urged, "for sooner or later you will start getting at us with your 'good news.' Only for us it will be bad news, because we know where it leads. We're alright: Christians, get over it!"[1]

It was an important lesson for the ministers in training to learn. It has been an important lesson for the churches to learn, though it has not yet been absorbed fully by all churches.

How others see us is hugely significant. Where Christians want to offer saving grace; others may experience intrusion, may be even aggression. Why is it that after five minutes in conversation with Muslims the accusation of the Crusades is slapped on to the table as though they happened only yesterday and as though I could be blamed for them so many centuries later? Why can we not lay the ghosts of the religious past to rest? Their present haunting is tellingly illustrated by Akbar Ahmed's fascinating anthropological travelogue, *Journey Into Islam*.[2] Taking postgraduate students with him across the Muslim world, he discovered the bottom-line question which preoccupied the vast majority of his fellow believers: "Why do they want to destroy our Islam?" It was not Afghanistan, Iraq, Crusades, western colonialism, economic globalization, and the like, which made ordinary citizens, educationalists, religious professionals, and those in high political office across the world angry, but an anxiety about a religious worldview under threat.

For some reason the paranoia virus seems all too prevalent. The faithful are feeling encroached upon by others who harbour unsavoury intentions: Jews fear anti-Semitism, Muslims Islamophobia, Christians the tauntings of New Atheists and putative Aggressive Secularists. Mental territory, it seems, is in danger of being invaded and that is more serious than the invasion of any slice of earth territory. Such is the anxiety behind paranoia, whether reasonably founded or menacingly imagined. Paranoia sometimes masquerades as the fear of survival. As one Muslim dialogue conversation partner once said to me: "I say to my children that you can be as western as you like, but don't give up your Islam." But could that Islam stand a better chance of being retained if it transmuted into a different shape for a different context? How changeable, adaptable, malleable can any religion afford to

---

1. Race, "Religious Absolutism," 183.
2. Ahmed, *Journey Into Islam*, (2007).

be? And is the experience of dialogue a new context which masks its own expectations of change? If so, it is small wonder that many remain cautious about it.

The rabbi and his congregation were incorrect, but not for the reasons they supposed. We're *not* alright. Only now, the "we" means all of us.

A PARADOX

I have long observed the following paradox for relations between religions: a world in desperate need unites the basic compassionate impulse of the varied religions as never before but the inherited worldviews of the religions themselves drive them apart (as they have always done, though perhaps with a few historical exceptions). If there is any truth in the rumor of a "clash of civilizations," then it has this paradox at its heart. But we don't need rumors; those of us involved in interfaith relations know it in our own experience: we are thrown together and have to make sense of it. Those involved in the problems theologically, academically, pastorally, and politically, know it as perhaps the most puzzling and challenging issue on their agenda.

So why be involved in interfaith relations? Many reasons can be proffered. Perhaps I want to know more about my religious neighbors' ritualistic and social habits, or the reasons for their moral advocacy on certain matters, or why they see the world as they do. If so, then getting to know neighbors more than superficially might help me figure out some answers. Or perhaps, in a more spirited civic mood, I might sign up for the social cohesion agenda, and I inevitably find myself having to unravel whether or not religious commitment is supportive of or inimical to social cohesion in a diverse society. Or, perhaps in a more politically resistant-minded mood, I join with others in protest, say, against aspects of foreign policy or home office immigration narrow-mindedness. In this instance, I observe that the dynamics of globalization are so intimately bound up with the history of civilizations, cultures, and religions that statecraft can no longer afford to bracket the issue of "ultimate commitment" out of the political reckoning. It seems that at every level of human interaction the business of what we think of and how we respond to people of different religious or ideological convictions matters.

Another way of entering into my fundamental paradox is to observe that we are creatures of both empathy and distancing in relation to those whose ways are not my ways. Empathy entails a sharing among human beings at existential levels where we experience, for example, joy, fear, anxiety, wonder, love etc. It leads to a mutual interest in discerning what constitutes a good and fulfilling life, and to a desire to be known, loved, and valued as we know, love, and value. These associations of empathy draw us into a common humanity and an ability to see the world as others see it. But then the opposite tendency follows close on empathy's heels. We are creatures who make distinctions: we distinguish between what is wholesome and what is demeaning, between good dreams and bad nightmares about the future, between what enhances our potential and what diminishes it. In empathetic mood my religious instinct might reach out to join with other traditions immersed in a common human quest. But in distinguishing mood I may be tempted to place the others in a negative light and see them as responsible for all things threatening.

In a post-psychoanalytic world we are familiar with the psychology of "splitting," the phenomenon whereby we project on to others, who are different in some cultural or religious sense, the unattractive or hated aspects of our own nature. These others become repositories of danger: they pollute our minds and morals, and they entangle us in their deceits. Is this what has been happening through our histories of religious intolerance, teachings of contempt and demonizing of others—the distancing overwhelming the empathizing?

The task for interfaith relations now, it seems to me, is to forge more creative ways of living existentially with the paradox of simultaneously being drawn together and yet thrust apart, and to do this with some self-conscious theological grounding. It won't do any more to perpetuate the splitting between other religions and Christianity conceived as a division between, say, "impersonal law" and "personal grace," or between "preparation" and "fulfilment," or between "types and shadows" and the "newer reality". (Other traditions will have their own versions of splitting). In the present globalizing context this looks simply like a strategic bid for superiority when the historical record affords no such evidence. Not that I am suggesting that we should adopt the attitude that "anything goes" in interfaith relations; clearly there remains a need to distinguish between good and bad, adequate and inadequate, and true and false religion. I am simply questioning why the line between these divisions should run between Christianity (or Islam, or Judaism) and the other religions and not right through all of them. Discerning the criteria for what counts as good and bad in religion is becoming a shared challenge in a globalizing world.

DIALOGUE AS THEOLOGICAL

The promotion of dialogue between faith-commitments has many motivations, as I noted above. We can correct stereotypical impressions of one another by the hard work of empathetic listening and we can create a sense of shared endeavour for the common good by committing ourselves to working together. But at its deepest religious level the motivation for dialogue is theological, that is, we expect that something of transcendent reality is encountered in dialogue. Without this we are simply behaving as all good neighbors should do to one another.

In dialogue we learn about the religious lives of others and we learn of their search for that truth which we intuit in experience as ultimate mystery. But how can we know when we have encountered something of that mystery in dialogue? As Christians, once we set aside the temptation to think that sheer difference between traditions automatically entails the rejection of the other, we are likely in dialogue then to measure others by their closeness to our own Christian outlook. In other words, we seek inevitably and naturally to interpret the other in terms of the framework of our own faith. A moment's reflection, however, will tell you that that strategy is impossible. Traditions are different—because of root experiences, history and geography, and politics, as well as philosophical speculations. To "measure" the other is already to place oneself at the apex prior to what might be learned from the other in dialogue itself. But then, the dialogue as such is presumably never-ending. This is one reason, at least, why dialogical theology represents something of a paradigm shift in religious belonging and believing.

Yet we continually shy away from the full implications of this new dialogical threshold. How do we do justice to the transforming power of universally-minded religions in the context of dialogue and plurality? This is the unavoidable task of the theology of religions. Yet it is my contention that this is precisely what is being side-stepped in the current social and political climate. The urgent need to address issues of religiously-motivated violence and religion in public life, for the sake of a society shaped by some sense of sustainable future hope, is entirely reasonable, even urgent. But the theological question presses: is "working for the common good" sufficient as a sole motive for interfaith dialogue? The religions, to be sure, will have their part to play in working for the common good. Dialogue, however, as I have already indicated, expects greater things than that.

But there is more. Already, the dialogue is producing positive fruits: the Abrahamic sibling rivalry is being addressed. We have begun to move forward from the position which was content simply to agree that our religious differences were a stubborn fact of history and tradition and that nevertheless this should not dissuade us from declaring a willingness to work together on common projects for the greater social good. Dialogue is demonstrating some fascinating interactions which are echoed in many projects, experiences, and theological explorations world-wide. First, for Christians in relation to Jews, the fruits have involved a root and branch reversal of the Christian doctrine of supersessionism. God does not renege on promises, the mainstream churches have declared (as Scripture has taught), and therefore the covenant with the Jews has not been overturned by the Christian dispensation. Then second, in relation to Islam, there are intense debates on "the meaning of prophethood," "the Qur'an as the word of God," or "religion as a whole way of life," and so on. The view of Christian faith as the final repository of revealed truth is becoming less plausible.

So a gap has opened up between the permission for dialogue, given and embraced more than four decades ago in the churches and academy, and the fruits of dialogue. There are some who say: let us at least keep our distinguishing finalities, our sense that divine reality has spoken definitively among us, for this is what motivates us at the deepest levels. Dialogue, the nervousness continues, should not be allowed to erode this sense of final connectedness with ultimacy, which represents the foundation of religious commitment as such. Yet the reality is that this is an assumption which the practice of dialogue in effect does seem to call into question. If dialogue leads us to expect to learn something of the reality of transcendent ultimacy from the other, then we should not be surprised if this is actually what transpires: surprisingly, we do learn! Yet the more this happens, the less our clinging to our different finalities makes sense. A form of cognitive dissonance between theory and practice opens up.

SEDUCED BY CONTEXT

Earlier I mentioned the twin features of our present-day western context as being dominated by concerns over "religiously-motivated violence" and "religion in public life." Both have come to the fore in relation mainly to the resurgent presence of Islam around the world. Islam has been burdened both with the image of violence as a result of the attacks in the USA on 11th September 2001, in London on 7th July 2005, and in other places around the world, and with the accusation of being the faith community least able to adapt to western democratic cultural habits and expectations. Rightly or wrongly, it is Islam which has thrust debate about the twin features of violence and religious relations with secularized culture into the public arena.

Yet there is every reason for seeing these twin features as functions of all religions in their negotiations with society as a whole. Christianity and Judaism continue to have their tangles with violence, and both exist, in varying degrees, in tension with perceived increasing secularity. Islam on its own deserves no demonizing. In fact, given our Abrahamic relationship, might it not be incumbent for Christians and Jews, precisely at this cultural moment, to join forces in solidarity, albeit critically, with a sibling under threat? Our shared dialogue could surely demand and embrace it.

Nevertheless, I contend that the allure of the maelstrom of both religiously-motivated violence and religion in public life is a convenient, if also understandable, distraction from the theological tasks. Yet theological tasks are also contextual. Therefore, if our dialogue is easily seduced by my twin features then let us be seduced and discover the theological challenges at the heart of the issues. If the horrors of religiously-motivated violence and the debates about religion in public life are faced head-on then it seems to me that the same theoretical issue will be raised within both arenas: what to say about absolutism in religious conviction in an age of dialogue? This remains, I believe, the bottom-line question for interreligious understanding. Therefore, let me take both issues in turn. It is my belief that the dialogical challenge to surrender our hold on doctrines of finality is brought into sharp relief in these two areas.

RELIGIOUSLY-MOTIVATED VIOLENCE

We know that religiously-motivated violence exists. Not only 9/11 and 7/7, but around the world it seems to erupt constantly. And we know it is not the preserve of one religion only but has examples in every tradition. (There is non-religious ideologically motivated violence too).

The explanations for this violence are harder to unravel. Social scientists analyze it in terms of injustice, poverty, globalization, political grievances, land, and so on. There is much credibility in these explanations. The problem, however, with these explanations is that the circumstances of religiously-motivated violence might be so different that valid explanations in one context might not be valid in another. Young suicide bombers, for instance, are often well educated and not necessarily stuck in poverty.

Other explanations involve us in cultural analysis. The work of Mark Juergensmeyer has been seminal here. His book, *Terror in the Mind of God* (2000), gave us not so much an explanation but an observation: much of present terrorism, he claims, is a form of "performative violence." That is to say, there is no rational strategy behind the acts, no masterplan with envisaged outcomes, but simply the desire to make a statement. They are, he says, "*dramatic events* intended to impress for their symbolic significance"[3]—a kind of ritual intended to alter how we view the world. And they have achieved that for many of us. Even so, there must be more to terrorism than theatre.

Closer to what I consider to be motivations behind religiously-motivated violence are explanations to do with cultural displacement and loss of identity. This is the likely explanation behind the UK's 7/7 bombers' actions, for example. Young Muslim men alienated from their elders because they have adopted elements of western lifestyles (especially the desire to choose their own marriage partners), and yet not fully accepted by indigenous British society either, find themselves occupying a cultural no-man's land, a land into which ideologues come and peddle their views.[4] It would not be too far wrong to call it a case of identity crisis.[5]

Therefore, it is not a sufficient explanation of religiously-motivated violence to say that religion is being used by criminal minds for non-spiritual purposes. If religion can be appealed to in support of violence then there must be something in the religions to allow it to be so misused. And there is: we call it "texts of terror." Our traditions are available for terror, because they contain stories of terror or recommendations about the rightness of terror.

What is the theological question arising from all this? Rowan Williams, as part of his response to the 38 Muslim scholars' *Open Letter* of 2007, "A Common Word Between Us and You,"[6] suggests that it relates to what we count as absolute, and that assuming responsibility for defending the absoluteness of God is not what faith intends. God's love or compassion is constant irrespective of human activities that measure up to it or fail it: "God does not fail," he says, "because we fail to persuade others or because our communities fail to win some kind of power."[7] Terror and religious wars stem, he believes, from precisely the opposite motivation. If we perceive that we are in competition with another faith and we go into the business of defending God, then violence will result. Dialogue, Williams goes on to suggest, could well be the mechanism for breaking cycles of violence and retaliation because it is not built on protecting God's interests.

All of which is wonderful grist to the dialogue mill. And yet, the defence of God is exactly what is embodied in our traditions. I take an example

3. Juergensmeyer, *Terror in the Mind of God*, 125.
4. Malik, "My Brother the Bomber," 30–41.
5. Kenney, "In Vain," 272–280.
6. Royal Aal al-Bayt Institute for Islamic Thought, "A Common Word," 2007.
7. Williams, "A Common Word," 2008.

from a colleague, Professor Perry Schmidt-Leukel, who has pointed out that even a major theological heavyweight such as Thomas Aquinas has a version of defending God. Aquinas makes the (to us) startling claim that heretics could be killed not because we might hate them but because of the command to love our neighbor. Loving the neighbor entails obliterating the heretic whose sole object is to lure the true believer away from true religion. God's offer of salvation needs protecting from the evil intentions of heretics. For the purposes of my argument here, instead of heretics read "other religions." (It is no accident that other religions have often been cast as Christian heresies. For example, this is why Dante placed the Prophet Muhammad [Peace be upon him] in the deepest regions of hell; and it is why the great twentieth century theologian, Karl Barth, once thought of Mahayana Buddhism as a kind of Lutheran heresy—they had a structure of grace-filled religion of sorts, but it was not the grace of Christ). Thus, it is the exclusive or finally superior hold on absolute truth which has given permission for religiously-motivated violence. As Schmidt-Leukel has written: ". . . the religious root of the potential for interreligious conflict . . . lies in the explicit or implicit intention to supersede all other religions and in the readiness to defend one's own religion against analogous ambitions on the part of the others."[8]

How does this account compare with that of Rowan Williams? Williams is clear that religions are not to be viewed as rival communities where "my" hold on God is pitted against "your" hold on God. Given this basis, Williams is then free to encourage dialogical interaction in order to find the best forms of living in a plural environment. The difference between Williams and Schmidt-Leukel is that Schmidt-Leukel wants to surrender supersessionist views and superiority claims as part and parcel of the theological appreciation of the religious other; Williams, on the other hand, is content simply not to concern himself with notions of superiority, as this in turn seems dependent on notions of interreligious competition which he has insisted are to be put aside. His real objection is to notions of neutrality in the weighing up of divine truth and human dialogue: ". . . we cannot expect to find some neutral positions beyond the traditions of our faith that would allow us to broker some sort of union between our diverse convictions." And further: ". . . our views are not just human constructions which we can abandon when they are inconvenient."[9] Yet this seems to me to be a potential weakness in the argument. Surely, whatever revelation we believe our tradition to be founded upon, our views are precisely our human

8. Schmidt-Leukel, "Struggle for Peace," 24.
9. Williams, "A Common Word," 2008.

constructions. The alternative would be that we hold the notion of revelation to be best envisaged as some propositional essence, and yet that runs counter to most Christian estimates of the meaning of revelation over at least the last hundred years. If we do not abandon notions of religious superiority and religious absolutism are we not landed with that competitive rivalry between faiths which Williams rightly deplores and which harbors the potential for violence which we are seeking to transform? It is the theological logic of religious absolutism that Schmidt-Leukel has so clearly put before us.

To sum up: having to deal with religiously-motivated violence could be thought to be, at one level, a distraction from the real business of interreligious dialogue. But once enquiry uncovers some of the religious factors at work within such violence it is far from a distraction. The real culprit, however, is that sense of religious superiority over the ownership of salvation, and which is generally thought to be intrinsic to religious identity and absolutism. The agonizing over the religious roots of violence leads the dialogue straight to the logic of absolutism which the churches had hoped to avoid by embracing the equally necessary pastoral practice of demonstrating solidarity in the face of societal atrocity.

RELIGION IN PUBLIC LIFE

My second example concerning the issue of religious absolutism in a dialogically mindful age centres on debates over what role the religions should or could play in the life of a pluralistic democracy. In a post-Christendom society the churches are freer than in previous ages to embrace the notion that a religiously plural society can be enriching for everyone, even if it is also rather messy. However, the spectre of different religions competing in the public square by responding to social change from out of very different sets of values and by being unwilling to restrain religious convictions to a private sphere, has unnerved some secularists. Therefore, we have witnessed in recent years some fairly bad-tempered polarised debates. These debates are variously portrayed as ones of Religion versus Secularism, Multiculturalism versus Integration, and Political Liberalism versus Theocratic Traditionalism.

One reason why the polarization of views has happened concerns the enormous success in western countries of political liberalism in theory combined with secular pragmatism in policymaking. But there is a feeling now that secular liberalism has not brought all of the benefits it perhaps once promised. For example, it has not had the strength to confront the corrosive effects of unrestrained economic globalization, or its half-hearted commitments to an ecologically sustainable future have become all too clear. More than that, in separating off the material bases of living from spiritual needs many wonder whether it has any convincing answers to the basic question of what goals we should be pursuing as human societies other than the satisfaction of individual self-expression for its own sake.

However, I do not wish to be overly negative: political liberalism has brought many benefits, not least an end to the over-weaning power of religious institutions and the opening up of a new sense of dignity for individuals. Nevertheless, wholesale accommodation to the processes of secularization which accompanied political liberalism was bound to remain problematic for the religious mind. The dispute is mainly with what is sometimes termed the Rawlsian contract theory of liberal democracy, from John Rawls the American political scientist. Theoretically speaking, Rawls proposed that our reasoning over public policy should be based on that which no reasonable person could reasonably reject. It is a sort of highest common factor or pragmatic approach: put simply, decisions are made according to what works and what citizens will accept.[10]

From a similar point of view, the philosopher Richard Rorty has said that when religion enters political/public debate it acts as a "conversation-stopper."[11] So when the religious person says that God commands this or that policy, it is difficult to know what sense can be made of it by citizens who do not subscribe to that particular framework. Therefore, religious believers ought to keep God's commands for their private selves. This is a familiar secularist argument. How else can pluralist societies hold together other than by secular politics and pragmatic policymaking?

The difficulty for many believers is that this immediately rules out religious beliefs as a basis for moral decision-making in relation to public policy. (Something similar could be said for ideological secularists whose worldview extends beyond policymaking based on simple pragmatism). Religious voices want to ask questions of purpose and meaning in the making of public policy, but a government shaped by Rawlsian assumptions has no mechanism for answering those questions. In law, government might maximise human liberties and even assist civil society in developing intermediate mechanisms for influencing public policy, but it is simply at a loss when it comes to policymaking from a single comprehensive point of view. In the debate between human goods and human rights, the religions are likely to

10. Rawls, *Political Liberalism*, 1993. Rawls claimed to have modified his view later, in "The Idea of Public Reason Revisited," 765–807. But many have not been persuaded that his basic argument has changed much.

11. Rorty, Richard, "Religion as a Conversation-stopper," 168–74.

be on the goods side and the governing powers of a liberal democracy on the rights side of the equation. Finding a decent balance between the two seems continually precarious, to say the least.

Furthermore, there may be a contradiction at the heart of the social contract theory. If the social contract is meant to allow freedom of expression and argument for all citizens and yet cuts out the reasons a great number of citizens give for arguing the way they do, then how can the social contract facilitate proper freedom?

There is a feeling, therefore, from many educated religious voices, Jews, Christians, Muslims, and others, that public debate requires deepening. Where are the virtues that create human character and habits of relating based on respect and dignity? Political arrangements must surely have some connection with what human life is for. Liberty is good but there is liberty "for" as well as liberty "from." Liberal democratic governments have no answer to what our liberty is for. This might be a standard religious riposte.

So what is to be done? We do not want to return to the theocratic state, yet a polarised stand-off between Religion and Secularism seems equally unattractive, not least because it oversimplifies everything. Ideological secularists want to confine comprehensive convictions to the private sphere and consider public debate about moral direction in society to be purely instrumental. Sometimes this is backed up with claims that secularism represents moral neutrality in the face of comprehensive convictions.[12] For the convinced Christian (and other) believer this seems insufficient: the claim to neutrality is intellectually mischievous. On the other hand, why can we not imagine a public square crowded with argument, which will be necessarily untidy and risky in terms of orderly debate, but where religious voices take their place alongside others in open exchange? As the Yale Law Professor, Stephen Carter, has it: liberalism needs to develop a politics based on "a willingness to *listen*, not because the speaker has *the right voice*, but because the speaker has *the right to speak*."[13]

What emerges from such an open exchange will not necessarily be the outcome of a kind of free-for-all ethical slanging match but, in the best possible world, the fruit of listening and rational persuasion—rational, that is, in the desired sense of seeing the persuasive reasons for something, even if one disagreed with the comprehensive view of life lying behind them.

So much is commendable. However, there still remains the increasingly unsettling issue of religious plurality. This brings me to a positive

---

12. Baggini, "Heavy Cross to Bear," 2012.

13. Carter, *Culture of Disbelief*, 230. See also, Stout, *Democracy and Tradition*, (2005).

proposal in trying to move beyond the stand-off between ideological secularists and convinced religionists.

What seems to be necessary is a model of participation in public democratic debate which allows for the particularities of religious and secularist voices and which relies on seeking common ground while respecting differences, and balancing compromise where necessary with critical solidarity, for the sake of a greater good. As we cannot know what that greater good might look like in advance, such a model must surely be dialogical at heart if the religions are to develop their democratic political relevance. Most of all, the model must involve the religions self-critically if they are both to overcome their historic mistrust of one another and to learn the values of provisionality and humility that are necessary in the context of interpreting and negotiating plurality. A report prepared by the Millennium Institute for the Third Parliament of the World's Religions in 1999 expressed the view that "the greatest single scandal in which Earth's faith traditions are now involved is their failure to practise their highest ethical ideals in their relations with one another."[14] Thankfully, this may be slowly changing, partly as a result of the permission for dialogue that has been hard-won over four decades of scholarship.

So, for religion in public life to be healthy what seems needed is not so much an empty public square but what we might call a dialogically filled public square. We accept critical reasoning which means that we explain to one another the reasons we have for believing the things we do and why we want to act on them, whether we are confessionally secularist or religious. Why can we not come to mutually agreed decisions based on that mutual listening and mutuality of respect?

This is why I believe our interreligious dialogue is so necessary. It is not only good for our own learning from one another; it could well pose itself as a kind of model for helping us to move beyond the stand-off between Religion and Secularism. Yet the religions should only be allowed their voices if they transcend their historic antagonisms and mistrust, and in the process become aware of the limitations of different worldview perspectives even as we might cherish them.

The public square should not be filled with theocratic religious voices or be left hostage to a liberal secularist absence of religious reasoning but be occupied by a dialogical conversation where each values the other even as it might disagree with them. This seems to me to be the next step in the religious support for liberty and democracy in a plural society. There is, however, one major problem in taking such a step. It will likely require us

---

14. Barney, *Threshold 2000*, 108.

to suspend, if not surrender, our religious senses of absolutism. And the trouble is, the religions do not generally recommend that.

To sum up this section: religion has not disappeared in the way that many predicted would happen in the modern period. During this same period we have also realised that pragmatism, which has served us well and is preferable to ideological or theocratic politics, too has limitations. Add to this the plurality which stems from globalization and increased immigration and the stage looks set for a change of direction. A politics which upholds pluralism requires a dialogue built not simply on respect or hospitality but on an acceptance which affirms separate identities even as it might not approve of everything those belonging to any particular tradition want to promote.

FINAL REMARKS

Interreligious dialogue, I suggest, is both what the world needs from the religions and what the religions at their best potentially offer the world. The dialogue between Jews, Christians, and Muslims has made enormous strides in recent years and can be a spur to extending dialogical encounters in a myriad of directions. As siblings in rivalry, they are learning to appreciate their shared ethos and their divergent differences. Their contribution to interreligious dialogue more broadly carries an enormous potential.

This essay has asked the awkward question whether the dialogue about the two preoccupations of religiously-motivated violence and the place of religion in public life can avoid the fundamental issue of whether or not Christian faith (or any faith) can for ever postpone the theology of religions question about the place of other faiths in God's purposes. I have argued that this question cannot be forever side-lined. More than that, I have suggested that the issues at the heart of religiously-motivated violence and religion in public life actually reveal what is at stake. Do we accept one another as theologically and religiously valid? And are we able to respond Yes to that question, even as we might be puzzled by some of the substantive matters that we each affirm?

10

Taking Democracy into a Global Ethic

The Christian Next Step

> THIS CHAPTER EXPLORES THE concept of Democracy as a contested site and unfinished project. Christian support for Democracy has not always been obvious but it is now accepted by most Christian ethicists as the preferred option of governance in modern times. However, if that support is to welcome the entry of other traditions into democratic participation in society there will need to be adjustments in how a religious voice might be heard. The idea of a Global Ethic is canvassed as an interreligious mediator in this process.

INTRODUCTION

In spite of the near-complete endorsement of the democratic vision by Christian theologians of all ecclesial persuasions in the contemporary world, the Christian relationship to democracy remains ambivalent. The reasons for this ambivalence derive not so much from the lack of intellectual consensus among political theorists about the meaning and scope of democracy as such, as from Christian faith's own theological engagement with the basic conceptual vision of it. There is a need to deepen the appreciation of this ambivalence if the contribution of Christian faith to the next phase of democratic development is to be clarified. The challenges to democracy arise from the growing multicultural and multifaith shape of religious persistence in democratic societies themselves. In the next phase of what the Catholic theologian, Charles Davis, called democracy's "narrative of an argument,"[1] the plurality of worldviews, religions and cultures raises distinct issues that arise from the struggle between competition and co-operation over the nature of the cultural values that are to inform democratic vision as such.

I shall comment briefly first on the historical and theological dimensions of the ambivalent relationship of Christian faith to democracy, highlighting its negative and positive sides in each case. Following this description of ambivalent relationships, I shall then discuss Christian involvement in the notion of a Global Ethic and the potential which this offers as a broker between the cluster of ideals at the heart of democratic vision and the roles open to religious and other communities as agencies of civil society in a pluralist context. My argument also recognizes that, after a long period of dominance in public affairs, secularity must come to realize its own limitations and boundaries, and that this too has profound implications for democratic government. I affirm this notwithstanding secularity's deepening global outreach.

HISTORICAL AND THEOLOGICAL LEGACIES

From a historical perspective, the facts are that Christian faith has acted as both an obstacle to and agent of democratic transformation. On the one hand, the obstacle mentality has been manifest in the Christian resistance to democracy at the beginning of the modern period in European history. Following the long reign of Christendom in Europe, the birth of democracy coincided with various versions of dissent, some religious, but much of it not so. Generally speaking, the churches were perceived as having been too entangled in social injustice, privilege, inequality and the *ancien régime*. Perhaps the nadir of the negative response to democracy was reached in the middle of the nineteenth century, when, in 1864, the encyclical *Syllabus Errorum* by Pope Pius IX condemned every call for liberty and democratic transformation. The reasons for this condemnation may have been complex, involving especially the memory of the Catholic downfall in the aftermath of the French Revolution. But the association in many Christian minds of democracy with the anti-religious thrust of Enlightenment secularity was made, and mistrust was sealed.

On the other hand, the positive history of Christian support for democracy can be traced to those religious groupings of political and religious

1. Davis, *Religion and the Making*, 108.

dissent, associated with various forms of Protestantism and Puritanism, that originated in England in the seventeenth and eighteenth centuries. These movements had their eventual fruits both in the English form of democracy, which retained political structural links with the Anglican Church, and in the American expression, which embraced radical separation between church and state. In more recent times, positive Christian support for democracy can be glimpsed in the role of the churches in many political arenas, and as different from one another as Nicaragua, East Germany and South Africa.[2] The momentum for democracy, moreover, has been such that, in a reversal of nineteenth century papal pronouncements, Pope John-Paul II's 1991 encyclical *Centesimus Annus* proclaimed that "the Church values the democratic system inasmuch as it ensures the participation of citizens in making political choices, and guarantees the governed the possibility of both electing and holding accountable those who govern them, and of replacing them through peaceful means when appropriate."[3] By the end of the twentieth century the negative suspicion about democracy, and therefore Christian ambivalence towards it, had subsided.

Other historical trajectories have also contributed towards the Christian support for democracy, chief among them being the victory over the totalitarian threats of Facism and Communism in the name of democratic freedom. This has led John De Gruchy to declare rightly that "There can be little doubt, then, that the long history of Christian antipathy towards democracy, which began with the Enlightenment and the birth of modernity, is largely at an end."[4] Furthermore, over the past two hundred years the Christian faith itself has been transformed in the wake of the rise of critical thinking and associated forms of life initiated by the Enlightenment—pursuing, for example, the values of individual freedom, rational (scientific) enquiry and religious toleration. This has also contributed towards dissolving the Christian ambivalence towards the democratic vision.

From a Christian theological perspective, democracy is valued, measured, and judged in relation to the key concept of the kingdom of God. However, this concept in Christian social ethics has proved highly elastic and is open to a wide variety of interpretations. These have ranged from emphasis on the inner life of the soul to the outer life of society, and from concentration on present this-worldly needs to eschatological other-worldly goals. Throughout Christian history it has been the futurist and otherworldly aspects of the concept of the kingdom of God that have largely been

2. De Gruchy, *Christianity and Democracy*, 129–224.
3. John Paul II, "Centesimus Annus," n. 46.
4. De Gruchy, *Christianity and Democracy*, 128.

emphasized. At the other end of the scale, the concept of the kingdom of God, relying on its Hebrew legacy, is interpreted as providing a mandate both for speaking and acting more inclusively in order to further the ends of a humane, just, and equal society, and for confronting oppressive relationships in social, political, and economic conditions when the political balance between the rulers and the ruled becomes distorted. In relation to democracy, the former emphasis disassociates Christian social thought more or less from the realities of political and civil society and therefore from any influential relationship to democracy; while the latter emphasis forms the basis for a critique of the realities of democracy in so far as these may fail to concur with the vision of inclusive human relationships inherent in the ideal notion of the kingdom of God.

Suffice it to say that the contemporary Christian engagement with democracy leans towards the latter emphasis in the concept of the kingdom of God. There may be differences between Christian theorists about how democratic interests are to be achieved, but the celebration of the prior democratic vision, as being consistent with the key ingredients of the kingdom of God, is shared by all.

A NAKED PUBLIC SQUARE?

The struggle to achieve Christian support for democracy does not mean that the Christian relationship to democracy presents no continuing problems. For a new ambivalence towards democracy has emerged just at the historic moment when Christian support seems guaranteed. It can be put simply as follows: while Christian support for democratic government is now fully apparent, the Christian voice in public debate struggles to receive a hearing. Some may be tempted to blame Christian complicity in what the Lutheran ethicist, Richard Neuhaus, once called the "naked public square" at the heart of secularized democracy. However, as there is no intrinsic link between democracy and the ideology of secularism, in spite of the historical entanglement of the two at the origins of modernity; the bluff of the sovereign myth of secular hegemony can be called. From a Christian perspective, the real issue is not Christian complicity in secularity, but how precisely the bluff might be called.

One strategy has been that of Neuhaus himself, who drives home the point that without a place for those institutions such as religious communities which act as vehicles of cultural values, the public square lacks moral seriousness and ethical direction. But more is at stake than that, for the vacuum at the heart of the secular dominance of the public square is ready to be filled by an alternative actor and Neuhaus offers the sober warning: "When the democratically affirmed institutions that generate and transmit values are excluded, the vacuum will be filled by the agent left in control of the public square, the state."[5]

Neuhaus may have exaggerated the absence of moral sensibility in the public square, for secularity has brought gains as well as losses. However, even if he is correct about the absence of informed ethical debate in public decision-making processes, there still remains the question of how Christian thought participates in debates about the democratic public square.[6] These questions are complicated by the facts of Christian diversity—there is no one Christian response to particular issues in democratic contexts—and by the increasingly complex web of contemporary global political relationships. Christians feel the need to explain that Christian truth does have a relevance beyond the privatization of conviction in a democratic state, but that is only part of the Christian dilemma. In the meantime, the case for strengthening the role of the organs of civil society in democracy can scarcely be gainsaid.

Knowing both some of the gains of democracy and observing also the state's proneness to dominance and control, Christian thought finds itself hovering between seeking to remind the democratic state of those ethical traditions and values within it which find an echo and, in some measure, have their roots in religious and Christian thought (e.g., personal liberty as a political expression and counterpart to religious freedom under God) and challenging the forgetfulness of the democratic state, in the name of prophetic criticism, when the needs of the poor and marginalized are disregarded. These roles are noble enough. Yet there are complicating factors that now present themselves in the light of our increasing global interconnectedness.

Among the new complexities that are presenting themselves in the post-Cold War world it is the rise of multifaith experience that challenges the debate over values and ethical direction in a democratic society. I have already pointed out that the substitution of secularity for religious values is

---

5. Neuhaus, *Naked Public Square*, 86.

6. An interesting illustration of the rise and fall of explicit ethical reference in political discourse can be supplied from the British context. In the initial period of the British New Labour government in 1997, the then Foreign Secretary, Robin Cook, announced that foreign policy was to have an "ethical dimension." Presumably, what was intended by this announcement was that foreign policy decisions would not be determined solely by pragmatic politics, historic obligations, and financial gain. The intention was noble, but as the pressures of *real politik* asserted themselves language about an "ethical dimension" came to be abandoned.

not a realistic solution to the problem of the absence of an ethical ethos in the public square. Again, as Neuhaus has warned:

> When particularist religious values and the institutions that bear them are excluded, the inescapable need to make public moral judgements will result in an elite construction of a normative morality from sources and principles not democratically recognized by the society.[7]

Yet in multicultural and multifaith societies, the values that are available for inclusion do not derive from a single tradition. In the context of seeking to inject democratic debate with ethical seriousness, and irrespective of any role that particular Christian traditions may have played in a state's history, it is not obvious that the democratic state should recognise the authority of one particular religious institution over other religious bodies or communities.

In these circumstances, how might Christian faith respond to religious rivalry over the values that inescapably inform the public square?

ROLE FOR A GLOBAL ETHIC

What seems needed is a model of participation in public democratic debate which allows for the particularities of religious and secular voices, seeking common ground while respecting differences, and balancing compromise where necessary with critical solidarity, for the sake of the common good. Such a model must surely be dialogical at heart if the religions are to develop their democratic political relevance. Further, the model must involve the religions self-critically if they are both to overcome their historic mistrust of one another and to learn the virtues of provisionality and humility that are necessary in the context of interpreting and negotiating plurality.

The model which readily suggests itself is one built around the notion of a Global Ethic, the most well-known of which was promulgated at the Parliament of the World's Religions, held in Chicago in 1993.[8] The Global Ethic is based on a four-step dynamic that moves from a diagnosis of the

---

7. Neuhaus, *Naked Public Square*, 86.

8. Both the Parliament text, drafted by Professor Hans Küng, and which was the result of extensive consultation among scholars and leaders of many religions around the world, and a text prepared by Professor Leonard Swidler, are available in Leonard Swidler, ed., *For All Life: Toward a Universal Declaration of a Global Ethic*. Oregon: White Cloud, 1998. The 1993 Global Ethic statement contained four Irrevocable Directives. Since the original publication of this chapter, I have added a fifth Directive here, in line with the Parliament's revision of the original version in July 2018.

world's condition towards the transcendent transformation of experience into a new ethical and spiritual consciousness, and can be represented diagrammatically as follows:

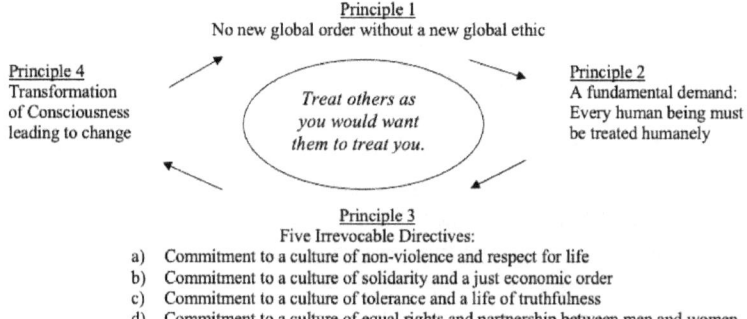

At the heart of the Global Ethic is the Golden Rule which is supported by all humane traditions, religious or secular: "Treat others as you would want them to treat you." The shared ethical seriousness is guaranteed by the five irrevocable directives or commitments. Cumulatively these commitments lead to the transformation of consciousness that is necessary for future ethical negotiation and co-operation within democratic nations and in a global environment.

The notion of a Global Ethic does not lay claim to being anything more than the search for "a fundamental consensus on binding values, irrevocable standards, and personal attitudes."[9] The hope is that it will supply a shared basis on which constructive debate over the future shape of ethical values will be able to maximize survival and global well-being. From a Christian perspective, I am suggesting that the notion of a Global Ethic provides the dialogical matrix whereby Christian faith might engage with the plurality of worldviews, cultures, and religions within national and international society as a whole, as a means for developing the next steps of democratic society.

The feasibility, even desirability, of a Global Ethic raises numerous issues. In the context of extending democratic vision, two can be mentioned here. First, does global ethic thinking in fact amount to a form of implicit imperialism which conceals a dominant single set of western politico-cultural values and thus jeopardizing the intentions of the framers of the Global Ethic? The complaint could be sharpened further: does the potential homogenizing thrust of the notion of a Global Ethic seem to ape too readily the globalizing pretensions of capitalist economics and libertarian politics?

9. Parliament of the World's Religions, "Towards," 3.

Second, in what sense can Christian thought support a Global Ethic? I shall offer a brief comment on each objection.

It is true that global ethic thinking occurs at the same historic moment as other globalizing pressures. But in itself this is scarcely a serious objection. Other movements—e.g., for justice and peace, for environmental protection, for an end to violence and war as a means of settling disputes—display similar globalizing tendencies and no-one doubts the value of their ethical idealism. At a deeper level, an argument for the potentially positive effect of global ethic thinking can be found by comparison with a related set of arguments from the human rights field. The 1948 Universal Declaration on Human Rights is often accused of reflecting purely a western agenda in international politics. While there may be some truth in this accusation, it is also true that the Declaration on Human Rights has established itself as an authoritative reference in virtually all human cultures. Further, a commanding world-wide study on Religion and Human Rights reported that peoples suffering from human rights abuses had no problem with the notion of a universal interpretation of human rights, and indeed thought that the importance of the universalism of rights strengthened the application of rights in particular cultural contexts. As one of the authors of the study, Sumner Twiss, has forcefully argued:

> . . . human rights set aspirational norms, and no persuasive case has been made to show that human rights as a goal for all peoples is either illegitimate or unattainable . . .
> Moreover, the group found that many oppressed peoples—regardless of their cultural locations and differences—have little difficulty accepting the ideas of universal rights.[10]

Why could the same not be said for the broader picture painted in terms of shared values? Participation in shared values, as represented by the notion of a Global Ethic, could also "set aspirational norms" and need not be "either illegitimate or unattainable."

What is required is close attention to how cultural and religious values might be protected and helped to participate in a democratic process which is accepted as a universal aspiration. "A correctly understood theory of rights," writes Jürgen Habermas, "requires a politics of recognition that protects the integrity of the individual in the life contexts in which his or her identity is formed."[11] The thrust of this argument is towards the develop-

---

10. Twiss, "Religion and Human Rights," 158.

11. Habermas, "Struggles for Recognition," 113. Habermas also notes that fundamentalist views cannot subscribe to participation on equal terms in the public square in so far as these are not open to scrutiny by reason, as he believes was demonstrated by

ment of democratic vision that ensures participation by different cultural and religious groupings, much as theories of individual human rights have been extended to include the rights of cultural communities and the life of the planet as a whole. My argument is that a mediating role played by a Global Ethic enhances the possibilities of participation by religious institutions by encouraging a focus on fundamental values and demands that are shared, while simultaneously stimulating "conversation, contention, and compromise among moral actors,"[12] necessary for the celebration of diversity without relativism.

SOME OBJECTIONS

The five directives of the Parliament's Global Ethic may strike us at first as being too generalized to be of use when it comes to the negotiation between particular religious values in the public square, and especially when it comes to disputes between religions. However, this objection moves too quickly. On the other hand, the Directives do not represent a bland acceptance of "things as they are," as some critics might suppose; neither do they propose a homogenizing approach. For: respect for all life (Commitment 1) is the basis for a critique of the wanton destruction of local cultures and the militarization of politics; a just economic order (Commitment 2) intrinsically questions the long-term benefits of democracy when it is too closely allied with *laissez-faire* global capitalism; a life of tolerance and truthfulness (Commitment 3) honours differences between histories and cultures without erasing distinctivenesses; for partnership between men and women (Commitment 4) sets the stage for a transformation of personal relationships in most cultures; and a culture of sustainability and care for the earth recognizes for (Commitment 5) the interdependence between life's eco-systems and human traditions of wonder and wisdom in the context of the sacred.

In other words, within the structures of global ethic thinking there is sufficient scope for both shared values and mutual criticism between traditions.

A Global Ethic is a shared statement of values and principles. If it is desirable and feasible it can only become so in so far as it continues to gain the support of different religious and humanist traditions and communities themselves, and simultaneously remain a self-critical open project. What support therefore might the evolving Christian tradition give to a Global

---

the example of Salman Rushdie: "As the Rushdie case reminded us, a fundamentalism that leads to a practice of intolerance is incompatible with the democratic state." 132–33.

12. Neuhaus, *Naked Public Square*, 128.

Ethic as an instrument for extending democracy? There are both epistemological and theological sides to this question.

Epistemologically, the requirement is laid on Christian thought to take with full seriousness the provisional nature of all its beliefs, practices, and ethos. Both the impact of modern knowledge in urging the symbolic and perspectival view of knowledge and the built-in biblical principle of safeguarding the sovereignty of God argue for greater humility in theological affirmation. At the very least this leads to an openness to different forms of truth and to a dialogical approach in relation to the diversity of traditions. No one group, religion, ideology, or confession has the final word. We learn from one another in respect, aware that the mystery that infuses us is greater than any one group or tradition can imagine. There is no contradiction between this and Christian principles, though the struggle to establish this might be a difficult task given the suspicion of the other in the history of Christian witness itself.[13]

Theologically, Christian support for democracy is built on the sovereignty or rule of God and the announcement of human freedom implied in the Christian ideas of creation and human fulfilment through the liberating impact of the figure of Jesus. Through a commitment to the transformation of human community, in line with the vision of the kingdom, it entails a notion of the common life (common good) which is inclusive and mutual. This mutuality seeks to balance different values over a broad field of achievements—equality of persons balanced with respect for differences, freedom of expression and association with social responsibility balancing self-interest, the right to economic self-determination balanced with a sense of social justice that protects the rights of the poor, the vulnerable and the disadvantaged. Finally, it entails a view of the rule of God, the heart of Jesus's message, as wider than the Christian instantiation of it, a factor which has long been recognized in dialogical circles. While Christian faith cannot endorse any one political system as being wholly reflective of the rule of God, many theologians nevertheless feel able to take the "reasonable risk" of endorsing certain particular political arrangements over others—and this is likely to be a *"presumption* in favour of democracy," as Philip Wogaman puts it.[14] As the Christian beliefs and values outlined here, albeit absurdly briefly, find a resonance in the "five irrevocable directives" of the Chicago Global Ethic, there is every reason to think that Christian faith can be aligned with its general thrust. In other words, Christian support for extending democracy through the possibilities offered in a Global Ethic can

---

13. Race, *Interfaith Encounter*, 124–43.
14. Wogaman, *Christian Perspectives*, 163.

be interpreted as a further reasonable risk in line with the *presumption* for democracy as a whole.

This essay began by noting the historic ambivalence of Christian faith towards the democratic vision. That ambivalence may seem to have been toned down in the light of history itself and Christian theological developments. But there is good reason for retaining a degree of ambivalence. It may be that the democratic vision can be celebrated for the gains it has brought, as Steven Rockefeller has urged:

> The democratic way means respect for openness to all cultures, but it also challenges all cultures to abandon those intellectual and moral values that are inconsistent with the ideals of freedom, equality and the on-going co-operative experimental search for truth and well-being. It is a creative method of transformation. This is its deeper spiritual and revolutionary significance.[15]

Yet if Christian faith has been transformed by interaction with that democratic way this does not mean that it remains captive to every proposition of democratic expression. Rockefeller's "experimental search for truth and well-being" needs also to develop a critical consciousness about democracy's relationship to other cultural products, particularly where these run roughshod over the needs of the poor and marginalized.

In this latter respect, the British political theorist, David McLellan, has drawn attention to the quite different origins of both the democratic and the religious outlook, and argues that the latter's grounding in community and connectedness offers a significant beginning for a critique of democracy's often unquestioned alliance with political liberalism and capitalism. Democracy, he avers, is essentially about "the ability of ordinary people to control their own lives and make meaningful decisions for themselves,"[16] thus connecting human purpose with other wider concerns such as the environment, but this vision has been hi-jacked by the corrosive effects of unbridled liberalism and capitalism. Cut loose from certain democratic principles such as participation and social inclusivity, economic and political powers easily become tyrannous. Yet it is precisely in this area of seeking authentic community that the religious outlook potentially offers most wisdom to democratic thinking and does so through prophetic criticism. As McLellan continues:

> The concern for universal human solidarity, the imperatives of social justice, the privileging of the poor, the oppressed and

---

15. Rockefeller, "Comment," 92.
16. McLellan, "Democracy," 32.

excluded which lie at the heart of the sacred texts of Islam, Judaism and Christianity point us in the right direction.[17]

Once decoupled from political liberalism and capitalism, democracy itself can be liberated to serve the needs of citizens and the whole community. McLellan's point is well made, and points towards a role for the religions of critical solidarity in relation to the democratic state. Moreover, the point is all the stronger for having been placed in an interreligious context.

CONCLUDING REMARKS

At one level, the Christian support for democracy, utilizing the notion of a Global Ethic in the context of plurality, is nothing exceptional. For Christian faith itself, at least in its modern self-critical form, has been hugely influenced by the impact of the Enlightenment values of liberty, equality, and toleration, and accompanying intellectual critical patterns of thought. Yet the Global Ethic points towards a further transformation of values both for democracy itself and for the religions in critical relationship with it. Moreover, the dialogical encouragement at the heart of a Global Ethic implies more than the values of toleration. If global ethic thinking is to influence the next phase of democratic life then the religions will need to become more interactive than toleration alone allows. As this begins to happen, we can again concur with John de Gruchy:

> Instead of religious pluralism being a problem for the building of common democratic values, it could become a source for the renewal of the democratic vision, as well as for human survival and world peace.[18]

In this way religious communities can make their contributions towards public debate and help to reverse the banishment of religion from the public square that was first inflicted during the installation of democracy in the early modern period. Christian support for democracy may have become the dominant persuasion among Christian theologians and the churches, but this does not mean that there is no place for the kind of continued ambivalence associated with notions of critical solidarity and prophetic criticism.

---

17. McLellan, "Democracy," 32.
18. De Gruchy, *Christianity and Democracy*, 266.

11

A Spirituality for Ecological Awareness

Contemplative Vision and Prophetic Discernment

THIS CHAPTER CONCENTRATES ON *what is probably the major big-picture concern of our present cultural times. It argues that understanding our ecological crises necessarily involves spiritual vision as well as scientific instrumental mechanisms for tackling them. I suggest that the prophetic wisdom of the Semitic traditions combined with the contemplative wisdom of Mystical traditions provides a template for what is needed in approaching our ecological crises.*

ALARMING PROSPECTS

We know that the climate emergency is not one issue among many facing the world. To be sure, there is degradation in many areas of life—environmental destruction, species loss, human rights abuses, political oppression, violence of many kinds, and so on—but it is climate emergency that hovers over everything. Ahead of the annual General Debate of the General Assembly of the United Nations (25th September–1st October, 2018) the Secretary General, António Guterres, alerted the world to what the climate emergency signalled: "If we do not change course by 2020 we risk missing the point where we can avoid runaway climate change, with disastrous consequences for people and all the natural systems that sustain us."[1] By any reckoning this is startling, and it would be surprising if we did not feel overwhelmed by such a picture.[2]

2020 has now passed.

The science documenting the climate emergency has been well-established over many years and a consultation with the reports of the International Panel on Climate Change provides us with the evidence.[3] It is easy to portray the evidence in apocalyptic terms. Again, from the United Nations:

> [A]fter more than a century and a half of industrialization, deforestation, and large-scale agriculture, quantities of greenhouse gases in the atmosphere have risen to record levels not seen in three million years . . .
> There is alarming evidence that important tipping points, leading to irreversible changes in major ecosystems and the planetary climate system, may already have been reached or passed.[4]

These apocalyptic type scenarios undermine the foundations of our psychological well-being, and they are multiplying. While such scenarios have always reared up from time to time throughout history, they are now informed by the kind of scientific evidence that was not available to our ancestors.

So, to ease the pressure slightly, let me recall a riddle. It comes from the late Anthony de Mello, a former Indian Jesuit, and features an encounter between a big and a little fish:

> "Excuse me," said an ocean fish, "You are older than I, so can you tell me where to find this thing they call the ocean?"
> "The ocean," said the older fish, "is the thing you are in now."
> "Oh this? But this is water. What I'm seeking is the ocean," said the disappointed fish, as he swam away to search elsewhere.[5]

De Mello's own commentary on his riddle runs as follows: "Stop searching, little fish. There isn't anything to look *for*. All you have to do is *look*."

---

1. Guterres, "Secretary-General's Remarks," lines 7–8.

2. Although the Covid-19 pandemic in 2020 eclipsed debate on the climate emergency for a time, its significance does not alter the status of the climate emergency as *the* overriding dilemma for the 21st century.

3. United Nations, "International Panel on Climate Change, Reports."

4. United Nations, "Peace, Dignity and Equality," lines 10–13, 44–45.

5. De Mello, *Song of the Bird*, 12–13.

Now, let me conjure up three equivalent issues to match De Mello's Water vs Ocean riddle. Hold in mind that Water was the presenting substance, while Ocean was the greater reality. So instead of Water vs Ocean, substitute the following:

a. Weather vs Climate: We talk Weather, but Climate is what we're in.
b. Immigration vs Multiculturalism/Multifaithism: We talk immigration policy but Multiculturalism/Multifaithism is what we're in.
c. Trade Wars vs Finitude of Resources: We talk Trade Wars but a Finite Planet is what we're in.

The crisis of ecology is a grand narrative and if the postmodern in you says there are not meant to be any grand narratives, then I suggest you have to think again.

The crisis is a grand narrative because it is manifest in our *total* environment—not only resident out there in the science of the seas, soil, and air, but also in our bodies. It is about the totality of who we are and our place in the cosmos. Two Christian authors put it like this over thirty years ago:

> Today's destruction of the environment differs from all earlier destruction of the environment because it is systematic, faster than the natural regulating mechanisms and is of world-wide dimensions.[6]

We are now becoming aware of the truth of this observation.

DENIALISM

You could be forgiven for feeling paralyzed by the enormity of what is at stake. But is feeling paralyzed a realistic option? It is one step away from the phenomenon known as Denialism. This is an ugly prospect which has been explored by the sociologist, Keith Kahn-Harris, in his recent book, *Denial: The Unspeakable Truth* (2018). Denialism is the disposition of the little fish refusing to recognize the ocean in which it swims.

Denialism, says Kahn-Harris, is an "intensification of our ordinary practices of denial," and he continues: "Denial is furtive and routine; denialism is combative and extraordinary. Denial hides from the truth, denialism builds a new and better truth."[7] For Denialism to succeed all it has to do is sow a tiny seed of doubt into an otherwise mass of incontrovertible

---

6. Duchrow and Liedke, *Shalom: Biblical Perspectives*, 16–17.
7. Kahn-Harris, "Denialism: What Drives People to Reject the Truth," lines 27–29.

evidence. It succeeds because the seed of doubt has the effect of undermining any urgent action for change. It also has the devastating effect of reinforcing the lie, as for example in holocaust denial. Holocaust deniers are not trying to set an historical record straight: their objective is the desire to maintain the anti-Semitic fabrications that Jews are pathological liars, intent on a world takeover, and busy stitching up the world's financial systems—and, most importantly, in order to combat this we have to rehabilitate the reputation of Nazi ideology.

Denialism therefore is many times more dangerous than our everyday small-scale denials. Denialism is not about evidence, it's about desire and the will. That is why those of us who get frustrated at the fact that deniers don't accept the clarity of evidence need to think differently. The driver of Denialism is the desire for something not to be true. The desires to claim that climate change is a hoax, that the holocaust is a fiction, that evolution is a lie, are just that—desires. Eventually, as we become mesmerized by our own delusionist desires, we tip over into a post-denialist world where you give yourself permission to see the world just however you like. Post-denialists need simply to draw attention to sufficient doubt about even a strongly agreed scientific position, such as the theory of evolution, in order then to erect an alternative, and the alternative might be bizarre or disturbingly ugly.

The climate emergency argument, ecological observations more generally, responses to immigration—are fast becoming issues about moral choices, independent of scientific evidence. That is why climate change is about economics, politics, and power. It is about how we see the world, ideologically if you will, and the action that flows from such seeing. In the face of Denialism what seems necessary is something like the religious idea of conversion. I do not mean conversion to a particular religion or spirituality but to seeing and acting aright. And religious and spiritual traditions do have some astute things to say about seeing and acting aright. The common paralysis of mind in the face of climate emergency is a luxury we cannot afford: our survival instinct cries out against succumbing to self-destruction and our spirituality should motivate us in a more positive direction of hope.

So what is our response? I want to suggest that at the deepest level we are required to balance a spirituality of *contemplative awareness*, as a remedy for Denial/Denialism, with *prophetic discernment*, as a remedy for shaking us out of inaction.

But before I give an outline of what I mean by those phrases, there seem to me to be two other options that are potentially alluring yet both distractive, and therefore unsatisfactory in their different ways. Let me highlight them very briefly before turning to my positive suggestion.

TWO UNACCEPTABLE SOLUTIONS

The first response is to succumb to apocalypticism, the notion that in the end we have run out of human responsibility and that solutions to problems lie only in the hands of some higher power. We look not to technical interventions to reverse the inevitability of ecological decline, but we seek a transformation that lies in the gift of the gods alone—a vision, moreover, that is usually preceded by suffering and the dissolution of the present order as punishment for wrong-doing. Our spiritual purpose before the apocalypse is reduced to an attitude of penitence and waiting on divine action.

The second response is to pretend that we can reclaim our lives as part of nature, as it were, prior to our human manipulation of it. All creatures and species are of equal worth, therefore what we need to do is "get back to nature," live off the land and forsake the technologies which have separated us from our place in the eco order. This seems to me to be a form of misplaced romanticism. It intends the resacralization of every rock, nook, and cranny of our natural environment. Our ancestors may have endowed the diversity of nature with different kinds of spirits and divine presences, but I believe that return to that kind of pre-Enlightenment life has been rendered unrealistic: we have drunk at the scientific well too deeply.

If we do not want either disempowering apocalypticism or anti-scientific romanticism, what other option is there that might connect our ecological interdependency with spiritual creativity, for the sake of hope in a sustainable future? Given that the climate emergency is one of grand narrative proportions, we are driven to the core of spirituality. As this is a broad term that encompasses people of different faiths and different beliefs, I suggest that we need a combination of *contemplative wisdom* and *prophetic discernment*. The contemplative attitude would serve to awaken us to an awareness of our connectedness with the whole of life—to the world being "charged with the grandeur of God," as the English Jesuit poet Gerard Manley Hopkins put it; where "nature is never never spent," because there lives "the dearest freshness deep down things."[8] Once this is grasped, the prophetic demand would then stimulate within us the ethical energy to take responsibility for our actions in creating a more sustainable future.

CONTEMPLATIVE AWARENESS

Let me set out now some elements of the contemplative-cum-prophetic approach I am advocating. To contemplate the natural world and our place in

---

8. Hopkins, "God's Grandeur," 288.

it is to see a system of intricately woven connections and dependencies and we can say this whether we view the world theistically or non-theistically. As one Christian scientist-theologian, has put it: "The character of the world-as-a-whole suggests that it is metaphysically plausible to perceive it as an *interconnected and interdependent System-of-systems...*"[9]

Consider now, as a relatively simple example of interconnectedness, the system governing the three-toed sloth observed by Ghillean Prance, formerly the Director of the world-renowned Royal Botanic Gardens, at Kew in London:

> The three-toed sloth (*Bradypus triactylus*) is not just a slow-moving, lazy mammal; it is a mobile, multi-organism ecosystem. It is well camouflaged because of the green algae which live on its grey fur, and this helps to protect it from its main enemy the harpy eagle (*Harpia harpyja*). However, the sloth is also host to beetles, ticks, and mites which live protected in its fur. The most interesting hitchhikers are a species of moth. The sloth descends from the trees to defecate only occasionally (once in three weeks). One species of moth lays its eggs in the sloth dung where the larvae develop until the mature moths link up to their home in the fur of the sloth on its next ground visit.[10]

Here we have the scientist as contemplative, pointing out the mutual dependencies of a multi-organism ecosystem.

But artists too can give us insight into the being of nature. In one of his sermons, the theologian Paul Tillich told of a Chinese emperor who asked a famous painter for a picture of a rooster. The painter agreed, but added that it would take a long time:

> After a year the emperor reminded him of his promise. The painter replied that after a year of studying the rooster he had just begun to perceive the surface of its nature. After another year the artist asserted that he had just began to penetrate the essence of this kind of life . . . Finally, after ten years of concentration on the nature of the rooster, he painted the picture—a work described as an inexhaustible revelation of the divine ground of the universe in one small part of it, a rooster.[11]

We learn from nature's revelatory potential.

---

9. Peacock, *Paths from Science*. 55. Italics original.
10. Prance, *Earth Under Threat*. 18.
11. Tillich, *Shaking of the Foundations*, 85.

Contemplating ourselves as part of the world's ecosystem is leading us to reassess our place in the totality of the system. We may have interventionist powers exceeding that of most other species but if we lose contemplative sight of our kinship with other species we contribute towards destruction and not flourishing. This has led some commentators to put all species on the same level of value—rocks, plants, animals, humans. I myself remain unconvinced about this equalising of value, for it supposes that all beings have equivalent levels of self-awareness and self-transcendence. There are grounds for claiming that evolution has endowed humanity with a greater degree of self-reflective awareness than what we discern in rocks, plants, and animals (though we are learning that animals share a greater degree of awareness and kinship with humans than we once assumed).

There is certainly a need to allow nature its own integral life, such that its fortunes are not simply viewed as objects to be manipulated or managed by human being, who, after all, are late-comers to the planet. All of the plant and animal species arose long before us and existed without us for millions of years, including most significantly the insect world. This was pointed out by the celebrated Harvard biologist, Edward O. Wilson, who once wrote:

> The truth is that we need invertebrates but they don't need us. If human beings were to disappear tomorrow, the world would go on with little change. Gaia, the totality of life on Earth, would set about healing itself and return to the rich environmental states of a few thousand years ago. But if invertebrates were to disappear, I doubt that the human species could last more than a few months.[12]

Human beings are both part of the intricate richness of planetary life and also bear some responsibility for sustaining it, especially the insects.

Still, the question remains: how do we exercise our contemplative ability in a manner that honours the interdependence of human beings with their environment?

There is an interesting passage from the Jewish philosopher Martin Buber which might help. Buber imagines a tree according to varying characterizations—the tree as (a) a picture; as (b) an instance of a certain species; as (c) an expression of nature's physical laws; as (d) one among any number. He says that the varying ways of approaching a tree are not mutually exclusive but are "inseparably fused." But then he switches to the following thought: "[I]t can also happen, if will and grace are joined, that as I contemplate the tree I am drawn into a relation, and the tree ceases to be an It . . . " And finally: "The tree is no impression, no play of my imagination, no aspect

12. Wilson, "Little Things," 345.

of a mood; it confronts me bodily and has to deal with me as I must deal with it—only differently."[13] When we cease to objectivise our place in the ecological scheme of things we establish patterns of relationship; we know our place *with* and not simply *over* the whole. The American psychologist and philosopher, William James, presses the same point for people of faith: "The universe is no longer a mere 'It' to us, but a 'Thou' if we are religious."[14]

For humans to *see* themselves as part of an ecological nexus of relationships is surely required if we are to become more responsible ecologically, though for many the irreversible damage has already been set in train. But Buber's summons to establish an "I-Thou" relationship with the earth goes beyond the pragmatic necessity of survival. There is that sense of self-transcendence which accrues to human beings and which instils in us a sense of responsibility for the way life goes. Perhaps other creatures and species have a similar or related sense; we do not know sufficiently to say, though it is becoming clear that many animals have a reflective capacity that exceeds the purely mechanical action-reaction model of behaviour that used to be assigned to them. My point here, however, is the simple one that human beings have been given a measure of responsibility for one another and for the earth, and this too is part of the meaning of the ecological nexus of relationships which is under threat.

PROPHETIC DISCERNMENT

The notion of responsibility leads us into an exploration of the prophetic side of my proposal for an ecological spirituality. If contemplation helps us to see how things are in the 'System of systems' then the prophetic summons helps us to transform the way things are for the sake of something better. That something better may remain elusive as a final goal, but it acts in the present as a spur to right action and right conduct. In relation to our fellow species, it entails that there is a responsibility, a caliphate, a stewardship which needs exercising. Yet it will not be a stewardship of domination but one which is consonant with the discovery, in our contemplative mood, of our interdependence with all living beings.

Interestingly, in the biblical tradition, it is the prophetic literature that resonates most with the idea that religious transformation entails a proper regard for the natural world and a sense of interdependence. So in the Book of the Prophet Isaiah we read:

---

13. Buber, *I and Thou*, 57–58.
14. James, *Will To Believe*, 86.

> I will put in the wilderness the cedar, the acacia, the myrtle, and the olive;
> I will set in the desert the cypress, the plane and the pine tree together,
> so that all may see and know, all may understand that the hand of the Lord has done this,
> the Holy One of Israel has created it. (Isaiah 41.19–20)

Part of the restoration of the people of Israel from captivity is the restoration of their place within the ecological order of things: plant, animal, and human life together. And in the Second Testament, Paul the Apostle speaks of the end-time vision of creation as being liberated from its subjection to futility: "The creation will itself be set free from its bondage to decay and will obtain the freedom of the glory of the children of God" (Romans 8:19–24). It is as though our human capability for destructiveness brings the created order down with it. Therefore, the transformation of the world involves the establishment of right relationships between all creatures, animate and inanimate.

However, as I said earlier, we must not become too romantic about notions of harmony. There are still the tapeworm, the malaria-carrying mosquito, viruses of many kinds, and so on. Part of the meaning of transformation is healing from disease, not simply living with it. Yet even the need to protect ourselves from threats, whether from disease or volcanoes, need not be an excuse for reasserting the model of human dominion over the natural world. We also know that a great deal of disease results from distorted life-style choices—obesity, for example. Is it the volcano's fault that humans build cities near it? Is it the animal's fault if its habitat is being consistently eroded and its food supply diminished? Therefore, when we contemplate the threatening side of nature and are tempted to reinstate notions of human dominion as a way of dealing with the threats, we have to remind ourselves of the aspiration to live in responsible harmony.

The following story illustrates this. It is a story from experience and is Buddhist in content. The historian of religion, Michael Carrithers, recounts how a Buddhist monk reacted to the threat of wild animals in the forests of Sri Lanka:

> On two occasions while on foot in the jungle there stood between me and a surprised and threatening animal—once a wild boar and once an elephant—only the slight body and unmoving equanimity of a monk. On both occasions the monk took a firm

but unaggressive stance and spoke calmly to the animal, which crashed off into the underbush.[15]

Living *with*, not living *over* or *against*—is it too romantic to claim the monk's actions as prophetic for our times?

Prophetic voices sound a warning but also point to renewal, restoration, and transformation. In order to achieve this they need to connect with what is perceived to be true about the totality of our ecological awareness. For the prophet, the "divine hand" draws us to an alternative future. Not that this "hand" overrides human freedom, but it draws the human community towards greater degrees of justice and peace for all creatures and towards harmony with the created world. The question arises therefore as to where we draw our inspiration from, in order to confront the human community with a more sustainable ecological awareness.

Other prophetic voices in our own day are alerting us to a marriage between scientific and religious consciousness as the way of the future. The universe itself is an emergent process, and for the eco-theologian, Thomas Berry, this includes not only its aspects described by the physical sciences but also its spiritual dimensions. He writes:

> This story of the universe is at once scientific, mythic, and mystical. Most elaborated in its scientific statement, it is among the simplest of creation stories. . .If until recently we were insensitive in relation to its more spiritual communication, this is no longer entirely true.[16]

This is an extraordinary statement—for it challenges scientists, theologians, and philosophers alike. It entails that the universe as such is the primary site for religious awakening. Here's how Berry explains it further:

> We have consistently thought of the human as primary and the earth as derivative. Only when the cosmos is acknowledged as the matrix of all value will we be able to solve the ecological crisis and arrive at a more comprehensive view of who we are in the community of the Earth.[17]

This is a challenge to all religions and philosophies. In order to understand and enter into it we shall need all the powers of listening and dialogue that we can muster. No one single tradition, it seems, has the totality of answers, yet all may have some insights and riches to bring. Both scientific and religious

15. Carrithers, "The Buddha," 69.
16. Berry, "Sacred Universe," 121–22.
17. Berry, "Sacred Universe," 128.

creation stories have their limitations and open-endedness. The prospects of a dialogue between them—based on their need of each other[18]—would potentially be a real source of inspiration and renewal for the whole world. This too is a prophetic call, championed urgently by Thomas Berry, that requires our engagement.

PROMOTING DOUBLE VISION AND DIALOGUE

In recent years, there have been innumerable statements and declarations about the interconnectedness of all life, from scientific, philosophical, and religious perspectives. In this chapter I have suggested that such declarations are best embraced when they combine a sense of contemplative awareness with prophetic discernment. From a Christian perspective no-one has promoted this double vision more urgently than Pope Francis. Regarding contemplative awareness, in his Encyclical Letter, *Laudato Si'*, he recalled some basic Catholic teaching:

> God wills the interdependence of creatures. The sun and the moon, the cedar and the little flower, the eagle and the sparrow: the spectacle of their countless diversities and inequalities tells us that no creature is self-sufficient. Creatures exist only in dependence on each other, to complete each other, in the service of each other.[19]

The interdependence of creatures as basic Christian teaching!

But, for a more complete response to our ecological interdependence, Pope Francis argued also for a deeper prophetic witness, by citing the final paragraph of The Earth Charter, which was first promulgated at the Parliament of the World's Religions in 1999 at Cape Town, South Africa:

> Let ours be a time remembered for the awakening of a new reverence for life, the firm resolve to achieve sustainability, the quickening of the struggle for justice and peace, and the joyful celebration of life.[20]

And in a final move, Pope Francis frames contemplative awareness with prophetic vision as a dialogical model:

> The majority of people living on our planet profess to be believers. This should spur religions to dialogue among themselves for

---

18. See Roger Haight, *Faith and Evolution*, 43–55; and Alan Race, "Two Truths."
19. Pope Francis, *Laudato Si'*, 86. Citing the *Catechism of the Catholic Church*, 340.
20. Earth Charter Commission, *Earth Charter*, 4.

> the sake of protecting nature, defending the poor, and building networks of respect and fraternity . . . Dialogue among the various sciences is likewise needed . . . An open and respectful dialogue is also needed between the various ecological movements . . . The gravity of the ecological crisis demands that we all look to the common good, embarking on a path of dialogue which demands patience, self-discipline and generosity. . .[21]

The pope's whole outlook situates the Christian response to the ecological crisis of our times within a wide-ranging prospectus balanced on the notion of dialogue as an over-arching necessity for both understanding and action, theory and practice.

Finally, it is worth noticing how the papal call for dialogue is reflected in the momentum and work of the Parliament of the World's Religions, especially through the incorporation of ecological concern into the "Irrevocable Directives" (Commitments) of the Global Ethic statement (See Chapter 10). But more than this, the Parliament has assembled, in an impressive parallel series, the spirituality, theology, ethical commitments, and activities of thirteen religious traditions regarding ecological principles and engagement. The traditions include: Indigenous, Judaism, Christianity, Islam, Zoroastrianism, Baháʼí, Hinduism, Jainism, Buddhism, Sikhism, Confucianism, Daoism, and Shinto. Risking the wrath of the postmodern critique that such a listing encourages misleading claims of generalized universality, the Parliament is happy to endorse 'Points of Agreement' between the traditions, first analyzed by Kusumita Pedersen, as follows:

1. The natural world has value in itself and does not exist solely to serve human needs.

2. There is a significant continuity of being between human and non-human living beings, even though humans do have a distinctive role. This continuity can be felt and experienced.

3. Non-human living beings are morally significant, in the eyes of God and/or in the cosmic order. They have their own unique relations to God, and their own places in the cosmic order.

4. The dependence of human life on the natural world can and should be acknowledged in ritual and other expressions of appreciation and gratitude.

5. Moral norms such as justice, compassion and reciprocity apply (in appropriate ways) both to human beings and to non-human beings.

---

21. Pope Francis, *Laudato Si'*, 96.

The wellbeing of humans and the wellbeing of non-human beings are inseparably connected.
6. There are legitimate and illegitimate uses of nature.
7. Greed and destructiveness are condemned. Restraint and protection are commended.
8. Human beings are obliged to be aware and responsible in living in harmony with the natural world, and should follow the specific practices for this prescribed by their traditions.[22]

Pedersen is aware of the dangers of over-generalization in the field of interreligious studies and that Points of Agreement might have limited applicability, but nevertheless it has some value in drawing religions into dialogical relationship. It remains a work-in-progress, with support from the United Nations Environment Programme and the Parliament of the World's Religions.

In terms of the two sides of my proposal for a spirituality of contemplative awareness coupled with prophetic discernment, it is clear that Pedersen's list contains elements of both. Yet within a dialogical framework, such as that sponsored by Pope Francis, its status as a work-in-progress could be strengthened by further work in dialogue studies, especially by reflections covering the exploration of complementarities between the types of religion represented in the list. Given that all of us are now united under one "universe story," traced through scientific cosmology, John D'Arcy May argues that "we are now in a position to explore the complementarity of traditions in the context of real and urgent problems which know no borders . . ."[23]

It has long been recognized that the push for complementarity struggles most sharply when two "metacosmic" religions are brought into focus. For example, Buddhism and Christianity are often said to be wholly incommensurable at metaphysical and spiritual levels, and it is true that a long history of antagonism has existed between them. But, in the context of Buddhist-Christian dialogue and under the umbrella of ecological needs and challenges, it could be said that the theme of "interconnectedness" through contemplative awareness is most forcefully and sharply depicted in Buddhist tradition, and the theme of "prophetic discernment" is most forcefully and sharply presented in Christian tradition. This is not to say that there is total discontinuity between them, for my two themes are present in both but

---

22. Pedersen, "Environmental ethics," 281. Reproduced also in United Nation, *Faith for Earth*, 71.
23. May, "Buddhists, Christians and Ecology," 102.

in their different major and minor keys.[24] Further, if we notice, as D'Arcy May does, that, "Both Buddhism and Christianity have benefitted from the assimilation of elements from the so-called 'nature religions', the 'primal' traditions of indigenous peoples for whom land is the 'place' where biological and social life assumes religious significance,"[25] then the stage is set for a significant dialogue and picture of complementarity between them. To this potential we could add Paul Knitter's remarks reflecting on *Laudato 'Si's* imperative for dialogue and collaborative working: as dialogue proceeds "[W]e will come to see that each of us has something to offer and that no one has the only or best answer . . . Talk of 'fullness' or 'finality' simply will not be relevant."[26] Combined with studies in complementarity, the theology of ecological ethics, it turns out, becomes one of the three bridges to a pluralist theology of religions.[27]

---

24. Arguments for antagonism or complementarity between Buddhism and Christianity have been explored more fully and intriguingly by Perry Schmidt-Leukel in *Transformation by Integration*, 107–123.

25. May, "Buddhists, Christians and Ecology," 106.

26. Knitter, "*Nostra Aetate*: Milestone," 57–58.

27. Hick and Knitter, *Myth of Christian Uniqueness*, 137–200.

PART FOUR

Epilogue

12

No Avoiding the Inevitable

A CONCLUDING ESSAY THAT engages with critics of the 3-fold typology of theology of religions and my advocacy of the pluralist model, and exploring why the views of the Naysayers in Religious Studies, Comparative Theology, Postmodern Theology and Dialogue-of-Life-Only cannot avoid theology of religions in the long run.

A poem by the same author who featured in the Introduction to this book captures some of the background ambiguity about the place of religion in modern/postmodern cultures that I have been exploring throughout this book:

Revision

The statues awe, not only as artefacts
But as gods. The reformation is not
To smash them, not to tip them into the
Abyss, but reinvent them, whilst
They stand, with human significance,
To admit that the divine has a
Worldly origin, that we cannot
Construct a universe of gods, without
Recourse to the world of our mortal

> Longings. The statues remain, but
> Turn their gaze from the heavenly
> Fields to the highways of time
> And chance. But they still inspire
> The dialectical dance: the need to
> Interpret experience, investigate
> Why people once gave them worship.
> They awe us now by a human holiness.
> They show us ourselves in a universal
> Setting, a human surrogate for the
> Divine likeness.[1]
>
> Raficq Abdulla

The poem reminds us that a religion's purpose is as much to do with—perhaps mostly to do with—the search for "human holiness" as it is with portraying a sacred world as a realm apart. If this is the case, then it is unlikely that religious awareness can be unmediated, despite the claim by some accounts of religious experience to the contrary.[2] The essays in this book have been based on this assumption.

In contrast, for some philosophers the religions are nothing more than human projections, misplaced pretensions claiming a transcendent origin as a way of either imposing their own power and control or compensating for the anxieties of living in a meaningless universe. The poem does not quite accept those conclusions: it leaves open the possibility—though only just—that we can admit the worldly origins of religions while believing that they might also have insight to offer and hope to instil—"they still inspire the dialectical dance." It is when religions turn their all-too-malleable, human experience of the sacred into representations as solid as statues that they forget "the need to interpret experience" and so lose their connection with "the highways of time and chance." The essays in this book are fully cognizant of the imperative to interpret. Indeed, they can imagine no other route by which we might comprehend religion as such, let alone come to some better view of what it is to be "a human surrogate for the Divine likeness" in a world of many likenesses.

SPIRITUALITY AND EXTERNAL FORM

The ambiguity, and therefore tension, inherent in the interplay between the spiritual core of a tradition and its external forms was neatly captured by

---

1. Abdulla, "Revision," 69.
2. Hick, *Fifth Dimension*, 142–160.

Sarvepalli Radhakrishnan (1888–1975), the Hindu philosopher and second President of India (1962–67), at the inaugural colloquy of the World Congress of Faiths, held in London in 1936:

> The true meaning of religion cannot be understood from the machinery of creed, cult, and symbol even as the individuality of a person cannot be understood from his dress, complexion and external behaviour. If we study the different religions which have played a part in the education of the human race, we will see that they are founded not on clear-cut comprehensible facts or simple moral apprehensions but on spiritual experiences, intuitive discernments, of which intellect gives practical definitions.[3]

Radhakrishnan did not advocate a spiritual life severed from institutional and historical forms, but he did insist that those forms should not overstep their role as pointers—what Buddhists might label as "skilful means"—in the service of coming to a more adequate grasp of transcendent truth.

Radhakrishnan offered, further, a collective list of what some of the religious traditions *qua* traditions, based on their experiential core, have contributed to civilizations:

- The pagan religions gave us a sense of the beauty and the largeness of life
- Hinduism has revealed to us profound spiritual possibilities
- Buddhism has shown us a way to be pure, gentle and compassionate
- Judaism and Islam teach us to be zealously devoted to God and faithful in action
- Christianity shows us the power of love and suffering.

Obviously, this is not an exhaustive list of religions, and the allocation of different religious goods made available through the traditions he cites seems rather phenomenologically contrived—for example, it is not only paganism that issues in "beauty and the largeness of life," or Buddhism that displays gentleness and compassion. I take it that the point of such a list, however, was to demonstrate that the religions have a central thrust, which is particular to them, yet they have a need of each other for a more holistic picture of the spiritual life and the practical impacts of religious witness. No one tradition can encompass the whole. Finally, embracing what that 1936 colloquy called a "fellowship of faiths" was tantamount, for Radhakrishnan,

---

3. Radhakrishnan, "Religion and Religions," 107.

to a "*spiritual evolution*" (his italics) in the perception of how the religions might now think of themselves appropriate for a dawning "one world" consciousness.

The announcement by Radhakrishnan of a "*spiritual evolution*" at the 1936 World Congress of Faiths' inaugurating colloquy sits midway between the dawning realisation of a religious evolution that had already been signalled by the charismatic Swami Vivekananda at the Chicago World Parliament of Religions in 1893, and the explosion towards the end of the twentieth century of various exploratory endeavours labelled as theology of religions, comparative theology, interreligious dialogue, interreligious theology. The *spiritual evolution*, it seemed, was destined over time to become many-sided.

At the World Parliament, Swami Vivekananda mesmerized the conference gathering with his yoking of hope for peace between the religions of the world with a Hindu conviction that "we accept all religions as true":

> I fervently hope that the bell that tolled this morning in honor of this convention may be the death-knell of all fanaticism, of all persecutions with the sword or with the pen, and of all uncharitable feelings between persons wending their way to the same goal.[4]

Inevitably, it has been that last phrase—"wending their way to the same goal"—that has proved the most problematic for theologians and religious studies scholars alike (though perhaps less so for advaita vedantists, Vivekananda's tradition), for the religions specify the purpose (salvation, liberation, eternal life etc.) of the spiritual path in manifestly different terms. However, a further intrigue arises from Vivekananda's problematic phrase: might it partially *explain* the rise of the many research endeavours that emerged at the end of the twentieth century? If not Vivekananda's assumption, then what or whose solution might best interpret religious diversity? In other words, at the dawn of the twentieth century a puzzling issue about interreligious relationships and the theological and philosophical interpretation of difference was emerging, and by the end of the century solutions and argumentations relating to theological and philosophical responses had begun to proliferate.

If Radhakrishnan's perception that, with the encounter between religions, a *spiritual evolution* was underway is correct, it is pertinent to ask: if this is the case, what do the new endeavours—theology of religions, comparative theology, interreligious dialogue, interreligious theology, each with

---

4. Vivekananda, "Response to Welcome." Final paragraph. The Parliament had assembled in Chicago as part of the Columbia Exhibition.

their own singular, yet overlapping *raison d'être*—really signify? And what is the relationship between them? This became the key question regarding diversity at the forefront of theological and religious enquiry as we entered the twenty-first century.

TWO WIDER CONTEXTS

I shall comment briefly on those endeavours shortly, but at this point pick up Radhakrishnan's phrase *"spiritual evolution"* and place it within two broader insights of historic evolutionary change. The first of these was highlighted in the German philosopher and psychiatrist Karl Jaspers' well-rehearsed notion of "axial consciousness," and the second refers to the idea of a "cultural evolution in values," which has been forcefully argued by Jim Kenney, who was for many years the Global Director for the Parliament of the World's Religions.

In his book, *The Origin and Goal of History*, Karl Jaspers (1883–1969) labelled the period 800–200 BCE the Axial Period because it was during this historic period "that we meet with the most deepcut dividing line in history. Man (*sic*), as we know him today, came into being. For short, we may style this the 'Axial Period.'"[5] The Axial Period heralded a momentous shift from a tribal (using that term descriptively, and not disparagingly) consciousness, where the dominant outlook was cosmic, mythic, ritualistic, and collective, to a greater sense of what we might term an individual consciousness, where the dominant characteristics are self-reflective, analytic, and critical. Pre-Axial religious consciousness was concerned with maintaining life on an even keel, upholding balance between humanity and the living world, and with religious ritual designed to reflect a harmonious sense of given life as an interconnected whole. Axial consciousness, in contrast, saw the development of a subject sense of self as being more indicative of humanity's relatedness to a transcendent otherness. The American scholar, Ewert Cousins, outlined how this was reflected through the world religions:

> "Know thyself" became the watchword of Greece; the Upanishads identified the atman, the transcendent centre of the self. The Buddha chartered the way of individual enlightenment; the Jewish prophets awakened individual more responsibility.[6]

Of course, elements of the pre-Axial period continued into later periods, often in unconscious ways, and although one could argue about the

---

5. Jaspers, *Origin and Goal*, 1; cited by Cousins, "Religions of the World," 10.
6. Cousins, "Religions of the World," 12.

legitimacy of the length of the 400-year time period, the central thrust describing historical evolutionary development seems accurate enough.

Axial developments emerged over a period, but did so, geographically speaking, more or less independently. This left the world with a legacy of separated religions, each with their own projection of universal-mindedness, and it is this that has fostered a sense of rivalry between them, especially when they became embedded as whole civilizations.

But axial development has not ceased. For some observers of cultural fortunes, humanity has entered a further (Second) Axial age. As Ewert Cousins again remarks:

> Although we have been conditioned by thousands of years of divergence, we now have no other course open to us but to cooperate creatively with the forces of convergence as these are drawing us toward global consciousness.[7]

Borrowing from the thought of the French Catholic palaeontologist, Teilhard de Chardin, Cousins conjectures that there is a law of "complexity consciousness" at work from the geosphere, through the biosphere, to the realm of human consciousness. Such complexity will not be constituted as a blended homogeneity but by what Teilhard called "centre to centre unions." Religious identity from now on will be forged through relationships of critical dialogue and mutual belonging-with-accountability. The religious future, if it is to be creative, will embrace a form of differentiated unity. Complexity consciousness, moreover, will necessarily need to recover some of the dynamic elements of pre-Axial awareness, as well as embracing a wider awareness of First Axial consciousness, for reclaiming our connectedness with the earth and respect for its natural rhythms of life is a desperate necessity, given the plunder and destruction of the planet's ecological systems by human greed, neglect and short-sightedness. (See my Chapter 11). This is the first evolving context in which the prospects for a shared religious future are being forged.

Cousins's estimate of axial change relates mainly to religious change and development. My second example of global context shares Cousins's account but takes an even wider perspective and proposes that the world in general is undergoing a cultural evolution of values. In his book, *Thriving in the Cross-current: Clarity and Hope in a Time of Cultural Sea Change* (2010) the former Global Director of the Parliament of the World's Religions, Jim Kenney, expresses the proposal in a nutshell as follows:

---

7. Cousins, "Religions of the World," 15.

> *Cultural Evolution* refers to a progressive movement of key human values toward a better fit with observed reality. Human observation of reality becomes more accurate and insightful. As a result, our conscious experience of the world grows clearer and our values tend to change accordingly.[8]

According to Kenney, the evolution of values is not a version of nineteenth century Progress as a philosophy of history but is inspired by the historical observation of large-scale developments in human awareness. In Kenney's estimate there have been four such large-scale developments throughout history: the move from hunter-gatherer societies in the palaeolithic period (beginning roughly 2.5 million years ago) to settled communities in the neo-lithic period (beginning roughly 12,000 years ago); the awakening within axial consciousness, mapped by Karl Jaspers; the establishing of the scientific outlook at the Enlightenment; and in our present-day with the move into a second axial age. In this way, the notion of *Cultural Evolution* is based on observations of significant times of tumultuous change throughout history and into the present.

In order to illustrate the present-day shape of *Cultural Evolution*, Kenney points to a number of emerging sentiments, which include at least the following:

a. the decline of patriarchy and the rise of feminist insight, giving way to a rise in new models of gender partnership

b. the belief in universal rights, applying both to individuals, groups, and whole communities, and extending beyond the human family

c. the aspiration to oppose war as an instrument of state power and policy

d. the realisation that Earth is a fragile living entity comprised of ecosystems which deserve respect and a sustainable future

e. the recognition that just solutions to problems (for example, poverty, inequity, violence, racist and imperial histories) require global cooperation involving governments, civil society, shared wisdom from the sciences and humanities acting in concert, and actors on many levels

f. the increasing openness to interreligious engagement, dialogue, and a rising interspirituality that seeks the integration of the best of the world's religious and spiritual traditions.

The list could be extended and some of it might strike us as simply aspirational—perhaps even beyond the bounds of possibility: after all, there

---

8. Kenney, *Thriving*, 35.

are sufficient examples of resistance to all of these evolutionary trajectories to make one doubt the plausibility of cultural evolution *per se*. But, again for Kenney, the forces of resistance to an emerging tide of progressive values are precisely part of a major reason for accepting the proposal in the first place. All change meets with resistance, but in principle the arguments for cultural value change have established themselves and will not be undone. Resistance is largely *institutional* resistance, a function of institutional hegemony and privilege that will eventually have to give way to the value systems that have already begun to shape the new perspectives of people and movements. We need only ponder the extent of civil society's in-principle support for the guiding values of peace, justice, and sustainability. The evolution of values yielding real institutional change is neither instantaneous nor historically smooth. But the directional sense of their evolution seems irreversible.

This defence of the notion of *cultural evolution* notwithstanding, it has been criticised for representing an inappropriate borrowing of terms: biological evolution is one thing but change in cultural perceptions is a different matter. This criticism, however, has been made too hastily. For not only does *biological* evolution favour increasing complexity and possibly even directionality—as was speculated by Ian Barbour, the doyen of Science-Religion debates: "There can be purpose without an exact predetermined plan,"[9]— but *cultural* evolution also seems intrinsically to unfold in a similar fashion. This point has been made by the science writer, Gaia Vince, who writes from an evolutionary anthropological perspective: "[W]e are continually making ourselves through a triad of genetic, environmental and cultural evolution, and . . . we've become an extraordinary species capable of directing our own destiny."[10]

If this is correct, then *Cultural Evolution* forms the wider background against which Christian faith and other religious traditions must face the realities of plurality.

PROTESTING THE TYPOLOGY

Over the last fifty years the impact of plurality has deepened but no single framework for interpreting this has found theological favour. At the same time, the framing of theology of religions in terms of the triadic typology of exclusive, inclusive and pluralist responses has been nervously protested. Various reasons have been given for this and, among others, they involve at least the following:

9. Barbour: *When Science Meets Religion*, 63.
10. Vince, *Transcendence*, 234.

- the typology was concerned only with the issue of "salvation," but this represents a limited approach to religious life and commitment as a whole
- the typology is biased towards a pluralist conclusion
- the typology is too abstract and too constraining in relation to the interactive promise imagined within the lived realities of interreligious relations and dialogue
- a more satisfying approach by means of Comparative Theology is needed for a longer period of learning to take place alongside other traditions, prior to any judgement in terms measured by theology of religions.

I would like now to offer some critical remarks in response to these objections and I consider that the first two anxieties can be addressed easier than the second two.

In relation to the complaint that the three options in theology of religions are limited to "salvation" only, my riposte is that "salvation" (and cognates, liberation and awakening) is what defines any religious response to human experience. "Salvation" is not a term defining one area of theological reflection but encompasses a religion's whole purpose. Among many descriptors, "salvation" signifies freedom from bondage (physical or mental); transformation of a negative or confining spiritual outlook on life by moving towards a more hopeful and open disposition; overcoming structural harms and injustices such as racism, patriarchy, poverty, violence, climate change denial; (re)discovering meaning in life through commitment to a presumed sacred source of life itself. Once the meaning of "salvation" is liberated from restrictive meanings (such as issues, say, of eternal life) the question of the salvific value of another tradition is no longer a narrow concern.

The objection that the typology is biased towards a pluralist conclusion equally misses the mark. Labelling certain views as exclusive, inclusive, or pluralist, not only describes possible theological options in response to other faiths but also frames arguments that lead in directions that seem more or less plausible in the light of evidence and the weight of experience. Inevitably there is bias, but this is a virtue and not a cause for dismissal. In other words, the bias is not of the "unconscious" type but arises out of the legitimate weighing up of arguments.

My suspicion is that the real reason for complaints based either on restrictions of focus or bias is that the hard (exclusivism) or soft (inclusivism) absolutism within Christian history (and also other religious histories) is not easily laid aside.[11] As a counter to pluralism there have been strong pleas to shift focus to the virtues of encounter and dialogue in order to facilitate both familiarity with a hitherto strange "other" and mutual learning for the sake of expanding knowledge. These goals for enhancing interreligious relations are laudable enough, but why should they be presented as alternatives to theology of religions? Let me cite two examples of what I think of as misplaced critique.

First, Ray Gaston, in his book *Faith, Hope and Love* (2017), acknowledges the value of the typology as an initial step in a pedagogical programme for trainee Christian clergy encountering other faith traditions. Asking ordinands to identify themselves as either exclusive, inclusive, or pluralist, prior to any meeting with those of a different religion, is, for Gaston the educator, unproductive as a learning opportunity. Therefore, the typology is of limited value and needs to be superseded. It is engagement that ought to take precedence if any theological reckoning with religious diversity is to yield both pastoral and intellectual fruit. As Gaston says, he is more concerned "with the practice of dialogue and encounter as the basis for theological reflection than with the construction of grand salvific theories. . ."[12]

At one level none of this can be gainsaid: approaching the "other" in the hope of establishing positive relationships in the spirit of respect, openness, and willingness to learn is grist to the mill of any dialogical intention. Gaston cites with approval the Hispanic-American theologian, Robert Goizueta: "the notion of transmodernity refers not so much to a new way of thinking as to a new way of living in relation to Others."[13] Needless to say, the substitution of theology of religions with the search for "a new way of living" is accompanied by much Enlightenment bashing and complaints about the legitimacy of seeking a Eurocentric grand narrative at the expense of cultural and local divergences.

What to say about these proposals? My main question is why "transmodernity" should want to drive a wedge between "living" and "thinking" in the Christian response to diversity. Learning to live with difference and deepening one's spirituality-in-relationship is an authentic Christian response for the second Axial period (Cousins) and in a time of cultural evolution (Kenney). But it is surely puzzling why this should accompany the reluctance to draw theological conclusions from the experience of pastoral encounter and living-with others. Interpreting the theological *results* of such encounters is surely a legitimate task. In this sense, forging grand narratives cannot be avoided—so long as they are counted as provisional,

11. "Pointers to Pluralism," forthcoming 2021/22.
12. Gaston, *Faith, Hope and Love*, 51.
13. Goizueta, "Locating," 189. Cited by Gaston, *Faith, Hope and Love*, 41.

work-in-progress, and open to continual revision. A theology resulting from real-life engagement includes both seeding and garnering—placing oneself vulnerably in the company of others and following through with the theological question of what we consider "God" to be up to through our encounters. It is not that the need for existential encounter invites us to "move on" from theology of religions, as Gaston and others would like to see happen, so much as return us to central issue of what "salvation" means in the light of encounter itself.

A similar refusal to engage with theology of religions in the forms articulated over the past fifty years or so is reflected in Michael Barnes's book, *Waiting on Grace: A Theology of Dialogue* (2020). Barnes is haunted by two realities: the unfinished inclusivity of Vatican II's *Nostra Aetate* and Christianity's relationship with Judaism, especially since the Shoah. Both of those hauntings have to wrestle with the residue of fulfilment thinking in Christian theology, highlighted, for example, in remarks by Claude Geffré:

> Personally, I fail to see how we can leave completely behind a certain inclusivism, that is, a theology of the *fulfillment* (to use a term present in Catholic theology since Vatican II) in Jesus Christ of all seeds of truth, goodness, and holiness contained in the religious experience of humankind.[14]

Part of the difficulty with the concept of fulfilment has been its failure to spell out precisely how it is that Christian faith brings other faiths to a greater spiritual and theological completion (see Chapters 3 & 4 above). In the past, this was largely envisaged through the lens of scriptural prophecy, or through identifying existential benefits in Christian spirituality, or through claims enshrined in affirmations such as the doctrine of the incarnation. However, most of these routes have been closed off by critical enquiry (see Chapter 6 above). What have come to take their place are recommendations for dialogue, solidarity, mutual witness, and a preparedness for refusing easy answers in the face of suffering humanity. Barnes does not pursue the term "fulfilment" and instead turns to notions such as "hospitality" (see Chapter 7 above), with its sense of welcome, openness, and hoped-for reciprocal learning through building relationships of trust and humility:

> My argument is that before any encounter develops into a conversation, raising questions about meaning and reference, it is grounded in a meeting of persons; before debating the coherence of propositions about God, it is necessary to attend to

---

14. Geffré, OP., "Paul Tillich," 268. The double 'l' in the spelling of "fulfilment" is from the original.

"dialogue-as-hospitality," that initial commitment to humble and patient waiting upon the other . . .[15]

Dialogue-as-hospitality intends a being-with, for its own sake, it seems, and not as a means to an end, be that end theological or other. Barnes enlists an array of luminaries in the fleshing out of what hospitality entails and means. Emmanuel Levinas's insistence that human identity is not possible apart from its reflection in the face of the suffering other; Johannes Metz's prophetic insistence that no Christian theology is worth it that does not insist on honouring its Jewish origins and Christianity's role in disfiguring its "elder sibling"; Abraham Heschel's belief in the relational God of pathos; and Edith Stein's embrace of Christianity without disowning her Jewish heritage—all, and more, assist Barnes in shaping and maintaining a rightful honesty at the heart of his notion of dialogue-as-hospitality.

Yet there remains an ambiguity: in what sense is dialogue-as-hospitality theological? If dialogue intends not simply that we do not judge the other from outside of a relationship of trust—where there is both honouring difference and deep receiving as well as giving, and that mutuality of valuing and learning for the sake of spiritual advancement is intrinsic to the new relationship—what theological architecture is at play?

According to Barnes, the architecture must necessarily be shaped in Christological terms:

> What grants coherence to patterns of engagement with the other, not just to everyday life but practices of hospitality and dialogue as well, is always the figure of Christ.[16]

Of course, a strong argument can be made that a Christian theologian cannot pretend otherwise. Yet the ambiguity involved in shaping dialogue-as-hospitality is not thereby removed. For are we to appeal to the historical figure of Jesus or the Christ icon of developed doctrine? In terms of historical teaching and impact there are many examples of overlap between Jesus and other seminal originating figures—the religions of the axial period share a sense of faith as both a pathway of individual pilgrimage and a means of holding political, economic, and social powers to account. But it is in doctrinal tradition where difficulties reveal themselves. Does the "incarnate Christ" fulfil other religious trajectories because God has uniquely involved Godself in person at a pivotal point in time, or is "Christ" simply the term used by Christians—but imagined metaphorically or symbolically (see Chapter 6 above)—to indicate Divine involvement with other histories,

---

15. Barnes, SJ., *Waiting on Grace*, 41.
16. Barnes, S.J., *Waiting on Grace*, 86.

even if the inspirational experience at the heart of other histories appears culturally in quite different forms?

Again, Barnes is not entirely clear. He is convinced that the "Word" and "Spirit" of Christian understanding is active throughout human history, but also that "Christians are, of course, given a *privileged* insight into the inner life of God through God's own self-revealing action in Christ."[17] And further:

> Christians [should] look to the way the Spirit of Christ is active in all religious communities as *revealing* the mystery of Christ—the mystery of what God is already doing in the world. In other words, the "comprehensive view" generated by the Mystery of Christ does not seek to impose a Christian set of answers but to raise for others the same possibility it holds out to the Church itself: to be touched and formed by the grace of God after the manner of Jesus's own obedience to the Father.[18]

Which is it to be? Is "the mystery of what God is already doing in the world" through other traditions complementary to or, in some final analysis, still inadequate in light of that "*revealing* the mystery of Christ"? Is there more than one "privileged insight into the inner life of God"? Dialogue-as-hospitality takes us to the threshold of this question; it is not a substitute for it.

Theologically motivated dialogue has become a growth industry in Academy and Church since the permission-giving decades of the 1960s and 1970s (especially with Vatican II's *Nostra Aetate*), but it has been far from easy to tabulate the real fruits of the enterprise. Initially set alongside theology of religions, it has, in some circles, come to function as an alternative to the theological quest. The genre known as Comparative Theology is the latest vehicle for delaying the theological reckoning.[19] In this regard, Paul Knitter made an astute observation and asked a searching question:

> As I survey the output of comparative theologians over the past 15 years, I have to conclude that comparative theology has been more comparison than theology. There have been intricate juxtapositions of Christian texts with Hindu texts, of Christian theologians/mystics with Buddhist scholars/mystics. Striking similarities and stark differences have been noted and examined, sometime meticulously. But where are the clear, creative, courageous conclusions as to what Christians can learn from these comparisons?[20]

17. Barnes, S.J., *Waiting on Grace*, 235. Italics mine.
18. Barnes, S.J., *Waiting on Grace*, 236.
19. Clooney, *Comparative Theology*, (2010).
20. Knitter, "Good Neighbours," 20. This article was first given as a lecture at the

Some might object that Knitter has over-egged his complaint here, and that comparative theology needs more time to establish itself more firmly as a kind of first cousin to dialogue itself. Still, if Knitter's observation is even partly correct then his question deserves a serious response. To my knowledge, none has been forthcoming since Knitter made his remarks.

TAKING STOCK SINCE *NOSTRA AETATE*

Given that both interreligious dialogue and comparative theology could well be considered to have arisen from what I have called "the permission-giving decades of the 1960s and 1970s," it is instructive to take stock of theological reflections since that period and especially those reacting, positively and negatively, to *Nostra Aetate* (1965). Luckily, a good example of this has been set out in the book, *The Future of Interreligious Dialogue: A Multireligious Conversation on* Nostra Aetate, compiled in commemoration of the fifty year anniversary.[21] The Christian responses in the book move in different directions: after rehearsing the recognized tension between *NA*'s affirmation of rays of truth in other religions combined with the full brightness of the truth of Christianity's orientation on Jesus Christ, the contributing authors differently argue for (a) a view that sees the seeds of a potential pluralism in *NA* that, following a dialogical period of 50 years, can now readily be embraced; (b) a reason for applauding *NA*'s inclusivism in its standing firm against any temptation towards pluralism by remaining clear about its basis in Christian orthodoxy; (c) a comparative theology perspective that seeks to combine Christian orthodoxy with the celebration of religious diversity as intrinsic to the will of God. Finally, regarding the responses of the non-Christian traditions in the book, most would desire that the Catholic Church embraces more of a pluralist outlook than has hitherto been grasped, for only then could their perceived second-class status—in spite of the dialogical overtures made to them—be overcome.

What can be said about each of these directions of travel? Let me engage with three of the contributors to this book, one from each category.

Regarding (a), Roger Haight argues for pluralism on the basis of a grace-filled theology of creation:

> Since God wills the salvation of all people, and this requires the grace of God, the effectiveness of God's salvific intent requires

---

Akademie der Weltreligionen, Hamburg, February 2014.

21. Cohen, Charles L. et al., *Future of Interreligious Dialogue*, (2017).

us to imagine that through one means or another God's grace is available to all persons.[22]

It is clear that "through one means or another" includes "other religions," being communities where a grace-filled creation intentionally displays salvific purpose. My own pluralist approach concurs with Haight's insights. I would add that for the effectiveness of God's grace to be fully acknowledged the surrender of Christian absolutism is a necessary requirement (see Chapter 5 above).

Regarding (b), from an Orthodox perspective, Peter Bouteneff argues the case that pluralism, unlike exclusivism and inclusivism, represents a significant step-change away from much of Christian tradition because it departs from orthodox affirmations of the divine-human Jesus, and I think that this is correct. However, from my perspective, "tradition" need not be the only necessary criterion for determining Christian identity in a world of many faiths, precisely because "tradition" is not a settled or easily identified notion (see Chapter 2 above). The challenge from religious diversity simply adds another layer of complexity to other pressures on orthodoxy, pressures for example arising from the insights of historical consciousness (See Chapter 1 above). When Bouteneff dissents from pluralist views because "Jesus Christ cannot properly be identified as the Truth, nor as the sole saviour or unique name by which we are saved," he is correct from an orthodox viewpoint. But the question is not whether pluralism represents a loss in Christian identity, so much as what "sole saviour" and "unique name" can mean in light of both history's flow of inter-connectedness and the Christian valuing of experience of authentic spirituality outside the Christian fold.

Regarding (c), John Thatamanil positively celebrates religious diversity as part of the providential will of God, an observation which he thinks is implicit in *NA*. But how does that fit with all that is implied by Christian orthodoxy, as Thatamanil intends it to? He pleads: "Only when the church acknowledges that it stands in permanent and holy need of the other traditions, even to understand the truth that has been entrusted to it, can the church move toward affirming that religious diversity is part of divine providence."[23] At first sight, this has resonance with pluralist views. But Thatamanil suffers from a similar tension as *NA*, when, on the one hand, he affirms religious diversity as being part of the "permanent will of God" and that other religions "afford not just truth but also salvation," but then, on the other hand, backtracks with "I do not affirm that traditions are

---

22. Cohen, et al, *Future of Interreligious Dialogue*, 97–98.
23. Thatamanil, *Future of Interreligious Dialogue*, 301.

"equally salvific."[24] Theologically, it is reasonable to ask: Does God then inspire truth and salvation in others but to a lesser degree of adequacy in relation to Christ and Christianity? And by what criteria could we discern that this is the case? How to resolve this conundrum? If this is the theology that underpins comparative theology then it surely suffers the same fate as NA, wonderfully innovative as that document was at the time and creatively developed since under the guise of comparative theology.

EPISTEMOLOGICAL ANXIETIES

In general terms, the seriously significant objections to the pluralist hypothesis that other traditions are "equally salvific" mostly come in one of two forms: (1) the belief and claim that God's incarnation in the person of Jesus is qualitatively superior to other claimed revelations (channelled through scriptures, other iconic figures, religious experiences, or relationships with natural world processes); and (2) the criticism that the epistemology required for a pluralist view robs traditions of any real—direct or indirect (e.g. through doctrines of analogy)—apprehension of religious truth in relation to the transcendence of ultimate reality. In other words, transcendent reality seems banished into a further dimension of unknownness as the price of having to "unify" different cultural religious philosophies. As Thatamanil has complained about Hick's reliance on the Kantian epistemological distinction between a thing-in-itself and a thing-known-in-human-perception: "Every religious tradition has access only to phenomena and not to the noumenon; what ultimate reality is in itself remains inaccessible to all."[25]

Both objections, however, have received numerous replies from pluralists. My Chapter 6 has addressed the issue of incarnation and I do not propose to add to it here. The second objection, concerning epistemology, was anticipated by John Hick and has been addressed by others numerous times. If the religions in their core experiences and spiritualities are counted as genuine—an assessment based on their practical ethical fruits, civilizational affects, philosophical sophistication, and dialogical engagements—then some distinction between "the Real in itself and the Real as variously humanly thought and experienced enables us to understand how this can be: namely, the differing belief-systems are beliefs about *different* manifestations of the Real."[26] We should emphasize that this is *not* a culturally relativist conception in postmodernist vein, as some critics have complained.

24. Thatamanil, *Future of Interreligious Dialogue*, 300.
25. Thatamanil, *Future of Interreligious Dialogue*, 294.
26. Hick, *Rainbow of Faiths*, 43.

Differences are related to manifestations of the Real and not simply the result of cultural histories. The epistemology underpinning such an account is "critical realism"—"realist" because the *experience* of ultimate reality is counted as authentic, but "critical" because we can only know this under conditions of limited human awareness. The "Real in itself" is "transcategorial" (to use Hick's term), and therefore strictly speaking unknowable, but "the Real as variously humanly thought and experienced" is transcendent reality responded to under conditions of human limitation. Without this distinction it is difficult to see how any theology of religions could make sense of religious diversity. The alternatives to the critical realist epistemology are either the reassertion of a straight realist single-tradition superiority or a view which likens ultimate reality to a jig-saw puzzle, where each of the religious traditions glimpse a part of transcendent truth reflected through their individual pieces—effectively, an arrangement of multiple ultimates. Both of these options seem deeply implausible.

Perry Schmidt-Leukel has trenchantly defended Hick against wilful misreadings of Hick's pluralist hypothesis:

> Hick is far away from ignoring the crucial significance of revelation or enlightenment to the constitution and ongoing formation of the religious traditions. But they can and need to be understood within the general epistemological constraints stated by critical realism.[27]

In an earlier response to critics, Hick had already laid down the challenge: "[W]e really do have to make a choice between a one-tradition absolutism and a genuinely pluralistic interpretation of the global religious situation."[28] One could argue that the growth of comparative theologies and truth-seeking dialogical encounters confirm the authenticity of different religious voices and, therefore, far from undermining the pluralist case, renders Hick's gauntlet-choice even starker.

ENTERTAINING THE INEVITABLE?

By way of bringing this chapter to a close, I would like now to mention two features of the current interreligious context that in their different ways add further reasons for welcoming the pluralist case—the first comes from the perspective of non-Christian scholars in dialogue with Christian faith and

---

27. Schmidt-Leukel, "Religious Pluralism and Critical Realism," forthcoming 2022.
28. Hick, *Rainbow of Faiths*, 43.

the second from a new perspective in comparative religious studies. Both examples relate to books in which I have shared the editing process.

The first relates to non-Christian responses to the call for dialogue from Pope Francis.[29] Unlike his two predecessors, Pope Francis appears to champion the case for dialogue beyond that of friendly relations:

> When leaders in various fields ask me for advice, my response is always the same: dialogue, dialogue, dialogue. The only way for individuals, families and societies to grow, the only way for the life of peoples to progress, is via the culture of encounter, a culture in which all have something good to give and all can receive something good in return. . . today, either we take the risk of dialogue, we risk the culture of encounter, or we all fall; this is the path that will bear fruit.[30]

This is the key affirmation in Francis's whole outlook, where dialogue presupposes that there is "something good" both to give and to receive. Again, Francis also speaks of dialogue as "in the first place a conversation about human existence" . . . "an ethical commitment which brings about a new social situation, a process in which, by mutual listening, both parts can be purified and enriched. These efforts, therefore, can also express love for truth."[31] And dialogue is "a path to truth."[32]

Respondents to the pontiff's pronouncements from outside of the Christian circle, however, while welcoming the invitation to dialogue, discern that Vatican II's unresolved inclusivist dilemma keeps reappearing in the form of reliance on Christian absolutism or finality. There is value in dialogical collaboration for the sake of the world's good—and Pope Francis has been a world leader in this respect—but at the truth-seeking end of dialogue reliance on the absolutism or finality of tradition becomes more problematic. There can be less than full integrity in a dialogue which conceals absolutism either for the sake of establishing friendly relationships only or for the purpose of sharing practical collaboration. So, for the Hindu scholar, Anantanand Rambachan, Pope Francis's welcome enthusiastic embrace of dialogue retains a shadow side. Rambachan raises the issue pointedly in relation to the Catholic church's theological commitment to evangelization:

---

29. Kasimow and Race, eds., *Pope Francis and Interreligious Dialogue*, (2018).

30. Pope Francis, "Meeting with Brazil's Leaders," 3. Cited also in Kasimow and Race, "In His Own Words," 78.

31. Pope Francis, *Evangelii Gaudium*, 250.

32. Pope Francis, "Address to Peace Conference."

> The evident tension between evangelization, interreligious dialogue, and diversity may not be problematic from the perspective of the Catholic Church, but it is certainly challenging for a Hindu dialogue partner who remains uncertain about the value of her tradition in the eyes of her dialogue partner. This tension between interreligious dialogue and evangelization is a consequence, in part, of the claim to religious self-sufficiency.[33]

By self-sufficiency Rambachan means the stance whereby a tradition has no need of insight from others in the quest for religious transformation and truth.

Interreligious dialogue is a hydra-headed animal and might not always yield consistency. What is fairly consistent, however, is the manner by which the contributors from different traditions resonate positively with the papal invitation to dialogue as a journey of discovery, as a shared enrichment, and as a universalising focus on the care of people and planet, but lament the theological brake on such enrichment when a less-than-pluralist theology of religions is applied. Only a pluralist theology of religions, they contend, has the potential to promote the "shared enrichment" that will cut through the Gordian knot identified by dialogical friends in other faiths.

My second example of recent developments relates to a new theory of how to comprehend religious diversity and is entitled "a fractal interpretation of religious diversity," proposed by the scholar of religious studies and theology, Perry Schmidt-Leukel. Borrowing from the fractal theory of Benoît Mandelbrot (1924–2010), who discerned that patterns of repetition on different scales are widespread within organic and inorganic matter, Schmidt-Leukel suggests that something comparable can be located in religious terms. A simple example of fractal patterning would be observing a cauliflower, where the shape and structure of individual florets is reflected in that of the whole plant. Such patterning is so widespread, no matter how uneven, that Mandelbrot concluded that "there is a fractal face to the geometry of nature."[34] Schmidt-Leukel applies this observation to religious diversity as follows:

> The nucleus of the theory is that the diversity that we observe *among* the religions globally is mirrored in the diversity that we find *within* each of the major religious traditions. And that we can also discern some patterns of this diversity—or elements thereof—*within the religious orientation of individual persons.*

---

33. Rambachan, "Religious Need?," 207.
34. Cited by Schmidt-Leukel, *Religious Pluralism and Interreligious Theology*, 225.

> In other words, religious diversity is neither chaotic nor entirely random. It rather follows to a significant extent a fractal structure.[35]

The proposal is that if this observation can be sustained then it not only restores an earlier interpretation of religious diversity that imagined lines of connection between religions on the model of "family resemblances," but also opens up new in-roads to what Schmidt-Leukel terms "interreligious theology." Under strict postmodern conditions, where only the particularities of human experience are counted as authentic, the idea of genuine similarities between religions had come under suspicion. A fractal interpretation renders that suspicion itself suspicious!

There have been fractal-style *hints* in the past in phenomenological studies, for example, in the allocation of spiritual emphases to different traditions after the manner of Radhakrishnan cited above (p. 159), though that kind of analysis now seems quite rudimentary. Perhaps better is Rosemary Radford Ruether's listing of traditions in terms of experience, as in the following:

> Although there is much overlap among religions, they also represent a broad spectrum of possible ways of experiencing the divine. Some may focus on the historical struggle for justice, some on the renewal of natural processes, and some on mystical ecstasy.[36]

But she then balances this judgement with a cautionary note:

> Each [tradition] has incarnated its way of symbolizing life and its relationship to the higher powers in unique ways that make it impossible simply to translate one religion to the other, or to create some abstraction of them all in to a universal, ethical faith . . ."[37]

The fractal theory would agree with Ruether's balance between "much overlap" and the impossibility "simply to translate one religion to the other," but also provides a more penetrating account of how traditions are, in a sense, mutually accountable to one another spiritually, theologically, and socially.

By way of illustrating the fractal theory further, and delving below surface comparisons, Schmidt-Leukel supplies a number of examples whereby a central belief or category sounded in a major key in one tradition finds its

---

35. Schmidt-Leukel, "A Fractal Interpretation," 3.
36. Ruether, "Feminism," 142.
37. Ruether, "Feminism," 142.

echo in a minor key in another. For example, in Buddhist-Christian-Muslim comparative studies, it is possible to discern how the Christian emphasis on "incarnation" is present in accounts of how Gautama and Muhammad come also, in some measure, to embody their transcendent messages; and how the Buddhist emphasis on "awakening" to ultimate truth applies also to Jesus and Muhammad in their experiences of divine commissioning; and how the Muslim emphasis on "prophethood" also runs through the life, teachings, and work of Gautama and Jesus.[38] The advantage of this analysis for Schmidt-Leukel can be summed up as follows: "A fractal perspective on religious diversity fosters an interreligious theological inquiry that tries to make sense of the differences between and within the religions."[39]

But Schmidt-Leukel also adds a further point, pertinent to both this book and theology of religions:

> However, within a religious interpretation of religion, a fractal interpretation of religious diversity will work best in conjunction with a pluralist theology of religions, that is, with the assumption that there is a diversity of different but in principle equally valid ways of experiencing and relating to ultimate reality, a diversity that reflects the diverse nature of humanity.[40]

These are intriguing suggestions and take us beyond debates about "commensurability" versus "incommensurability" in religious studies. Should the fractal theory gain substantial traction then a fresh impetus will be injected into debates within theology of religions.[41] In particular, the postmodern-determined view that religions cannot be compared or be subject to an overview such as reflections in theology of religions seek, can be laid aside. It will not be the case that theology of religions should be superannuated for the sake of comparative theology and interreligious dialogue, but that the promised mutuality between all three partnered dimensions will be strengthened.

---

38. Schmidt-Leukel, "A Fractal Interpretation," 21–22.

39. Schmidt-Leukel, "A Fractal Interpretation," 22.

40. Schmidt-Leukel, *Religious Pluralism and Interreligious Theology*, 245. A full account of a Christian pluralist theology can be found in Schmidt-Leukel's masterly *God Beyond Boundaries: A Christian and Pluralist Theology of Religions*, Münster and New York: Waxmann, 2017.

41. My own support for the fractal theory can be found in "The Fractal Proposal and Its Place in the Christian Theology of Religions." In *New Paths for Interreligious Theology: Perry Schmidt-Leukel's Fractal Interpretation of Religious Diversity*, edited by Alan Race and Paul Knitter, 145–161. Maryknoll: Orbis, 2019.

CONCLUDING REMARKS

At an official dialogue occasion between Hindu and Christian traditions centred on ethical concerns and practical collaborations, I once witnessed a frustrated Hindu participant voice his concern to the Christian leader of the event: "Joint working together is all well and good, but what I *really* want to know is what you think of my religion?" In other words, questions of theology of religions keep surfacing whenever persons of different religious convictions encounter one another. Religious toleration in the civic space is not sufficient as an answer to living with religious difference, fundamental as toleration undoubtedly is for a healthily functioning polity.

Unfortunately, theology of religions can be dismissed in a single sentence, such as that by the disingenuous negative comment of John Tilley on Perry Schmidt-Leukel's defence of the 3-fold typology by logical formalising the choices, that Schmidt-Leukel "saves the triad only by making it so abstract as to be useless."[42] For others, theology of religions is said to have outlived its usefulness as an analytic tool for understanding the place of religious diversity within a theological framework: the construct "religion" is said not to correspond well with how people live their religion in real time, so how can there be a "theology" of it? From my perspective these objections seem wide of the mark. First, there seems nothing abstract about people being either exclusivist, inclusivist, or pluralist, as generally most reply in one of these terms when asked about their overall view of other religious persuasions. And this is as true for people from other religions as it is for Christians.[43] Second, "religion," while remaining to a degree elusive as a category defining an orientation in life, there is nevertheless a sense in which we understand what is being alluded to. There is practice, reflection, and living at the heart of any religious disposition, and there seems no reason to abandon completely the category of "family resemblance" in seeking to describe what religion entails. "Religion" does not have to be a neatly defined entity for there to be a theology of its plurality.

My overwhelming suspicion is that calls to set aside theology of religions—for a greater emphasis on comparative studies or on interreligious learning and living through encounter—are an unconscious reaction to what is felt as a challenge to abandon Christian absolutism.[44] This is particularly so in many an expressed animus against pluralist theologies.

---

42. Tilley, *Religious Diversity*, xii.

43. Schmidt-Leukel has begun the task of outlining how the 3-fold typology applies also for other major religious tradition, in his *Religious Pluralism and Interreligious Theology*, Part 1, 17–106.

44. Race, "Pointers to Pluralism," 2022.

Commitment to the historical finality of Christ and Christian faith does not sit well with developing interreligious dialogue and relations, even in the broadest terms, and the same could be said for reflections on plurality from other religious perspectives. This is what was intuited with the Hindu's question, "What I *really* want to know is what you think of my religion." It is also at the heart of discussion about the meaning of Christian mission, even when missiology renounces unethical proselytizing.

Chapter 1 of this book told the story of Christian development through history as one of continuous inventiveness and enlargement. By that I not only meant that Christian faith has been shaped differently according to historical times and geographical places, but also that with each phase something new has been summoned from the interaction between circumstances and basic faith—understanding faith in the comprehensive formulation of Wilfred Cantwell Smith as "a way of seeing the world and of handling it . . . to see, to feel, to act in terms of, a transcendent dimension."[45] In our own time the circumstances for enacting faith as a "way of seeing the world and handling it" have become ineradicably plural. That inevitably entails greater complexity in respect of what it means to see, feel, and act "in terms of a transcendent dimension." The pluralist view is that negotiating that complexity theologically and ethically is best undertaken as a joint venture—an "interreligious theology" venture—discerning all the while that at the heart of our particularities resides a call to recognize those truths which are the possession of all of us.

---

45. Smith, *Towards*, 113–14.

13

"Whose God is it anyway?"

*Sermon preached at Great St. Mary's
University Church, Cambridge
Sunday 10th May 1987*

IT IS SOMETIMES CLAIMED *that pluralist theologies undermine the Christian appeal within preaching and the liveliness of commitment necessary for ecclesial community. This sermon refutes both claims and demonstrates how commitment in Christian faith relates positively to other religious ways of commitment.*

I once worked on the campus of the University of Kent at Canterbury as a Christian chaplain and was asked on one occasion to mediate in a love-dispute between two Muslims. I brought what pastoral counselling skills I knew to bare on the matter, as best as I could, but it soon became clear that the situation was hopeless. The two of them never really stood a chance: one was from a strict Muslim background, the other from a liberal one. Their expectations of one another and the pressures of their different cultural backgrounds presented too high a barrier for either of them to leap over.

That experience taught me the simple point that we cannot understand how the world is today without understanding how religion has shaped its searchings and aspirations, its boundaries and conflicts, its civilizations and cultures. I say this is a simple point, but how to respond to it is far from simple or clear. In modern times we have often supposed that we could pursue the human good without recourse to religion. I suspect that now we are more hesitant about leaving religion out of a total picture of what it means to be human. Nevertheless, we remain unsure how religion might serve the human endeavor in the future. Certainly, we cannot understand the past and therefore most of the world's present regional and ideological disputes—not to mention failures in personal passions—without taking account of the role of religion. But the shape of things to come: where might religion feature in that prospect?

Here is another story of Christian-Muslim encounter. I once asked a Muslim at the University how he knew which way to turn to face Mecca so that he could say his prayers. He responded: "It's quite simple, I face the Cathedral, and its East-West orientation tells me which way is East." Here indeed I thought was a starting point for conversation, helped by a structure resonant with the theme of pilgrimage and things of the spirit, a point of potential mutuality where two human beings might engage their traditions in new encounter. But my delight was short-lived, as further reflection drew a puzzle: the Cathedral which for me as a Christian was a resting place for the eye, had become for him a point of departure. Not a place for meeting, but a place to pause before moving on. This is a simple story, but again one that raises the most profound issues about human beings and their search for God. We are nourished by particulars—by particular places and practices, by particular historical figures and Scriptures which record their impact, by particular warmth and emotional ties. How are we to remain loyal to our particularities and yet within our vision do justice to the others' particularities, the evident spirituality springing from other geographies and other histories?

Whose God is it anyway? This is the question raised in the mind of Gershon, the Jewish Chaplain in Chaim Potok's wonderful novel, *The Book of Lights*, when he came across an old man praying fervently and reverently at a Buddhist shrine in Tokyo. Remember his musings in our reading this evening with his companion?

> "Do you think our God is listening to him, John?"
> "I don't know, chappy, I never thought of it."
> "Neither did I until now. If He's not listening, why not? If He is listening, then—well, what are we all about . . . ?"[1]

Meeting spirituality elsewhere shatters the illusion that God is known by only one reference point in the world, the one which just happens to be

---

1. Potok, *Book of Lights*, 248.

important to me or my part of the globe. Human beings need particularity, but that is no reason for practising exclusivity. The one does not imply the other. God hears our prayers, so we believe, it's God's job, as it were. But if that listening is not limited to one section of the human race—and there is nothing in Christian faith which suggests that it should be—then what is my relation now to those millions of others whose prayers are different and whose history is not mine?

The encounter of Christian faith with secularism over the last decades has produced many cul-de-sacs, but also many good results. It has pruned the Church of superstition and caused many Christians to reappraise their faith in the light of new knowledge and new experiences. Change has brought new discoveries of the spirit, even if for some it has been accompanied by much pain. (Religious people seldom give up their cherished habits without a struggle). The encounter with secularism will doubtless proceed. But today we have a new encounter, which one writer has said will make faith's encounter with the scientific spirit seem like child's play. When faith meets faith in a spirit of openness and respect, we have another new potential for yet further discoveries of the spirit.

How are Christians to respond to the strange and often perplexing faith of their neighbors and their friends? We were taught to think that the heathen bowed down to wood and stone, as the old hymn had it. But really that was a piece of ideology, a means of saying that to belong to God is to belong to my group. It was the classic religious put-down. Professing religious faith we now realize is about how a person uses material reality as a pointer towards another deeper reality. It is to do with what motivates a person, with how a person sees and feels the universe around him or her in the largest perspective possible, with vision and aspiration at the horizons of human possibility. When a Buddhist bows down before a statue of the Buddha, she is not giving her life to wood and stone as such, but to the Buddha nature which is potential in all of us and is the goal of human living. When a Christian partakes of the sacramental food of bread and wine and calls it Christ's body and blood, he is not literally eating body and blood, but participating in the self-giving action of Jesus which is also potential in all of us and the goal of human living. Rituals, doctrines, community, all exist to inform the faith of a believer of what it means to be human in relation to a higher reality. They are pointers and provide a context; they are not themselves to be confused with that higher reality that Christians and others call God. Therefore, the first Christian response to the person of another faith is humility: trying to listen to what is being said and enacted through the other, trying to hear the music they hear.

And this is not so platitudinous as at first it sounds. We are not generally trained in Western culture to listen. We are so used to announcing to the world our own importance, and that happens religiously as well as politically. Listening to the other involves emptying ourselves of prejudice; it involves the breaking down of stereotypes—e.g., Hindus and Buddhists are fatalistic, or Sikhs are just warriors under another name, or Jews follow a purely legalistic religion. It involves owning up to our own shadows. It is quite salutary to discover that the Japanese name the Hiroshima bomb as the Christian bomb! Listening should lead us to expect that God was in other places before our arrival. It should also chasten our capacity for thinking our religion is the purest one on offer.

In making their response to other religious traditions Christians are likely to search their past for clues as to how to go about it. The past of course does not yield one answer, but an ambiguous set of answers. There are both closed and open ways of relating to unfamiliar others. There is the closed mind of the exclusivist, the one who like the disciple of St. Augustine, Fulgentius, in the sixth century, said, "There is no doubt that not only all heathens, but also all Jews and all heretics and schismatics who die outside the church will go into that everlasting fire prepared for the devil and his angels." But there are also more open voices, such as that of the second century Christian philosopher, Justin Martyr, who said that "It is our belief that those who strive to do the good which is enjoined on us have a share in God." So those who think that the only Christian voice from the past is a highly negative one cannot be supported from the facts. Yet the negative one did come to dominate, mainly due to the encounter with the fervent missionary religion of Islam, an encounter which undoubtedly played a large part in the hardening of attitudes.

These hardened attitudes are resurfacing today again in many parts of the world. But the Christian voices for a more open response are also growing, and there is emerging a wave of dialogue and co-operation between religious traditions. It represents a new phase in the history of the human religious quest; and it stands to affect the future of the human race in countless untold ways. Because of it, religious traditions are bound to be changed. For this reason, some Christians will shun the dialogue venture. They will suspect it of watering down the gospel, and thereby robbing it of its vibrant center. They might even suspect it of giving up on the question of truth in a quick bid for global religious agreement. Others will welcome the new moves, feeling that it is like coming into open territory where the human quest for truth can be more adventurous and breathe the fresh air denied to them by the isolationist spirit and the ghetto mentality. They will see that their commitment to God in Christ does not involve them in compromise with the gospel, but that the Christian mission in a world of many religions cannot be anything other than the process of dialogue itself. Change always poses both a threat and a promise. The ghetto mentality reacts out of threat; the dialogue community sees the possibilities of promise.

It is interesting to look again at some of the New Testament stories with the dialogue filter before us. In the reading this evening from Mark's gospel, there was an encounter between Jesus and a Gentile woman, a Phoenician of Syria. It is a dialogue between Jesus and a foreigner, and it indicates how the Jesus mission was to be a Gentile mission as well as a Jewish one. The woman, who is far from passive—for she has to bargain with Jesus and drag the healing power out of him—recognizes in Jesus the compassionate presence of God so abundantly that it could not be confined to one race or one group. By the same token Jesus recognizes in her a faithfulness and a trust that deserves respect and honor, and his response which he gives in the act of healing for her daughter. But notice that he does not insist that she follow him. She goes home and in the healing for her child discovers the knowledge that God is not to be confined to one nation alone. By winning Jesus's respect her anxiety about being left out of God's care drains away.

Now I am not suggesting for a moment that this story of encounter between Jesus and a foreigner is concerned to promote dialogue in the modern sense of that word. That would be anachronistic. Yet as we seek to relate positively to those of different traditions, we may find that we have to have respect dragged out of us by those not of our group, as the woman had to drag it out of Jesus. And there is no reason why this ought not to apply also for those Christians who think that on the whole they are open-minded and tolerant. Religious beliefs and practices, often being so bizarre and ridiculous, can harbor many layers of prejudice inside us.

So how are we to proceed with the new openness in dialogue? I have already mentioned the preparation in listening and in trying to see the world as others see it. All this is necessary as part of growth in mutual respect and trust. There must be this respect and trust if we are to achieve any new deepening of the spirit. But what of the relationship between commitment and openness: is it possible for the two to belong together? Does not belief in Jesus as God's final savior automatically involve supersession over others; or, if that offends, perhaps a gentle superiority? Some Christians at this point wish to speak of meeting Christ in dialogue with people of other traditions. Christ, as the Christian touchstone of truth is capable of meeting us in various guises. As the first Christians looked for evidence of Christ in the Hebrew Scriptures, so today we might look for it in other Scriptures, in other lives, in other cultures. Christ, being eternal, is not the property of any one group, let alone the Christians. We have to enlarge our understanding and perception of Christ, they say. This expectation is certainly more satisfactory than the one which thought deceit resided only within the non-Christian traditions. But I wonder, though, if it is satisfying enough in a pluralist world. It feels judgmental still, an arbitrary method of raising one's own norms and criteria above those of others before the dialogue is underway. One French theologian has said of this view that what we would have is a dialogue between an elephant and a mouse—and we know which religion is meant to be the elephant and which the mouse! For this reason, I prefer to speak of Christ being one norm among other religious norms, each being informed by the ultimate reality upon which all our lives can be built. On this view, each tradition has its own uniqueness which it must assert, but it must do so together with a belief in its partial and provisional nature. Christians know the unique manifestation of God in the person of Jesus and their response to him; others know God's manifestation in other uniquely different ways, under uniquely limited forms. To be a Christian today means knowing the uniqueness of God in Jesus and knowing the complementary uniqueness of God elsewhere.

This need not be seen as a variation on the view that all religions are the same underneath or share a common essence. The dialogue which embraces uniqueness and complementarity knows both how one religious uniqueness needs the other for its stimulation and development and how a practice of mutual criticism can be embraced as part of the journey together. For example, we might say that Christianity's use of symbols and metaphors needs the critique of transcendent Islam in case it forgets that its descriptions of God are just that, humanly created symbols and metaphors. Islam, in turn, needs the Christian critique of leaving God too remote in utter transcendence, the Christian critique that brings God down to earth. Religions need each other for their mutual development and their mutual correction. Without the last component we end up in a common soup, forgetting the question of truth. Perhaps the newness of our present circumstances can be summed up by saying that in a world of religious pluralism we cannot be Christian by living out of our Christian resources only. In our personal relations we know how individual uniqueness can be both stimulated and complemented by the other. It is the same for relations between religions.

Whose God is it anyway? Referring back to the Potok novel, if God listens to the prayers of people of different religious traditions, then that is a pointer to the dialogue that we must now undertake together as part of the exploration into God on a global scale. It is a vulnerable process with many potential and real pitfalls. But vulnerability might in the end be its best recommendation. For, if this was the pattern of Jesus our savior, it is our pattern too. Only in our religiously plural world this vulnerability has its own shape and special direction in dialogue.

Bibliography

Abdulla, Raficq. "Serious Pursuit." *Interreligious Insight* 3 1 (January 2005) 75.
——— "Revision." *Interreligious Insight* 4 4 (October 2006) 69.
Ahmed, Akbar. *Journey Into Islam: The Crisis of Globalization*. Washington D.C.: Brookings, 2007.
Ariarajah, S. Wesley. *Strangers or Co-Pilgrims? The Impact of Interfaith Dialogue on Christian Faith and Practice*. Minneapolis: Fortress, 2017.
Baggini, Julian. "A Heavy Cross to Bear," *The Guardian* g2, 15 February 2012.
Barbour, Ian. *When Science Meets Religion*. San Francisco: HarperSanFrancisco, 2000.
Barnes, Michael, SJ. *Waiting on Grace: A Theology of Dialogue*. Oxford: Oxford University Press, 2020.
Barney, Gerald O. *Threshold 2000: Critical Issues and Spiritual Values for a Global Age*. Millennium Institute. Ada, MI: CoNexus, 2000.
Barth, Karl. *Church Dogmatics* I/II. Edinburgh: T. & T. Clark, 1956.
Bayfield, Tony. "Response." In *Christian-Jewish Dialogue: the Next Steps*, authored by Marcus Braybrooke, 113–126. London: SCM, 2000.
———. With signatories: Jewish—Michael Hilton, Jonathan Magonet, Norman Solomon, Elizabeth Tikvah Sarah; Christian—Eric Allen, John Bowden, Marcus Braybrooke, Alan Race, Jenny Sankey; Muslim—Rumman Ahmed, Roger Abdul Wahhab Boase, Abdul Jalil Sajid, Ataullah Siddiqui. "The Platform Statement." In *Beyond the Dysfunctional Family: Jews, Christians and Muslims in Dialogue With Each Other and With Britain*, edited by Tony Bayfield et al., 269–74. London: The Manor House Abrahamic Dialogue Group, 2012.
Berry, Thomas. *Sacred Universe: Earth, Spirituality, and Religion in the Twenty-first Century*. New York: Columbia University Press, 2009.
Buber, Martin. *I and Thou*. Translated by Walter Kaufman. London: T. & T. Clark, 1970.
Carrithers, Michael. "The Buddha." In *Founders of Faith*, edited by Michael Carrithers et al., 1–88. Oxford: Oxford University Press, 1989.
Carter, Stephen. *The Culture of Disbelief: How American Law and Politics Trivialize Religious Devotion*. New York: Basic, 1993.
Chaplin, Jonathan. *Talking God: The Legitimacy of Religious Public Reasoning*. London: Theos, 2008.

Chillingworth, William. *Religion of Protestants a Safe Way to Salvation* (1638). Facsimile reprint. White Fish, Montana: Kessinger, 2010.

Clooney, Frank, SJ. *Comparative Theology*. Chichester: Wiley-Backwell, 2010.

Cobb, John B, Jr. *Beyond Dialogue: Toward a Mutual Transformation of Christianity and Buddhism*. Minneapolis: Fortress, 1982.

Cohen, Charles L., Paul F. Knitter, and Ulrich Rosenhagen, eds. *The Future of Interreligious Dialogue: A Multireligious Conversation on* Nostra Aetate. Maryknoll: Orbis, 2017.

Congregation for the Doctrine of the Faith Declaration. "*'Dominus Iesus'* On the Unicity and Salvific Universality of Jesus Christ and the Church." https://www.vatican.va/roman_curia/congregations/cfaith/documents/rc_con_cfaith_doc_20000806_dominus-iesus_en.html.

Cornille, Catherine. *The im-Possibility of Interreligious Dialogue*. New York: Crossroad, 2008.

Cousins, Ewert. "Religions of the World: Teilhard and the Second Axial Turning," *Interreligious Insight*, 4 4 (2006) 8–19.

D'Costa, Gavin. *The Meeting of Religions and the Trinity*. Edinburgh: T. & T. Clark, 2000.

D'Costa, Gavin, Paul Knitter, Daniel Strange, *Only One Way?: Three Christian Responses on the Uniqueness of Christ in a Religiously Plural World*. London: SCM, 2011.

Davis, Charles. *Religion and the Making of Society: Essays in Social Theology*. Cambridge: Cambridge University Press, 1994.

De Gruchy, John W. "Part III: Churches and the Struggle for Democracy." In *Christianity and Democracy: A Theology for a Just World Order*, 129–224. Cambridge: Cambridge University Press, 1995.

DeLillo, Don. *Mao II*. New York: Penguin, 1991.

De Mello, Anthony. *The Song of the Bird*. New York: Image, 1984.

DiNoia, J. A., OP. *The Diversity of Religions: A Christian Perspective*. Washington: The Catholic University of America Press, 1992.

Driver, Tom F. "The Case for Pluralism." In *The Myth of Christian Uniqueness*, edited by John Hick, et al., 203–18. Maryknoll: Orbis, 1987.

Duchrow, Ulrich, and Gerhard Liedke. *Shalom: Biblical Perspectives on Creation, Justice and Peace*. Geneva: WCC, 1987.

Dulles, Avery. *The Catholicity of the Church*. Oxford: Clarendon, 1985.

Dupuis, Jacques. *Toward a Christian Theology of Religious Pluralism*. Maryknoll: Orbis, 1997.

Earth Charter Commission. *Earth Charter*. https://earthcharter.org/wp-content/uploads/2020/03/echarter_english.pdf?x79755.

Eusebius, *Demonstratio Evangelica III*, 7, 30–33.

Flannery, Austin, OP., ed. *Vatican Council II, The Conciliar and Post-Conciliar Documents*. Dublin: Dominican Publications, 1975.

Gangadean, Ashok. *Meditations of Global First Philosophy: Quest for the Missing Grammar of Logos*. New York: SUNY, 2008.

Gaston, Ray. *Faith, Hope and Love: Interfaith Engagement as Practical Theology*. London: SCM, 2017.

Geffré, Claude, OP. "Paul Tillich and the Future of Interreligious Ecumenism." In *Paul Tillich: A New Catholic Assessment*, edited by R. F. Bulman and F. J. Parrella. Minnesota: The Liturgical Press, 1994.

Goizueta, Roberto S. "Locating the Absolutely Absolute Other: Toward a Transmodern Christianity." In *Thinking from the Underside of History: Enrique Dussel's Philosophy of Liberation*, edited by Linda Martín Alcoff et al., 182–193. Lanham, MD: Rowman & Littlefield, 2000.

Goulder, M. D. *Midrash and Lection in Matthew*. London: SPCK, 1974.

Green, Vivian. *A New History of Christianity*. Gloucestershire: Sutton, 1998.

Guterres, António. "Secretary-General's remarks on Climate Change." https://www.un.org/sg/en/content/sg/statement/2018-09-10/secretary-generals-remarks-climate-change-delivered.

Habermas, Jürgen. "Struggles for Recognition in the Democratic Constitutional State." In *Multiculturalism: Examining the Politics of Recognition*, edited by Amy Gutmann, 107–48. New Jersey: Princeton University Press, 1994.

Haight, Roger, SJ. *Faith and Evolution: A Grace-Filled Naturalism*. Maryknoll: Orbis, 2019.

———. *Jesus: Symbol of God*. Maryknoll: Orbis, 1999.

Harris, Sam. *Letter to a Christian Nation*. New York: Knopf, 2006.

Hastings, Adrian, ed. *A World History of Christianity*. London: Cassell, 1999.

Hedges, Paul. *Controversies in Interreligious Dialogue and the Theology of Religions*. London: SCM, 2010.

Hick, John. *Disputed Questions in Theology and the Philosophy of Religion*. Basingstoke: Macmillan, 1993.

———. *The Fifth Dimension: An Exploration of the Spiritual Realm*. Revised edition. Oxford: Oneworld, 2004.

———. *An Interpretation of Religion: Human Responses to the Transcendent*. Second Edition. Basingstoke: Palgrave Macmillan, 2004.

———. *The New Frontier of Religion and Science: Religious Experience, Neuroscience, and the Transcendent*. Reissue. Basingstoke: Palgrave Macmillan, 2010.

———. *The Rainbow of Faiths: Critical Dialogues on Religious Pluralism*. London: SCM, 1995.

———. "Religious Pluralism." In *The World's Religious Traditions*, edited by F. Whaling, 147–64. London: T & T. Clark, 1984.

———. and Paul F. Knitter, eds. *The Myth of Christian Uniqueness: Toward a Pluralistic Theology of Religions*. Maryknoll: Orbis, 1987.

Hirudayam, Ignatius. "My Spiritual Journey Through the Highways and Byways of Interreligious Dialogue." In *Inter-religious Dialogue: Voices from a New Frontier*, edited by M. Darrol Bryant. New York: Paragon, 1989.

Houlden, J. L. *Backward Into Light*. London: SCM, 1988.

———. *Connections: The Integration of Theology and Faith*. London: SCM, 1986.

Hume, David. *Enquiries Concerning Human Understanding and Concerning the Principles of Morals*. Reprint, 3rd revised edition. P. H. Nidditsch. Oxford: Clarendon, 2000.

Hurtado, L. *One God, One Lord*. London: SCM, 1988.

Isaac, Jules. *The Teaching of Contempt*. New York: Holt, Rinehart and Winston, 1964.

James, William. *The Will to Believe and Other Essays in Popular Philosophy*. New York: Longmans Green, 1937.

Jaspers, Karl. *Vom Ursprung und Ziel der Geshichte*. Translated by Michael Bullock as *The Origin and Goal of History*. New Haven: Yale University Press, 1953.

Johns, Jeremy. "Christianity and Islam." In *The Oxford Illustrated History of Christianity*, edited by John McManners, 163–195. Oxford: Oxford University Press, 1990.

Juergensmeyer, Mark. *Terror in the Mind of God: The Global Rise of Religious Violence.* California: University of California Press, 2000.

———. *God at War: A Meditation on Religion and Warfare.* Oxford University Press (USA), 2020.

Kahn-Harris, Keith. "What Drives People to Reject the Truth." *The Guardian*, The Long Read. https://www.theguardian.com/news/2018/aug/03/denialism-what-drives-people-to-reject-the-truth?fbclid=IwAR3qmFt2SzhxiW5uFKPkNPCpwO uc_Kc50JGzYyAvOPGunResHY5iRHuWaNo.

Kasimow, Harold, John P. Keenan, and Linda Klepinger Keenan, eds. *Beside Still Waters: Jews, Christians, and the Way of the Buddha.* Somerville: Wisdom, 2003.

———, Harold. *Interfaith Activism: Abraham Joshua Heschel and Religious Diversity.* Eugene, Oregon: Wipf and Stock, 2015.

Kasimow, Harold, and Alan Race, eds. *Pope Francis and Interreligious Dialogue: Religious Thinkers Engage with Recent Papal Initiatives.* Switzerland: Springer Nature, Palgrave Macmillan, 2018.

Kaufman, Gordon D. *The Theological Imagination.* Westminster: John Knox, 1981.

———. "Religious Diversity, Historical Consciousness, and Christian Theology." In *The Myth of Christian Uniqueness*, edited by John Hick et al., 3–15. Maryknoll: Orbis, 1988; London: SCM, 1988.

Kenney, Jim. *Thriving in the Cross-current: Clarity and Hope in a Time of Cultural Sea Change.* Illinois and Chennai: Theosophical, 2010.

———. "In Vain: Violence in God's Name." In *A Non-Violent Path to Conflict Resolution and Peacebuilding*, edited by Kamran Mofid et al., 272–280. Istanbul: Fatih University Press, 2008.

Knitter, Paul F. "Catholic Theology of Religions at a Crossroads." *Concilium* 183 (1986) 99–107.

———. "Good Neighbours or Fellow Seekers? Dealing with the plurality of religions in the twenty-first century." *Interreligious Insight* 12 1 (June 2014).

———. *Introducing Theologies of Religions.* Maryknoll: Orbis, 2002.

———. "Nostra Aetate: *A Milestone in the History of Religions?*" In *The Future of Interreligious Dialogue: A Multireligious Conversation on* Nostra Aetate, edited by Charles L. Cohen, et al., 45–58. Maryknoll: Orbis, 2017.

———. *No Other Name? A Critical Survey of Christian Attitudes Toward the World Religions.* London: SCM, 1985.

———. *One Earth, Many Religions: Multifaith Dialogue and Global Responsibility.* Maryknoll: Orbis, 1995.

———. and Roger Haight. *Jesus and Buddha: Friends in Dialogue.* Maryknoll: Orbis, 2015.

Kraemer, Hendrik. *The Christian Message in a Non-Christian World.* London: Edinburgh House, 1938.

Küng, Hans. *On Being a Christian.* New York: HarperCollins Fount, 1978.

———. *Christianity and the World Religions.* London: Collins, 1987.

———. *Global Responsibility.* London: SCM, 1991.

Kuschel, Karl-Josef. "'Faithful' to the New Testament?" In *The Uniqueness of Jesus: A Dialogue with Paul F. Knitter*, edited by Leonard Swidler and Paul Mojzes, 85–93. Maryknoll: Orbis, 1997.

Lindbeck, George, A. *The Nature of Doctrine.* London: SPCK, 1984.

Loisy, Alfred. *The Gospel and the Church*. Translated by Christopher Home. London: Sir Isaac Pitman & Sons, 1904.
Malik, Shiv. "My Brother the Bomber." *Prospect* (June 2007) 30–41.
May, John D'Arcy. "Buddhists, Christians and Ecology." In *Buddhism, Christianity and the Question of Creation: Karmic or Divine?*," edited by Perry Schmidt-Leukel, 94–107. Aldershot: Ashgate, 2006.
McLellan, David. "Democracy: reflections of a political theorist among theologians." *World Faiths Encounter* 8 (1994) 29–32.
McTernan, Oliver. *Violence in God's Name*. London: DLT, 2003.
Mojzes, Paul. "The What and the How of Dialogue." In *Inter-religious Dialogue: Voices from a New Frontier*, edited by M. Darrol Bryant et al., 199–206. New York: Paragon House, 1989.
Moltmann, Jürgen. *The Way of Jesus Christ: Christology in Messianic Dimensions*. Translated by Margaret Kohl. London: SCM, 1990.
Neuhaus, Richard John. *The Naked Public Square: Religion and Democracy in America*. Grand Rapids: Eerdmans, 1986.
Nineham, D. E. "Ye Have Not Passed This Way Heretofore." *Theology* LXXXVII (1984) 361–367.
Ott, Heinrich. "The Dialogue Between the Religions as a Contemporary Theological Responsibility." In *Dialogue in Community: Essays in Honour of S. J. Samartha*, edited by C. D. Jathanna, 178–198. Mangalore: Karnataka Theological Research Institute, 1982.
Parliament of the World's Religions. "Towards a Global Ethic: An Initial Declaration." file:///C:/Users/Alan/Downloads/Global%20Ethic%20PDF%20-%202020%20Update%20(1).pdf.
Peacock, Arthur. *Paths from Science to God: The End of All Our Exploring*. Oxford: Oneworld, 2001.
Pedersen, K. P. "Environmental Ethics in Interreligious Perspective." In *Explorations in Global Ethics: Comparative Religious Ethics and Interreligious Dialogue*, edited by Sumner Twiss et al., 253–290. Boulder, CO: Westview, 1998.
Phan, Peter. *The Joy of Religious Pluralism*. Maryknoll: Orbis, 2017.
Pontifical Council for Inter-Religious Dialogue. *Dialogue and Proclamation*. 17. https://www.vatican.va/roman_curia/pontifical_councils/interelg/documents/rc_pc_interelg_doc_19051991_dialogue-and-proclamatio_en.html.
Pope Francis. "Address to the International Peace Conference." http://www.vatican.va/content/francesco/en/speeches/2017/april/documents/papa-francesco_20170428_egitto-conferenza-pace.html.
———. *Apostolic Exhortation Evangelii Gaudium*. http://w2.vatican.va/content/francesco/en/apost_exhortations/documents/papa-francesco_esortazione-ap_20131124_evangelii-gaudium.html.
———. "In His Own Words." In *Pope Francis and Interreligious Dialogue*, edited by Harold Kasimow and Alan Race, 7–82. Springer Nature, Switzerland: Palgrave Macmillan, 2018.
———. *Laudato Si': On Care for Our Common Home*. London: Catholic Truth Society, 2015.
———. "Meeting with Brazil's Leaders." http://w2.vatican.va/content/francesco/en/speeches/2013/july/documents/papa-francesco_20130727_gmg-classe-dirigente-rio.html.

Pope John Paul II, "Centesimus Annus," *Encyclical Letter*, 46. http://www.vatican.va/content/john-paul-ii/en/encyclicals/documents/hf_jp-ii_enc_01051991_centesimus-annus.hyml.

Potok, Chaim. *The Book of Lights*. London: Penguin, 1983.

Prance, Ghillean. *The Earth Under Threat: a Christian Perspective*. Wild Goose, 1996.

Race, Alan. *Christians and Religious Pluralism: Patterns in the Christian Theology of Religions*. London: SCM, 1983. Revised and Enlarged, SCM, 1993.

———. "Christianity and Other Religions: Is Inclusivism Enough?," *Theology* LXXXIX, 729 (1986) 178–186.

———. "The Fractal Proposal and Its Place in the Christian Theology of Religions." In *New Paths for Interreligious Theology: Perry Schmidt-Leukel's Fractal Interpretation of Religious Diversity*, edited by Alan Race and Paul Knitter, 145–161. Maryknoll: Orbis, 2019.

———. *Interfaith Encounter: The Twin Tracks of Theology and Dialogue*. London: SCM, 2001.

———. *Making Sense of Religious Pluralism: Shaping Theology of Religions for Our Times*. London: SPCK, 2013.

———. "Pointers to Pluralism Not Relativism." In *John Hick's Religious Pluralism in Global Perspective*, edited by Sharida Sugirtharajah. Switzerland, Springer Nature: Palgrave Macmillan, 2022.

———. "Prospects for a Global Ethic?." In *Interfaith Encounter: The Twin Tracks of Theology and Dialogue*, 124–143. London: SCM, 2001.

———. "Religious Absolutism, Violence, and the Public Square." In *Beyond the Dysfunctional Family: Jews, Christians and Muslims in Dialogue With Each Other and With Britain*, edited by Tony Bayfield et al., 183–200. London: The Manor House Dialogue Group, 2012.

———. "Rethinking Revelation, Exclusivity, Dialogue and Mission." In *Deep Calls To Deep: Transforming Conversations Between Jews and Christians*, edited by Tony Bayfield, 175–188. London: SCM, 2017.

———. "Taking Democracy into a Global Ethic: The Christian Next Step." In *Religions in Dialogue: From Theocracy to Democracy*, edited by Alan Race and Ingrid Shafer, 73–82. Aldershot: Ashgate, 2002.

———. *Thinking About Religious Pluralism: Shaping Theology of Religions for Our Times*, Minneapolis: Fortress, 2015.

———. "Truth is Many-Eyed." In *God's Truth*, edited by Eric James, 177–190. London: SCM, 1988.

Radhakrishnan, Sarvepalli. "Religion and Religions." In *Faiths and Fellowship: The Proceedings of the World Congress of Faiths*, edited by A. Douglas Millard, 104–121. London: J. M. Watkins, 1936.

Rahner, Karl. *Theological Investigations* Vol. 4. New York: Crossroad, 1992.

Rambachan, Anantanand. "Do We Have a Religious Need for Each Other? Pope Francis and Interreligious Dialogue." In *Pope Francis and Interreligious Dialogue: Religious Thinkers Engage With Recent Papal Initiatives*, edited by Harold Kasimow and Alan Race, 199–218. Switzerland, Springer Nature: Palgrave Macmillan, 2018.

Rawls, John. *Political Liberalism*. New York: Columbia University Press, 1993.

———. "The Idea of Public Reason Revisited." The University of Chicago Law Review 64 3 (1997) 765–807.

Robinson, Bob. *Jesus and the Religions: Retrieving a Neglected Example for a Multicultural World*. Oregon: Cascade Books, 2012.
Robinson, John A. T. *Honest to God*. London: SCM, 1963.
———. *The Roots of a Radical*. London: SCM, 1980.
———. *Truth is Two-Eyed*. London: SCM, 1979.
Rockefeller, Steven C. "Comment." In *Multiculturalism: Examining the Politics of Recognition*, edited by Amy Gutman, 87–98. New Jersey: Princeton University Press, 1994.
Rorty, Richard. "Religion as a Conversation-stopper." In *Philosophy and Social Hope*, 168–74. London: Penguin, 1999.
Rose, Kenneth. *Pluralism: The Future of Religion*. London: Bloomsbury, 2013.
Royal Aal al-Bayt Institute for Islamic Thought. "A Common Word." Open Letter. http://www.acomonword.com/the-acw-document.
Ruether, Rosemary Radford. "Feminism and Jewish-Christian Dialogue," In *The Myth of Christian Uniqueness: Toward a Pluralistic Theology of Religions*, edited by John Hick et al., 137–148. London: SCM, 1987.
———. *Women-Church: Theology and Practice of Feminist Liturgical Communities*. Reissue Edition. Eugene, OR: Wipf and Stock, 2001.
Samartha, Stanley. *Between Two Cultures: Ecumenical Ministry in a Pluralistic World*. Geneva: WCC, 1996.
Samartha, Stanley. *One Christ—Many Religions*, Maryknoll: Orbis, 1991.
Schillebeeckx, Edward. *The Church: The Human Story of God*. New York: Crossroad, 1990.
Schmidt-Leukel, Perry. ed. *Buddhism and Christianity in Dialogue: The Gerald Weisfeld Lectures 2004*. London: SCM, 2005.
———. ed. *Buddhism, Christianity and the Question of Creation: Karmic or Divine?*, Aldershot: Ashgate, 2006.
———. "Exclusivism, Inclusivism, Pluralism: the Tripolar Typology—Clarified and Reaffirmed." In *The Myth of Religious Superiority: a Multifaith Exploration*, edited by Paul F. Knitter, 13–27. Maryknoll: Orbis, 2005.
———. "A Fractal Interpretation of Religious Diversity, An Overview." In *New Paths for Interreligious Theology: Perry Schmidt-Leukel's Fractal Interpretation of Religious Diversity*, edited by Alan Race and Paul Knitter, 3–22. Maryknoll: Orbis, 2019.
———. *God Beyond Boundaries: A Christian and Pluralist Theology of Religions*. Translation by Ulrike Guthrie, Carolina Weening, Charlie Cahill, and Perry Schmidt-Leukel. New York: Waxmann, 2017.
———. "Religious Pluralism and Critical Realism." In *John Hick's Religious Pluralism in Global Perspective*, edited by Sharida Sugirtharajah. Switzerland, Springer Nature: Palgrave Macmillan, 2022.
———. *Religious Pluralism and Interreligious Theology: the Gifford Lectures—An Extended Edition*. Maryknoll: Orbis, 2017.
———. "The Struggle for Peace: Can Religions Help?" In *Transformation By Integration: How Inter-faith Encounter Changes Christianity*, 13–29. London: SCM, 2009.
Schweitzer, Albert. *The Quest of the Historical Jesus*. London: SCM, 1981. First English Edition, 1910.
Senior, Donald, and Carroll Stuhlmueller. *The Biblical Foundations for Mission*. London: SCM, 1983.

Shapiro, Rami Mark. "Moving the Fence: One Rabbi's View of Interreligious Dialogue." In *Inter-religious Dialogue: Voices from a New Frontier*, edited by M. Darrol Bryant et al., 31–40. New York: Paragon House, 1989.

Sherwin, Byron L. and Kasimow, Harold, eds. *John Paul II and Interreligious Dialogue*, Maryknoll: Orbis, 1999.

Smith, Wilfred Cantwell. *Faith and Belief*. New Jersey: Princeton University Press, 1979.

———. *The Meaning and End of Religion: A Revolutionary Approach to the Great Religious Traditions*. New York: Macmillan, 1962.

———. *Towards a World Theology*. London and Basingstoke: Macmillan, 1981.

Stout, Jeffrey. *Democracy and Tradition*. New Jersey: Princeton University Press, 2005.

Sullivan, Francis. *Salvation Outside the Church?: Tracing the History of the Catholic Response*. London: Geoffrey Chapman, 1992.

Swidler, Leonard. *After the Absolute: The Dialogical Future of Religious Reflection*. Minneapolis: Augsburg Fortress, 1990.

———. John B. Cobb Jr, Paul F. Knitter, and Monika K. Hellwig. *Death or Dialogue: From the Age of Monologue to the Age of Dialogue*. Philadelphia: Trinity, 1990.

———. ed. *For All Life: Toward a Universal Declaration of a Global Ethic*. Oregon: White Cloud, 1998.

———. "Interreligious Dialogue: its Origin and Meaning." *Interreligious Insight* 12 2 (2014) 10–33.

———. and Paul Mojzes. *The Study of Religion in an Age of Global Dialogue*. Philadelphia: Temple University Press, 2000.

———. and Ashok Gangadean. "The Technology of Deep-Dialogue/Critical Thinking." *Theoretical Principles Underlying Deep-Dialogue/Critical-Thinking*. Key Documents 1–6. Global Dialogue Institute, Philadelphia, 2000. http://www.globaldialogueinstitute.org/category/document.

———. ed. *Toward a Universal Theology of Religion*. Maryknoll: Orbis, 1987.

Tempest, Kae. "Words on a page are incomplete." *The Guardian (Review)* 142 (2020) 24–25.

Thatamanil, John, J. "Learning From (And Not Just About) Our Religious Neighbours, Comparative Theology and the Future of *Nostra Aetate*." In *The Future of Interreligious Dialogue: A Multireligious Conversation on Nostra Aetate*, edited by Charles L. Cohen et al., 289–301. Maryknoll: Orbis, 2017.

Theological Advisory Commission of the Federation of Asian Bishops' Conferences. "Seven Theses on Interreligious Dialogue: An Essay in Pastoral Theological Reflection." *International Bulletin of Missionary Research* 13 3 (1989) 108–110.

Thompson, William M. *The Jesus Debate*. New Jersey: Paulist, 1985.

Tilley, Terence W. (with others). *Religious Diversity and the American Experience: A Theological Approach*. London & New York: Continuum, 2007.

Tillich, Paul. *The Shaking of the Foundations*. Pelican, 1962.

Traer, Robert. *Faith in Human Rights: Support in Religious Traditions for a Global Struggle*. Washington: Georgetown University Press, 1991.

Troeltsch, Ernst. "Historiography." In *Encyclopedia of Religion and Ethics*, edited by James Hastings, VI: 716–23. New York: Charles Scribner's Sons; Edinburgh: T & T Clark, 1908–27.

Twiss, Sumner B. "Religion and Human Rights: A Comparative Perspective." In *Explorations in Global Ethics: Comparative Religious Ethics and Interreligious*

Dialogue, edited by Sumner B. Twiss et al., 155–175. Boulder, Colorado: Westview, 1998.

United Nations Environment Programme and Parliament of the World's Religions. *Faith for Earth: A Call for Action*. Nairobi: UNEP, 2020. https://www.unenvironment.org/resources/publication/faith-earth-call-action.

Vince, Gaia. *Transcendence: How Humans Evolved Through Fire, Language, Beauty and Time*. London: Penguin, Allen Lane, 2019.

Vincent of Lérins. "*Commonitorium*." New Advent, 2 6. https://www.newadvent.org/fathers/3506.htm.

Vivekananda, Swami. "Response to Welcome. Addresses at the Parliament of Religions." https://ramakrishna.org/vivekanandaparliament.html.

Ward, Keith. *Is Religion Dangerous?* London: Lion, 2006.

Wiles, Maurice. *Christian Theology and Inter-Religious Dialogue*. London: SCM, 1992.

Wilken, Robert. *The Myth of Christian Beginnings*. London: SCM, 1979.

Williams, Rowan. "A Common Word." Response to Muslim scholar's Open Letter, 2008. http://rowanwilliams.archbishopofcanterbury.org/articles.php/1107/a-common-word-for-the-common-good.

Wilson, Edward O. "The Little Things That Run the World (The Importance and Conservation of Invertebrates)." *Conservation Biology*, 1 4 (1987) 344–346.

Wogaman, J. Philip. *Christian Perspectives on Politics*. London: SCM 1988.

———. *What Christians Can Learn From Other Religions*. Louisville: Westminster John Knox, 2014.

World Council of Churches. "Religious Plurality and Christian Self-Understanding." *Current Dialogue* 45 (July 2005). http://wcc-coe.org/wcc/what/interreligious/cd45-02.html.

———. "Theological Perspectives on Plurality" II, 1990. https://www.oikoumene.org/en/resources/documents/wcc-programmes/interreligious-dialogue-and-cooperation/christian-identity-in-pluralistic-societies/baar-statement-theological-perspectives-on-plurality.

Index

Roman numerals refer to pages in the Introduction.

7/7 terrorist attacks, UK, 122
9/11 terrorist attacks, US, 103–105, 106–107, 109–110, 114, 120

Abdulla, Raficq, xvii, xx–xxi, 157–158
Abélard, Pierre, 30
absolutism, xxv–xxvii, 113–114, 121, 122–124, 128
AD dating system, 5–6
Ahmed, Akbar, 116
Aikiya Alayam, 53–54
"anonymous Christians" (Rahner), 61, 88
anti-Semitism, 17
apocalypticism, 145
Aquinas, Thomas, 123
Augustine, 81
authority of the past, 13–15, 32–33, 183
awakening, 177
axial consciousness, 70–71, 161–162

Baar Statement, 74, 97
Baha'is, xxiv
Barbour, Ian, 164
Barnes, Michael, 167–169
Barth, Karl, 85–87, 123
Bayfield, Tony, 59
Bede, the Venerable, 6
belief, 13–15, 25–26, 34–35

Berry, Thomas, 150–151
Bible, 41, 71–73, 82–83. *See also* gospel traditions
Bouteneff, Peter, 171
Buber, Martin, 55, 147–148
Buddhist–Christian relations, 153–154
Buddhists and Buddhism, xxii–xxiii, xxiv, 86–87, 123, 149–150, 177

caricatures, going beyond, 26, 76, 98
Carrithers, Michael, 149–150
Carter, Stephen, 126
Catholic Church, 14, 15. *See also Dominus Iesus;* Francis, Pope; International Theological Commission; John-Paul II, Pope; *Nostra Aetate;* Pius IX, Pope; Roman Catholic Federation of Asian Bishops' Conferences
Centesimus Annus (papal encyclical), 131
Christ. *See* Christology; Jesus Christ
Christendom, 11–12, 17
Christian Fundamentalism, 22
Christian universalism, 11–13, 21, 71, 74–75, 87–89, 99
Christianity
    cultural success of, 6–8, 11–13

Christianity (continued)
  democracy and, 130–134, 135, 137–140
  inventiveness of (historical diversity), 3–27
  missionary activity, 12–13, 41, 96–98, 99, 101–102, 174–175, 183–184
  political power and, 7
Christian-Jewish relations, xxiv, xxv–xxvi, 7–8, 17, 59–60, 72–73, 115–116, 120
Christian-Muslim relations, 17–19, 59–60, 100, 116–117, 120, 181, 185
Christology, 6–7, 42–43, 45, 61–62, 80–91, 168–169. *See also* Jesus Christ
Church Fathers, 31, 81–82, 183
climate emergency, 141–154
colonialism, 13
comparative theology, 169–170, 172
competitive spirit, 52, 122–124
complexity consciousness, 162
contemplative awareness, 145–148, 151–152, 153–154
contextuality, 40–41, 69
conversion, 144
Cousins, Ewert, xix, 70, 161, 162
covenant, 59, 60
Creeds, 14
critical realism, 173
critical thinking, xxv–xxvi, 74–75, 84, 113, 131
crusades, 18, 116
cultural evolution, 162–164

Dante, 123
dating system, 5–6
D'Costa, Gavin, 63
De Gruchy, John, 131, 140
De Mello, Anthony, 142–143
DeLillo, Don, 104
democracy, 16, 107, 124–125, 126, 129–140
Denialism, 143–144
Denys the Short (Dionysius Exiguus), 5–6

dialogue, xxv–xxvii, 19–20, 27, 51–59
  Christian approach to, 183–185
  definition, 110
  ecological awareness and, 150–154
  guidelines for, 55–56
  as hospitality, 167–169
  mission and, 96–98, 99, 101–102, 174–175, 183–184
  non-Christian responses to, 23–24, 173–175
  philosophical versus ethical framing, 106
  as providential rather than pragmatic, 66
  public democratic debate, 127–128
  religiously-motivated violence and, 103–106, 110–114, 122, 124
  theological motivation, 119–120
difference, 54, 77, 100–101
DiNoia, Joseph, 62–63
Dionysius Exiguus (Denys the Short), 5–6
diversity, 29–30, 175–177. *See also* strangeness with resonance; unity and diversity
Dominus Iesus (declaration by the Congregation for the Doctrine of the Faith), 58–59, 60
Dulles, Avery, 31
Dupuis, Jacques, 58–59, 62

Earth Charter, 151
ecological spirituality, 141–154
empathy, 117–118
encounters with other faiths, xxi–xxiv
enlightenment (awakening), 177
Enlightenment (historical period), 15–20, 130, 131, 140
epistemology, 22, 172–173
eschatology, 61–62, 63, 84
Eusebius of Caesarea, 11–12
evangelization, 174–175
exclusivism, xxvii, 40–41, 60–61, 85–87, 99–100, 113–114, 164–166, 183
experience, trust in religious, xx, 64, 75–76, 101

Fathers of the Church, 31, 81–82, 183
fear, 116–117
fractal theory, 175–177
Francis, Pope, 151–152, 174–175
fruits, spiritual, 64, 75, 76
Fulgentius, 183
fundamentalism, 22

Gandhi, Mahatma, 105
Gangadean, Ashok, 66
Gaston, Ray, 166–167
Geffré, Claude, 167
Global Ethic, 134–140
God, 75, 87, 122–123, 181–182. *See also* ultimate reality
Goizueta, Robert, 166
gospel traditions, 9–10, 33, 71–73, 82–83, 87, 184
Greco-Roman empire, 11–12
Green, Vivian, 18
Guterres, António, 141–142

Habermas, Jürgen, 136
Haight, Roger, 65, 170–171
Harris, Sam, 107–108, 110
Hastings, Adrian, 8
heretics, 113–114, 123
Hick, John, viii, 47, 64, 114, 172, 173
Hindus and Hinduism, xxiii, xxiv, 174–175, 178
Hirudayam, Ignatius, 53–54
historical consciousness, 3–8, 25–27, 30, 44–46
Holocaust, 17
holy figures and saints, 76
Hopkins, Gerard Manley, 145
hospitality, 96–98, 101, 102, 167–169
Houlden, J. Leslie, 30n4
human rights, 16, 136
Hume, David, xxi

imperialism, ethical, 135–136
incarnation, 6–7, 42–43, 80–90, 172
inclusivism, xxvii, 61–62, 63, 73–74, 87–89, 99, 100, 164–166, 167, 184–185
ineffability, 57, 100

interconnectedness of all life, 145–149, 151
interfaith relations, paradox of, 117–118
International Theological Commission, 97–98
interreligious conflict. *See* violence, religion and
interreligious dialogue. *See* dialogue
Isaiah, Prophet, 148–149
Islam and Muslims, xxii, xxiv, 120, 121, 122, 177. *See also* Jameelah, Maryam; Muhammad, Prophet; Muslim–Christian relations

Jainism, xxiii–xxiv, 54
Jameelah, Maryam, 23–27
James, William, 148
Jaspers, Karl, 70, 161
Jesus Christ
  compared with Gautama and Muhammad, 177
  encountering after death, 61–62, 63, 100
  encountering in dialogue with people of other faiths, 184–185
  as parable, 89–91
  supremacy (priority, finality) of, 42–43, 45, 61–62, 63, 84
  and the Syrophoenician woman, 184
  universal message of, 65, 71–73
  See also Christology
Jewish–Christian relations, xxiv, xxv–xxvi, 7–8, 17, 59–60, 72–73, 115–116, 120
John, gospel of, 9, 82, 83, 87
John-Paul II, Pope, 131
Johns, Jeremy, 18
Juergensmeyer, Mark, 105, 121–122
Justin Martyr, 183

Kahn-Harris, Keith, 143
Kaufman, Gordon, 44–45
Kenney, Jim, xi–xiv, 162–164
kingdom of God, 131–132, 138

INDEX

Knitter, Paul, viii, 47, 57, 65, 154, 169–170
knowledge, 22, 172–173
Kraemer, Hendrik, 100
Küng, Hans, 105, 114
Kuschel, Karl-Josef, 56

Laudato Si' (papal encyclical), 151–152, 154
liberal democracy, 124–126
listening, 182–183
Loisy, Alfred, 3
Luke, gospel of, 9–10

Mark, gospel of, 9–10, 83, 184
Matthew, gospel of, 9–10, 33
May, John D'Arcy, 153, 154
McLellan, David, 139–140
mission, 12–13, 41, 96–98, 99, 101–102, 174–175, 183–184
modern period, 15–20
modernist crisis, 4–5
Mojzes, Paul, 56, 105, 110
Moltmann, Jürgen, 84
monotheism, 11
Muhammad, Prophet, 59–60, 123, 177
multi-religious statements (examples), 110–113
Muslim–Christian relations, 17–19, 59–60, 100, 116–117, 120, 181, 185
Muslims and Islam, xxii, xxiv, 120, 121, 122, 177. *See also* Jameelah, Maryam; Muhammad, Prophet; Muslim–Christian relations
mutuality, 49, 55–56, 57, 68, 185

natural world, interconnectedness of, 145–149, 151
Neuhaus, Richard, 132–133, 134
New Testament studies, 9–10, 33, 71–73, 82–83, 87, 184
9/11 terrorist attacks, US, 103–105, 106–107, 109–110, 114, 120
Nineham, Dennis, 32
non-competitive spirit, 52
non-violence, 105

Nostra Aetate (Declaration on the Relation of the Church with Non-Christian Religions), 73, 167, 170–172

Origen, 73
Orthodox Christianity, 14, 15
orthodoxy (right belief), 13–15, 171

paranoia, 116–117
Parliament of the World's Religions, 127, 134–135, 137, 151, 152–153, 160
particularity(ies), xxi, 79–81, 89, 91, 99, 181–182
past, authority of the, 13–15, 32–33, 183
patristic period, 31, 81–82, 183
Paul, Apostle, 149
peace, 111, 114. *See also* violence, religion and
Pedersen, Kusumita, 152–153
"people of the book," 18
Pius IX, Pope, 130
Plato, 14
pluralism
  criticisms of, 47, 48, 64–65, 77, 101, 172–173
  definition, xxvii, 42
  model of, 46–50, 75–78
  mutual criticism in, 49, 68, 185
  as response to plurality of religions, 60–61, 63–66, 99, 100–101, 170–171
  roots of Christian, 71–75
political liberalism, 124–126, 139–140
political power, Christianity and, 7
post-colonial period, 106–107
postmodernism, 62, 66
Potok, Chaim, 181, 185
Prance, Ghillean, 146
prayer, 181–182, 185
prophetic discernment, 148–151, 153–154
Protestant Christianity, 14, 15–16
providence, 51–52, 60–61, 66
public life, religion in, 120–121, 124–128, 132–140

Qur'an, 109

Radhakrishnan, Sarvepalli, 159–160
Rahner, Karl, 61, 88
Rawls, John, 125
reality, xx–xxi, 22, 182. *See also* ultimate reality
Reformation, 15–16
relativism, 48, 49, 76
religion
    definition, 69–70, 178
    distinguishing good and bad, 76, 118
    in modern and postmodern culture, 157–158, 180–181
    in public life, 120–121, 124–128, 132–140
    revelation versus, 85–86
    spirituality and external form, 158–161, 182
    violence and, 103–114, 120–124
    See also theology of religions
Religious Plurality and Christian Self-Understanding (World Council of Churches), 95–98
religious truth. *See* truth
revelation, 41, 45, 85–86, 123–124, 146
Robinson, John A. T., 39–44, 83, 88
Rockefeller, Steven, 139
Roman Catholic Church, 14, 15. *See also Dominus Iesus;* Francis, Pope; International Theological Commission; John-Paul II, Pope; *Nostra Aetate;* Pius IX, Pope
Roman Catholic Federation of Asian Bishops' Conferences, 87
romanticism, 145
Rorty, Richard, 125
Ruether, Rosemary Radford, 7, 176

saints and holy figures, 76
salvation
    Christ and, 84–85, 88, 90, 171
    definition, 165
    pluralist view, 46, 170–171
    religious plurality and, 62, 75, 170–172

    threats to, 113–114, 123
    tradition-specific view, 62
Samartha, Stanley, 61, 64, 68, 102
scandal of particularity, 79–81, 89, 91
Schillebeeckx, Edward, 60
Schmidt-Leukel, Perry, viii, 123, 173, 175–177, 178
Schweitzer, Albert, 4
science, 150–151
secularism, xxv, 107–108, 113, 124–128, 132–134
Senior, Donald, 72, 73
7/7 terrorist attacks, UK, 122
Shapiro, Rami Mark, 54–55, 57
Siddiqui, Ataullah, xvii
Smith, Wilfred Cantwell, 46, 47, 67–68
Spirit, 63
spiritual evolution, 160–161
spiritual fruits, 64, 75, 76
splitting, psychological, 118
statements, shared (examples), 110–113
strangeness with resonance, xxiii–xxv
Stuhlmueller, Carroll, 72, 73
suffering, 65
Swidler, Leonard, xxv, 77, 105
Syllabus Errorum (papal encyclical), 130

Teilhard de Chardin, 162
terrorism, 103–105, 106–107, 109–110, 114, 120, 121–122
Thatamanil, John, 171–172
theology of religions, xix–xxvii, 59–66, 98–102, 164–170, 178–179
Thomas Aquinas, 123
Thompson, William, 48–49
Tilley, John, 178
Tillich, Paul, 146
Timothy I (Nestorian patriarch), 18–19
tradition, 13–15, 22–23, 28–36, 68–69, 171
tradition-specific approach, 62–63
Traer, Robert, 16
Trinity, 61
Troeltsch, Ernst, 44, 80
trust in religious experience, xx, 64, 75–76, 101

truth
    and the authority of the past, 13–15
    contextuality of, 69
    dialogical approach, 54–55
    epistemology and, 172–173
    as human construct, 10, 44–45, 80, 123–124
    two-eyed (Robinson), 41–44
    as unchanging, 14, 25
    welcome and unwelcome, 111–113
Twiss, Sumner, 136

ultimate reality, 76, 100, 172–173, 182
United Nations, 141–142
unity and diversity, 41–42, 54, 57, 65–66

universalism, 11–13, 21, 71, 74–75, 87–89, 99

Vatican II. *see Nostra Aetate*
Vince, Gaia, 164
Vincent of Lérins, 29–30
violence, religion and, 103–114, 120–124
Vivekananda, Swami, 160

Ward, Keith, 109
Wilken, Robert, 15
Williams, Rowan, 122, 123–124
Wilson, Edward O., 147
World Council of Churches: "Religious Plurality and Christian Self-Understanding," 95–98

www.ingramcontent.com/pod-product-compliance
Lightning Source LLC
Chambersburg PA
CBHW070736160426
43192CB00009B/1459